HOW WILL THIS HELL TURN INTO HEAVEN?

A POLITICAL AND ECONOMIC REVIEW

SAJID MOLLAH

I dedicated this book to all democratic socialists worldwide.

I dedicate this message to those who relentlessly fight for justice, equality, and the uplifting of the common people; to those who oppose the forces of oppression and division; and to those who envision a world in which 99% of mankind may thrive in prosperity, dignity, and peace.

May this work be a call to action, a lighthouse of truth, and a guide to transforming the hell of the present world into the heaven it can become.

Contents

Contents

Foreword

• • •

*Sajid Mollah's *How Will This Hell Turn Into Heaven: A Political and Economic Review* is a vital and insightful piece in a world growing more defined by sharp divisions and economic uncertainty. Emphasising the complex interaction of politics, economics, and social justice, this book provides a thorough study of the modern global scene. Mollah's sharp criticism explores the urgent problems of our day: the crisis in cost of living, inequality, corruption, and the inability of present economic models to benefit most people. By means of painstaking research and careful analysis, he reveals how a tiny fraction of the world's population gains from policies that cause the others to suffer financially. Drawing on a variety of case studies, including thorough analyses of India's present problems and comparisons with other countries, Mollah offers a whole picture of how governmental shortcomings prolong suffering. His investigation of British Fabian Socialism and democratic socialism provides perceptive analysis of how these ideas might direct us towards a more fair and rich future. The book is divided into two sections: the first describes the issues afflicting our planet, and the second offers doable remedies and policy suggestions meant to benefit most people and solve structural inequalities. Mollah's vision is clear: to turn our present "hell" into a "heaven" of justice, stable economy, and better quality of living for all. Working as a political correspondent, I have seen personally the hardships people all around experience. The work of Sajid Mollah offers a road map for significant change in addition* *to a diagnosis of our present problems, so offering hope. His commitment to expose the truth and support of the common people is admirable and required. Readers will find a call to action and inspiration source on these pages. Mollah's relentless belief in the ability of change is shown by his dedication to build a better world by wise, compassionate policy. This book is a potent manifesto for a time when everyone can reach justice and prosperity, not only a political and economic analysis.*"

Martina Bet
Political Correspondent, *The Sun*
London, England

• • •

• • •

"*As a sociologist at Sheffield Hallam University, I have spent my career studying the complexities of societal structures and the forces that shape our world. With great enthusiasm, I present Sajid Mollah's *How Will This Hell Turn Into Heaven: A Political and Economic Review*. This book is an important scholarly contribution that provides both a profound critique and a hopeful outlook for the future. In an era when global inequalities and socioeconomic challenges appear more pronounced than ever, Mollah's work provides an essential analysis of the systemic flaws that perpetuate suffering for the vast majority of people. His investigation into radical nationalism, historical revisionism, and the intersection of capitalist interests and dictatorial power provides a compelling look at the forces that shape modern governance and economic policies. Mollah's book* *stands out not only for its rigorous analysis, but also for its ambition to find solutions. The in-depth examination of the flaws in current economic models, as well as the impact of these systems on everyday life, is both informative and thought-provoking. His critique of capitalism's role in promoting fake economic growth and perpetuating inequality is based on empirical research and provides a new perspective on these pressing issues. What stands out about Mollah's approach is his commitment to not only diagnosing problems but also proposing practical solutions. His support for democratic socialism and a humane economy is bolstered by practical recommendations aimed at addressing the underlying causes of economic and social injustice. The case studies from India and other countries demonstrate the global significance of his arguments and the potential for transformative change. *How Will This Hell Turn Into Heaven* is more than a critical review; it is a rallying cry for policymakers, academics, and citizens alike. Mollah's vision for a fairer, more equitable world is based on a thorough understanding of socioeconomic dynamics and provides a road map for navigating today's complexities. Sajid Mollah's book is a must-read for anyone looking for a thorough and insightful analysis of the forces that shape our world and potential paths to a better future. It encourages us to question the status quo and work towards a more just and prosperous society.*

"

Russ Jackson
Sociologist, Sheffield Hallam University

• • •

. . .

. . .

. . .

*"In a time when political and economic obstacles appear insurmountable, Sajid Mollah's *How Will This Hell Turn Into Heaven: A Political and Economic Review* stands as a beacon of confidence and clarity. To be a Scottish Labour MP, I have personally experienced the profound influence that well-researched and thought-provoking analyses can have on influencing public discourse and bringing about policy change. Sajid Mollah's book is a critical contribution to this dialogue, providing a comprehensive examination of the systemic issues that are currently affecting our world and articulating a compelling vision for change. Sajid Mollah's ambitious work decodes the complex dynamics of contemporary economic systems and governance. He meticulously investigates the many ways in which current policies fail to serve the majority, the cost-of-living crisis, and the pervasive inequalities. His critique of capitalist frameworks, in conjunction with a comprehensive examination of the ways in which these systems perpetuate economic disparity, is both enlightening and alarming. A sobering yet essential perspective on the state of global affairs is provided by Mollah's insights into the dangers of radical nationalism, historical revisionism, and the entanglement of dictatorial power with capitalist interests. This book is distinguished by its practical solutions and comprehensive analysis. Mollah does not merely emphasise issues; he also provides practical suggestions for how governments can enhance their services to their constituents. His emphasis on British socialism and*

*democratic socialism, particularly in the context of human economic thought, provides a guide to a more equitable and prosperous future. The potential for reform and the universality of these issues are underscored by the detailed case studies from India and other countries. This book is a testament to Sajid Mollah's dedication to promoting the common good and enlightening the truth. His vision for transforming the current state of our world from "hell" to "heaven" is both ambitious and attainable, as it is based on a profound understanding of socio-economic principles and rigorous research. *How Will This Hell Turn Into Heaven* is an indispensable read for anyone who is concerned with the future of our societies and the welfare of the many over the few. It prompts us to reconsider our preconceived notions, confront uncomfortable realities, and envision a more equitable world. Sajid Mollah has not only offered a critique of existing systems, but also a practical and optimistic approach to the future.*"

Alison S. Taylor
Scottish Labour MP for Paisley & Renfrewshire North
For casework and assistance,
please email alison.taylor.mp@parliament.uk

• • •

Preface

*The global majority—99% of mankind—is caught in a cycle of deprivation and suffering in an increasingly complicated world when inequality, unemployment, corruption, and the cost of living crisis rule headlines. The situation is dire and it is obvious that government policies mostly bear responsibility. Still, layers of false information and misguided priorities serving just the privileged few obscure the road to a better future. My attempt to expose the truth by removing those layers is this book, *How Will This Hell Turn Into Heaven: A Political and Economic Review*. My name is Sajid Mollah and I have spent my life trying to understand the complex web of political and financial influences forming our planet. By means of this book, I aim to share that knowledge with you, the reader, so that together, we can light the road towards a more equitable society. This book opens with exploring the issues afflicting our planet today. It is very important to carefully analyse these issues—be it the rise of radical nationalism, the dangers of historical revisionism, or the insidious effects of capitalism on our societies—because without a clear understanding of the problem, solutions will remain elusive. In the second section, I explain particular, realistic policies meant for 99% of the population. These policies have their roots in the ideas of a humane economy and in a strong dedication to democratic socialism as British Fabian Socialism envisioned it. My analysis goes beyond surface-level critiques to offer a comprehensive roadmap for transforming our current world—from a hellish landscape of inequality and despair into a heaven where fairness, prosperity, and human dignity prevail. Throughout the book, I have included case studies from India and other nations to explain how these global problems manifest in different contexts, while also emphasising that the struggles of people across the world are interconnected. If we are to produce significant change, I have sought to expose the harsh reality we must face by removing the veil of truth long covered. My hope is that this book will not only enlighten you but also inspire you to join in the effort to build a better world. By forming a collective public opinion* *grounded in truth and justice, we can push for the implementation of policies that will uplift the many, rather than enrich the few. In the pages that follow, you will find not just an analysis of the world's problems, but a vision for a future where 99% of people can live in prosperity, equality, and peace. This is our chance to turn hell into heaven—let's seize it together.*

———————— ————————— ————————— ———————— Sajid Mollah

.

• • •

Saligram, Nadia
West Bengal, India
15th August, 2024

Acknowledgements

*"I would want to especially thank those who helped to create *How Will This Hell Turn Into Heaven: A Political and Economic Review*.*

First of all, I really owe my editors, Mark Serwotka and Chris Hanalky, thanks. This book was shaped into what it is today in great part by your sharp observations, painstaking attention to detail, and relentless commitment. I much appreciate your efforts; your direction has been priceless.

A particular thank you to Aoife Burke, whose exceptional and provocative thoughts helped the ideas in this book to come to life. Your work gives this book a dimension not possible with just words.

Furthermore much appreciated is the help I got during the book's research and development phases. Your activism and writings, Sam Pallis, have been a lighthouse of inspiration and clarity. Toby MacDonnell, your thorough grasp of political economy has given this work vital background and analysis.

At last, for Jamie Lewis and Lucy Sweetman, your encouragement, remarks, and support have been absolutely essential over this road. I really value your work.

This book is a team effort, thus I really appreciate all those who helped to produce it. I appreciate your enabling me to realise this vision."

---- Sajid Mollah

• • •

CHAPTER I

Nationalism: A Force for Division and Exclusion

Nationalism is a historical and controversial practice in society and politics. In a general sense, when a community of people is organised politically and economically, driven by imagination and sentiment, it is called a nation. The nation is organised for purely mechanical purposes. A society becomes increasingly mechanised when it is manipulated for the purposes of political and economic power. It is through him that such a people become addicted to proving themselves powerful and superior. National interest is of utmost importance to them. The sense of justice and injustice does not always find a place in the Political Agenda to protect that national interest. Instead, there is mutual jealousy, competition for power.

Nationalist ideologies, while varying in their precise manifestations, strive to define and support the interests of a certain nation, which is frequently distinguished by shared ethnicity, language, religion, or cultural history. At their foundation, nationalist ideologies seek to instill a sense of belonging and unity among members of the nation, promising safety, pride, and collective strength. However, the process of nation-building and identity construction is inherently exclusionary and divisive because it requires determining who belongs to the nation and who does not. The inherent exclusivity and divisiveness of nationalist beliefs present substantial difficulties to societal cohesiveness, equality, and world peace.

The appeal of nationalism lies in its ability to offer individuals a sense of identity, purpose, and solidarity. In times of uncertainty, economic distress, or social upheaval, nationalism often becomes a rallying cry, offering simple solutions to complex problems by uniting people around a common cause or perceived threat. However, this sense of unity often comes at the cost of excluding those who do not fit the national ideal, whether due to differences in ethnicity, religion, language, or cultural practices. The resulting divisions can manifest in various forms, from social discrimination and marginalization to outright violence and conflict.

The following piece looks at the different ways in which nationalist ideologies are inherently exclusive and divisive. I will discover how, despite its potential to unite, nationalism can also be a powerful force for division and exclusion by investigating the dynamics of ethnic and cultural exclusivity, ingroup versus outgroup mentality, territorial claims, cultural homogenisation, social hierarchies, exclusionary policies, and inter-national conflicts. I will use historical and contemporary case studies to demonstrate the real-world effects of nationalist ideology on societies and the global order, ultimately calling nationalism into question in a world that increasingly values inclusivity, diversity, and cooperation.

Ethnic and Cultural Exclusivity

Many nationalist ideas centre on the concept of ethnic and cultural exclusion. Often, nationalism describes the country as a cultural or ethnic community rather than only as a political entity. This description naturally leaves out people who do not share the dominant ethnicity, language, religion, or cultural legacy. Nationalist ideas marginalise and devaluate the identities of minority populations by raising one group's identity as the norm of national belonging. Many times, nationalist ideas claim that a shared ethnic or cultural legacy ties the country together. Seen as the markers of national identity, shared genealogy, language, religion, or cultural practices can all form the basis for this concept.

In the case of ethnic nationalism, for instance, the country is sometimes understood as a homogeneous group with a shared bloodline or lineage. This viewpoint naturally labels those who do not possess these traits as outsiders or dangers to national purity, therefore excluding them. Many times, the national identity is also strongly correlated with a dominating religion, therefore accentuating exclusion. Hindu nationalism in India, for instance, aims to establish the country as essentially Hindu, therefore excluding other religious groups including Muslims and Christians. Analogously, Jewish nationalism in Israel is frequently based on the concept of a Jewish state, which affects the rights and position of non-Jewish people and inhabitants.

Ethnic and cultural exclusivity has been a driving force in some of the most horrific and deadly events throughout history. Driven by Nazi nationalism, the Holocaust aimed to create a pure Aryan country by eradicating Jews, Roma, handicapped people, and other groups judged to be either culturally or genetically inferior. Hutu nationalism drove the 1994 genocide against Tutsis in Rwanda; nationalist ideas positioned Tutsis as foreign invaders needing to be exterminated in order to defend the Hutu country. The emergence of ethno-nationalism in several countries around modern times still threatens minority communities. Under government and military motivated by Buddhist nationalist discourse, Rohingya Muslims have suffered terrible persecution and ethnic cleansing in Myanmar. White nationalist movements seeking the exclusion of immigrants and people of colour in order to maintain the cultural and racial identity of the country have gathered steam in the United States and Europe.

For minority populations, ethnic and cultural exclusivity has significant and broad effects. Minority groups sometimes suffer systematic discrimination, violence, and exclusion when nationalist ideas define one group's identity above others. Their languages, faiths, and customs could be denied or devalued, therefore erasing cultural legacy and identity. Further isolating these groups would be denial of equal rights, political representation, and resources, hence strengthening their marginalisation. Sometimes the exclusion turns into violence and genocide as the dominant group tries to eradicate or deport anyone who deviate from the national ideal. The social and psychological effects of being deprived of the national identity can cause alienation, resentment, and social disturbance even in less extreme circumstances, therefore compromising the stability and cohesiveness of the society as a whole.

Nationalist Movements and Ethnic Cleansing

- The Holocaust (Germany): The Nazi regime's pursuit of an ethnically pure Aryan nation resulted in the systematic extermination of six million Jews, as well as millions of other individuals, including Roma, disabled individuals, and political dissidents. The fatal repercussions of extreme ethnic nationalism are exemplified by this horrific example.

- Rwandan Genocide (Rwanda): Under the influence of nationalist and ethnic exclusivity, the Hutu Power movement incited the mass murder of an estimated 800,000 Tutsis and moderate Hutus. The genocide was incited by the conviction that the Tutsis were foreign invaders and a menace to the Hutu nation.

- Myanmar's Rohingya Crisis: Buddhist nationalist ideologies have portrayed the Rohingya Muslims as unlawful immigrants and a threat to the nation's cultural and religious identity, resulting in severe persecution, displacement, and violence.

Ingroup vs. Outgroup Dynamics

Nationalist ideologies often rely on the creation of a dichotomy between the ingroup (members of the nation) and the outgroup (outsiders or perceived enemies). This dynamic fosters a sense of solidarity and unity within the nation, but it also promotes distrust, hostility, and violence towards those outside the ingroup. The us-versus-them mentality is a powerful tool for nationalist leaders, but it is also a significant source of division and conflict.

The Us vs. Them Mentality —

The ingroup vs. outgroup dynamic is a fundamental aspect of nationalist ideologies. By defining the nation in exclusive terms, nationalism inherently divides the world into those who belong and those who do not. This division creates a strong sense of ingroup solidarity, as members of the nation are encouraged to see themselves as part of a collective whole, united by a common identity and purpose.

However, this sense of unity often comes at the expense of the outgroup, who are depicted as threats, enemies, or inferiors. Nationalist rhetoric frequently portrays the outgroup in negative terms, using fear, suspicion, and prejudice to justify their exclusion or persecution. This us-versus-them mentality can lead to the scapegoating of minority groups, immigrants, or other outsiders, who are blamed for the nation's problems or portrayed as obstacles to national progress.

The psychological impacts of ingroup vs. outgroup dynamics are significant. By fostering a sense of ingroup identity, nationalism can create strong bonds of loyalty and solidarity among members of the nation. However, it also reinforces negative attitudes and behaviors towards the outgroup, including prejudice, discrimination, and hostility. These attitudes can be deeply ingrained, leading to long-term social divisions and conflicts.

On a social level, the ingroup vs. outgroup dynamic can contribute to the marginalization and exclusion of minority populations, who are seen as less legitimate members of the society. This exclusion can lead to social and economic disparities, as well as tensions and conflicts between different groups within the nation. Moreover, the us-versus-them mentality can undermine social cohesion and trust, making it difficult to build inclusive and harmonious societies.

Xenophobia and scapegoating are common manifestations of the ingroup vs. outgroup dynamic in nationalist ideologies.

Xenophobia, or the fear and distrust of foreigners or outsiders, is often fueled by nationalist rhetoric that depicts immigrants, refugees, or minority groups as threats to the nation's identity, security, or economic well-being. This fear can lead to exclusionary policies, discrimination, and even violence against those who are perceived as outsiders.

Scapegoating is another common tactic used by nationalist movements to rally support and deflect blame for social or economic problems. By blaming the outgroup for the nation's difficulties, nationalist leaders can unite the ingroup around a common enemy and distract from other issues. This can lead to the persecution of minority groups, who are unfairly held responsible for problems that are often systemic or unrelated to their presence.

Nationalism and Inter-group Conflict

- The Balkans (Yugoslavia): The breakup of Yugoslavia in the 1990s was marked by intense nationalist conflicts between different ethnic and religious groups. The ingroup vs. outgroup dynamics played a central role in the violence, as nationalist leaders used ethnic and religious identities to justify acts of genocide, ethnic cleansing, and war.

- The Israeli-Palestinian Conflict (Middle East): The longstanding conflict between Israelis and Palestinians is deeply rooted in nationalist ideologies on both sides. The us-versus-them mentality has fueled decades of violence, mistrust, and failed peace efforts, as both groups assert their national identity and territorial claims.

- The United States (Modern): The rise of white nationalist movements in the United States has been accompanied by increasing xenophobia, racism, and anti-immigrant sentiment. The ingroup vs. outgroup dynamic is evident in the rhetoric of these movements, which portray people of color, immigrants, and other marginalized groups as threats to the nation's identity and security.

Territorial Claims and Expansionism

Nationalist ideologies often assert territorial claims based on historical grievances, ethnic ties, or cultural connections. These claims can lead to disputes over borders and territorial sovereignty, fueling conflicts and aggression between nations. The territorialism inherent in many nationalist ideologies is a significant source of international instability and violence.

Territorial sovereignty is a central tenet of nationalist ideologies, as the nation-state is often defined by its control over a specific geographic territory. Nationalist movements frequently emphasize the importance of defending or expanding this territory, particularly when there are historical grievances or disputes over borders. This emphasis on territorial sovereignty can lead to aggressive policies, including military interventions, annexations, or efforts to reclaim lost lands.

In some cases, nationalist ideologies may also justify territorial expansionism, as leaders seek to create a larger or more ethnically homogeneous nation. This expansionism can be driven by a desire to unite all members of the national or ethnic group within a single state, or by the belief that the nation has a historic or divine right to certain territories. However, these territorial ambitions often come into conflict with the sovereignty and rights of other nations or groups, leading to disputes and conflicts.

Nationalist territorial claims are often based on historical grievances or ethnic ties to a particular region. Leaders may argue that the nation has a historical right to certain lands, based on past borders, cultural heritage, or ancestral connections. These claims can be particularly potent when they are tied to a sense of victimization or injustice, as nationalist movements seek to rectify perceived wrongs by reclaiming lost territories.

Ethnic ties are another common justification for territorial claims, as nationalist ideologies often seek to unite all members of a particular ethnic group within a single state. This can lead to irredentist movements, which aim to reclaim territories inhabited by members of the nation's ethnic group, even if those territories are currently part of another country. However, these claims can be highly contentious, as they often involve redrawing borders or challenging the sovereignty of neighboring states.

Irredentism and expansionist nationalism are significant drivers of territorial conflicts. Irredentism refers to nationalist movements that seek to reclaim territories inhabited by members of the national or ethnic group, often based on historical or cultural ties. This can lead to disputes with neighboring countries, as nationalist leaders assert their right to territories that are currently under foreign control.

Expansionist nationalism, on the other hand, involves efforts to expand the nation's territory beyond its current borders, often through military conquest or annexation. This type of nationalism is particularly dangerous, as it can lead to wars of aggression and colonialism, as nationalist leaders seek to create a larger or more powerful state.

Nationalist-driven Conflicts over Territory

- Nazi Germany (World War II): The Nazi regime's expansionist nationalism led to the annexation of Austria, the invasion of Poland, and the subsequent outbreak of World War II. The regime's territorial ambitions were driven by a desire to create a greater German state and to unite all ethnic Germans under one rule.

- The Kashmir Conflict (India-Pakistan): The Kashmir region has been a flashpoint for nationalist-driven conflict between India and Pakistan since their independence in 1947. Both countries assert territorial claims based on ethnic, religious, and historical ties, leading to decades of violence and instability in the region.

- The South China Sea (China): China's nationalist-driven territorial claims in the South China Sea have led to disputes with neighboring countries, including Vietnam, the Philippines, and Malaysia. China's claims are based on historical grievances and cultural ties, but they have been challenged by international law and the sovereignty of other nations.

Cultural Homogenization

Nationalist ideologies often promote cultural homogenization as a means of achieving national unity and cohesion. This involves the suppression or assimilation of linguistic, religious, or cultural diversity within the nation, leading to the marginalization of minority cultures and the erosion of cultural pluralism. The push for cultural homogenization is a significant source of tension and conflict in many nationalist movements.

Nationalist movements frequently emphasize the importance of national unity and cohesion, arguing that a strong and unified nation is necessary for political stability, economic prosperity, and social harmony. To achieve this unity, nationalist ideologies may promote the adoption of a common language, religion, or cultural practices, often at the expense of diversity and pluralism.

This push for cultural homogenization can take various forms, including language policies that promote the use of a single national language, religious policies that favor a dominant religion, or cultural policies that elevate certain traditions or practices as the standard of national identity. While these policies may create a sense of shared identity and belonging among members of the dominant group, they can also alienate and marginalize those who do not conform to the national ideal.

Cultural homogenization often involves the suppression of linguistic, religious, or cultural diversity within the nation. Minority languages may be discouraged or banned, religious practices that differ from the dominant faith may be restricted, and cultural traditions that do not align with the national identity may be stigmatized or outlawed. This suppression can lead to the erosion of cultural heritage, as minority groups are pressured to assimilate or abandon their traditional practices.

In some cases, cultural homogenization may also involve the forced assimilation of minority groups, as nationalist governments seek to create a more homogeneous society. This can include policies of forced relocation, reeducation, or even violence against those who resist assimilation. The result is often the loss of cultural diversity and the creation of a more uniform but less inclusive society.

The impacts of cultural homogenization on cultural pluralism and individual identity are significant. Cultural pluralism, or the coexistence of multiple cultures within a society, is a key component of social cohesion, creativity, and innovation. However, when nationalist ideologies promote cultural homogenization, this pluralism is often undermined, leading to a loss of diversity and a reduction in the richness of the cultural landscape.

For individuals, the pressure to conform to the national identity can lead to a sense of alienation and loss of identity. Minority groups may feel that their cultural heritage is devalued or erased, leading to resentment and resistance. Moreover, the suppression of cultural diversity can create social divisions and tensions, as those who do not conform to the national identity are seen as outsiders or threats to national unity.

Case Studies: Nationalist Policies and Cultural Suppression

- Turkey (Kurdish Language Ban): In an effort to promote Turkish nationalism and cultural unity, the Turkish government implemented policies that banned the use of the Kurdish language in public life. This policy, along with other measures aimed at suppressing Kurdish identity, led to significant tensions and conflict between the Turkish state and the Kurdish population.

- China (Uyghur Cultural Suppression): The Chinese government's efforts to assimilate the Uyghur Muslim population in Xinjiang have included restrictions on religious practices, language use, and cultural traditions. These policies, driven by a desire for national unity and control, have led to widespread human rights abuses and the erosion of Uyghur cultural identity.

- France (Laïcité and Religious Expression): France's strict secularism, or laïcité, has led to policies that restrict religious expression in public life, particularly for Muslim women who wear headscarves. While these policies are intended to promote national unity and secular values, they have been criticized for marginalizing religious minorities and undermining cultural diversity.

Social Hierarchies and Exclusion

Nationalist movements often reinforce social hierarchies based on ethnicity, race, religion, or other identity markers. These hierarchies privilege certain groups while marginalizing others, perpetuating systemic inequalities and discrimination. The exclusionary nature of nationalist ideologies is a significant obstacle to social justice and equality.

Nationalist ideologies often elevate one ethnic, racial, or religious group as the true or rightful members of the nation, creating a hierarchy that privileges this group over others. This hierarchy can be based on various factors, including ancestry, skin color, religious affiliation, or cultural practices. By defining the nation in exclusive terms, nationalism legitimizes and perpetuates these social hierarchies, leading to the marginalization and exclusion of those who do not fit the national ideal.

For example, in many cases of ethnic nationalism, the dominant ethnic group is seen as the true embodiment of the nation, while other groups are viewed as inferior or less legitimate members of the society. Similarly, religious nationalism often elevates the dominant religion as the core of national identity, marginalizing those who follow different faiths. These hierarchies can be deeply entrenched, leading to systemic inequalities in access to resources, political power, and social status.

Nationalist ideologies play a significant role in perpetuating systemic inequalities within society. By privileging certain groups over others, nationalism reinforces existing social divisions and power imbalances. These inequalities can manifest in various ways, including disparities in education, employment, housing, and political representation. Moreover, the exclusionary nature of nationalist ideologies can lead to discrimination and violence against marginalized groups, further entrenching their disadvantaged position.

Systemic inequalities are often justified by nationalist rhetoric that portrays the dominant group as the rightful or superior members of the nation. This rhetoric can be used to legitimize discriminatory policies, such as segregation, apartheid, or exclusionary immigration laws. In some cases, nationalism may also be used to justify violence or repression against marginalized groups, as a means of maintaining social order or protecting the national identity.

Case Studies: Caste, Race, and Nationalist Movements

- India (Hindu Nationalism and the Caste System): Hindu nationalism, or Hindutva, has been linked to the perpetuation of the caste system in India. Despite legal efforts to abolish caste-based discrimination, nationalist rhetoric often reinforces traditional social hierarchies, privileging upper-caste Hindus and marginalizing lower-caste and Dalit communities.

- South Africa (Apartheid and Afrikaner Nationalism): The apartheid system in South Africa was driven by Afrikaner nationalism, which sought to maintain white supremacy and racial segregation. The nationalist ideology of the ruling Afrikaner minority justified systemic racial inequalities, leading to decades of oppression and violence against the black majority.

- The United States (Jim Crow and White Nationalism): The Jim Crow era in the United States was marked by the rise of white nationalism, which sought to maintain racial hierarchies and segregation. Nationalist rhetoric was used to justify discriminatory laws and practices that disenfranchised and marginalized African Americans, leading to systemic inequalities that persist to this day.

Exclusionary Policies and Practices

Nationalist governments and movements have historically implemented exclusionary policies and practices that target minority groups, immigrants, or other perceived outsiders. These policies often violate human rights and undermine principles of equality and inclusion, leading to social and political instability.

Nationalist ideologies frequently lead to the implementation of discriminatory laws and policies that exclude or marginalize certain groups within society. These policies can take various forms, including immigration restrictions, assimilationist agendas, and laws that target specific religious or ethnic communities. The goal of these policies is often to preserve the national identity or protect the interests of the dominant group, at the expense of others.

Immigration restrictions are a common manifestation of nationalist exclusion, as governments seek to limit the entry of foreigners who are perceived as threats to the nation's cultural or economic well-being. These restrictions can be based on ethnicity, religion, or nationality, and they often result in the exclusion or mistreatment of refugees, asylum seekers, and migrant workers.

Assimilationist policies are another form of exclusion, as they seek to force minority groups to conform to the national identity. These policies may include language requirements, religious conversion, or the suppression of cultural practices. While these measures are often justified as necessary for national unity, they can lead to the erasure of minority identities and the violation of individual rights.

The impact of exclusionary nationalist policies on human rights and equality is profound. By targeting specific groups for exclusion or assimilation, these policies undermine the principles of equality and non-discrimination that are fundamental to human rights. Minority groups may be denied access to education, employment, healthcare, and other basic services, leading to social and economic disparities.

Moreover, exclusionary policies can lead to the violation of fundamental rights, such as freedom of religion, freedom of expression, and the right to participate in political life. In some cases, these policies may also result in violence, displacement, or even genocide, as nationalist governments seek to eliminate or expel those who do not fit the national ideal.

Case Studies: Nationalist Governments and Exclusionary Policies

- The United States (Immigration Restrictions and the Muslim Ban): The Trump administration's immigration policies, including the Muslim Ban, were driven by nationalist rhetoric that portrayed immigrants and refugees as threats to national security and cultural identity. These policies led to the exclusion of individuals based on their religion or nationality, raising concerns about human rights violations and discrimination.

- France (Burqa Ban and Religious Expression): France's ban on the wearing of full-face veils, or burqas, in public spaces is an example of exclusionary nationalist policies targeting religious minorities. The policy, justified as a measure to promote secularism and national unity, has been criticized for violating the rights of Muslim women and undermining religious freedom.

- China (Reeducation Camps and Uyghur Assimilation): The Chinese government's policies targeting the Uyghur Muslim population in Xinjiang, including the establishment of reeducation camps, are driven by nationalist and assimilationist goals. These policies have led to widespread human rights abuses, including forced detention, cultural suppression, and violations of religious freedom.

Inter-National Conflicts

Nationalist ideas sometimes put the needs of the nation-state ahead of those of other countries, which fuels rivalry and strife among states. As countries strive to establish their dominance or defend their sovereignty, this can lead to diplomatic tensions, trade conflicts, and even wars. Since nationalist ideas sometimes give the nation-state's interests top priority over world cooperation or multilateralism, they greatly influence international relations. This focus on national sovereignty and self-interest can result in a zero-sum approach to world affairs whereby countries see one another as rivals rather than allies. Under these circumstances, nationalist leaders might pursue military interventions, trade protectionism, or territorial expansion among other aggressive foreign policies. Although these laws are sometimes justified as required for the defence or advancement of the national interests, they can also cause diplomatic problems, economic strife, and even wars. As each country strives to establish its supremacy or defend its interests, the rivalry and competition inherent in nationalist ideas can cause problems between national boundaries. Territorial conflicts, trade wars, and military confrontations are among the several ways this might show up. Sometimes nationalist leaders will mobilise domestic support by depicting the country as under danger from outside enemies, so leveraging foreign conflicts. Furthermore since nationalist ideas sometimes entail historical grievances, territorial claims, or cultural differences, they can aggravate already existing conflicts between countries. These disputes can be challenging to settle since they usually stem from strongly felt nationalist ideas and identities. Consequently, a cycle of rivalry and conflict results that compromises world peace and stability. Many of the major wars and conflicts of history have been driven by nationalist ideas. For instance, as countries sought to assert their dominance on the world scene and pursue territorial expansion, the emergence of nationalist movements in Europe in the 19th and 20th centuries helped to spark World Wars I and II. Modern nationalism still fuels diplomatic tensions and trade conflicts between countries. Under the Trump administration, for instance, the nationalist-driven trade policies of the United States resulted in a trade war with China, so causing economic disturbance and damaged relations between the two nations. Likewise, nationalist rhetoric and policies have stoked tensions between Russia and its neighbours, so sparking wars including the annexation of Crimea and the continuing conflict in Ukraine.

Nationalism as a Catalyst for War —

- World War I (Europe): The rise of nationalist movements in Europe in the late 19th and early 20th centuries was a significant factor in the outbreak of World War I. Nationalist leaders sought to assert their nation's dominance, leading to a web of alliances and rivalries that ultimately culminated in the conflict.

- World War II (Europe and Asia): The aggressive nationalism of Nazi Germany, Imperial Japan, and Fascist Italy was a key driver of World War II. These regimes pursued territorial expansion and sought to create ethnically homogeneous states, leading to the devastation of the war and the genocide of millions of people.

- The Yugoslav Wars (Balkans): The breakup of Yugoslavia in the 1990s was marked by intense nationalist conflicts between different ethnic and religious groups. Nationalist leaders used ethnic and religious identities to justify acts of genocide, ethnic cleansing, and war, leading to the fragmentation of the country and the loss of countless lives.

• • •

CHAPTER II

Radical Nationalism in Modi's India

To understand how radical nationalism has played a role in Modi's leadership, it is essential to examine the specific strategies and policies that have been used to promote this ideology and consolidate power.

1. Hindu Nationalism and the RSS

Modi's political career and ideology are deeply rooted in the RSS, which has been instrumental in shaping his vision of India as a Hindu nation. The RSS promotes the idea of Hindutva, or "Hinduness," which seeks to define Indian culture in terms of Hindu values and traditions. This ideology is exclusionary, as it views other religious communities, particularly Muslims and Christians, as outsiders who do not belong to the "true" Indian nation. The RSS and its affiliates, collectively known as the Sangh Parivar, have been at the forefront of promoting Hindu nationalist policies and mobilizing support for the BJP. They have also played a key role in spreading radical nationalist narratives through their extensive network of schools, media outlets, and social organizations. Under Modi's leadership, the influence of the RSS on government policy has grown significantly. This is evident in the promotion of Hindu cultural and religious symbols, the rewriting of history textbooks to reflect a Hindu nationalist perspective, and the increasing marginalization of minority communities.

2. The Politics of Exclusion

One of the central strategies of radical nationalism is the creation of a sense of unity among the majority population by excluding and demonizing certain groups. In Modi's India, this has been achieved through a combination of legal measures, propaganda, and violence. The CAA and NRC are perhaps the most significant examples of how the Modi government has sought to exclude Muslims from the national community. The CAA, which grants citizenship to non-Muslim refugees from neighboring countries, has been widely criticized as discriminatory. The NRC, which was first implemented in the state of Assam, requires citizens to prove their citizenship through documentation, a process that has disproportionately affected Muslims. These policies have been accompanied by a broader campaign of vilification against Muslims, who are often portrayed in government and media narratives as outsiders, invaders, or terrorists. This has led to an increase in hate crimes and violence against Muslims, as well as a growing sense of fear and insecurity within the community. The exclusion of Muslims from the national narrative is also evident in the government's response to the protests against the CAA and NRC. The protests, which were led by students, activists, and civil society groups, were met with a heavy-handed crackdown by the police and security forces. Protesters were labeled as "anti-national" and "terrorists," and many were arrested or harassed. The politics of exclusion is not limited to Muslims. Other minority communities, such as Christians, Dalits (formerly known as "untouchables"), and Adivasis (indigenous peoples), have also faced increasing marginalization and violence under Modi's government. This has been accompanied by efforts to suppress dissent and criticism from civil society, the media, and opposition parties.

3. Centralization of Power

Another key aspect of radical nationalism is the centralization of power in the hands of a single leader or ruling party. Modi's leadership has been marked by a significant centralization of authority, with power increasingly concentrated in the Prime

Minister's Office (PMO) and a small group of trusted advisors. This centralization of power has been accompanied by the weakening of democratic institutions and checks and balances. The independence of the judiciary has come under question, with allegations of political interference in judicial appointments and decisions. The autonomy of state governments has also been eroded, with the central government increasingly asserting its authority over state-level policies. Modi's government has also used state institutions, such as the police, intelligence agencies, and tax authorities, to target political opponents, activists, and journalists. These actions have created a climate of fear and self-censorship, where dissenting voices are increasingly silenced. The centralization of power has been justified by the need for strong leadership to address the nation's challenges, including economic development, national security, and social harmony. However, this has come at the cost of democratic norms and civil liberties, raising concerns about the erosion of India's democratic institutions and the emergence of authoritarianism.

4. Cult of Personality

Radical nationalist movements often rely on the creation of a cult of personality around the leader, who is portrayed as the embodiment of the nation's values and aspirations. Modi has successfully cultivated such a cult of personality, positioning himself as a strong, decisive leader who is dedicated to the welfare of the nation. This cult of personality is evident in the extensive use of Modi's image and name in government propaganda, social media, and public events. Modi is often portrayed as a "man of the people," who understands the struggles of ordinary citizens and is committed to their upliftment. His humble beginnings as a tea seller are frequently highlighted as a symbol of his connection to the common people. Modi's speeches and public appearances are carefully choreographed to reinforce his image as a strong leader. He regularly uses populist rhetoric, citing themes of nationalism, growth, and cultural pride, while presenting himself as the savior of the nation. The cult of personality around Modi has been reinforced by the loyalty and devotion of his supporters, who often see him as a messianic figure. This has created a political environment where criticism of Modi is often equated with disloyalty to the nation, further stifling dissent and opposition.

5. Media Control and Propaganda

Control of the media and the dissemination of propaganda are essential tools for radical nationalists to shape public opinion and maintain power. Under Modi's leadership, there has been a considerable increase in government influence over the media, with many news outlets matching their coverage with the government's narrative. The government has also used social media aggressively to convey its message and generate support. Modi's social media presence is among the largest of any international leader, and his online followers are typically extremely organized and aggressive in defending his image and assaulting his adversaries. At the same time, journalists and media organizations that are critical of the administration have experienced harassment, legal action, and violence. This has generated a climate of fear and self-censorship in the media, where critical voices are increasingly repressed. The use of propaganda and media control has allowed the Modi government to mould the public narrative, depict itself as the champion of national interests, and delegitimize its opponents. This has been crucial in preserving popular support for the government, even while it pursues policies that erode democratic norms and civil rights.

6. International Implications

The growth of radical nationalism under Modi's leadership has not only changed India's domestic politics but has also had important repercussions for its international relations. Modi's foreign policy has been characterized by a more forceful and nationalist approach, notably in interactions with neighboring countries such as Pakistan and China. The Modi government's emphasis on Hindu nationalism has also altered India's relations with the Muslim world. While India has always maintained strong ties with countries in the Middle East, there have been concerns regarding the influence of the Modi government's domestic policies on these partnerships. At the same time, Modi has pushed to depict India as a global leader and a protector of democratic norms. However, this has been hampered by the increasing authoritarian tendencies of his government, which have generated fears about the future of democracy in India. The international community has taken note of these trends, with certain countries and organizations expressing worry about the deterioration of democratic principles and the rise of intolerance in India. However, Modi's government has mostly disregarded these complaints, characterising them as intervention in India's domestic affairs.

My friends, Narendra Modi's leadership in India is a modern example of how radical nationalism may be utilised to consolidate power and foster authoritarian tendencies within a democratic framework. Modi's dedication to Hindu nationalism, centralisation of authority, use of populist rhetoric, and cultivation of a personality cult have all contributed to the deterioration of democratic norms and marginalisation of minority groups. As history has demonstrated, the growth of radical nationalism and the establishment of totalitarian regimes can have disastrous effects for both the country and the international community. It is critical to recognise warning indicators and take action to defend democratic institutions, civil liberties, and human rights. Only by doing so will we be able to prevent the rise of authoritarianism and uphold democratic, tolerant, and human rights ideals.

• • •

CHAPTER III

Historical Revisionism

Historical revisionism—the selective interpretation or distortion of historical events done so as part of a national narrative—is a common activity of nationalist organisations. This approach sometimes minimises or totally ignores the darker sides of the nation's past, including injustices, crimes, and failures, while elevating its accomplishments, heroes, and symbols. For nationalist leaders, historical revisionism may be a useful tactic since it helps to build a coherent and romanticised national identity that can be used to defend present policies and promote unity among the people.

But this selective presentation of history can also reinforce negative preconceptions and falsehoods. Nationalist movements can impede attempts to recognise and redress historical injustices including colonialism, genocide, and systematic discrimination by either neglecting or distorting previous events. This lack of recognition can hinder healing and reconciliation between many groups inside a country or between countries, therefore extending divisions and feeding continuous strife.

Historical revisionism can greatly affect collective memory and national identity. Nationalist groups can inculcate in the people a feeling of superiority and exceptionalism by supporting a narrative of history that stresses the achievements and values of their country. This can lead to a mistaken view of the nation's involvement in world history, whereby the country is seen as a continuous victim or hero rather than as a participant in a complicated web of historical events including both positive and negative actions.

Additionally supporting current social structures and inequality is this idealised national identity. For instance, nationalist movements can hide the historical foundations of racial and ethnic inequalities by downplaying the effects of colonialism or slavery, therefore complicating current efforts to solve these problems. Furthermore, the focus on some historical personalities and events could marginalise the experiences and efforts of minority groups, hence strengthening their exclusion from the national story.

Case Studies: Historical Revisionism in Nationalist Movements —

Japan (War Crimes and National Identity): In Japan, nationalist movements have often engaged in historical revisionism by downplaying or denying the atrocities committed by Japanese forces during World War II, such as the Nanking Massacre and the use of "comfort women." This revisionism has been reflected in school textbooks, public statements by nationalist politicians, and the veneration of war criminals at sites like the Yasukuni Shrine. This selective portrayal of history has strained Japan's relations with its neighbors, particularly China and South Korea, and has hindered efforts at reconciliation.

Turkey (The Armenian Genocide): In Turkey, nationalist leaders have long denied the Armenian Genocide, a systematic campaign of mass murder and forced deportation carried out by the Ottoman Empire during World War I. This denial is a cornerstone of Turkish nationalist identity, with the government and nationalist organizations actively working to suppress recognition of the genocide both domestically and internationally. The refusal to acknowledge this historical atrocity has perpetuated tensions between Turkey and Armenia, as well as within Turkey itself, where minority groups continue to face discrimination.

The United States (The Lost Cause and Confederate Monuments): In the United States, the "Lost Cause" narrative, which emerged after the Civil War, is a prime example of historical revisionism in service of nationalist ideology. This narrative glorifies the Confederacy, portraying it as a noble cause fought for states' rights rather than the preservation of slavery. This revisionist history has been perpetuated through monuments, school curricula, and popular culture, contributing to the ongoing racial divisions in the country and the resistance to addressing the legacy of slavery and segregation.

The Glorification of Nationalist Leaders and Symbols

Nationalist movements often glorify certain leaders, symbols, and events as embodiments of the nation's virtues and values. This glorification serves to reinforce the nationalist narrative and create a sense of continuity between the past and the present. However, this practice can also perpetuate divisions and hinder reconciliation efforts, as it often involves the elevation of figures and symbols associated with controversial or oppressive actions.

For example, the veneration of Confederate leaders in the United States, such as Robert E. Lee, has been a point of contention in recent years, with critics arguing that these figures represent a legacy of racism and oppression. Similarly, the celebration of colonial-era leaders in former European empires has been challenged by those who seek to acknowledge the injustices and violence associated with colonialism. The continued glorification of these leaders and symbols can prevent societies from fully coming to terms with their histories and from fostering a more inclusive and equitable national identity.

My friends, Historical revisionism is a potent tool for nationalist movements, allowing them to construct a cohesive and glorified national identity that supports their ideological goals. However, this selective interpretation of history comes at a significant cost. By ignoring or distorting the past, nationalist movements can perpetuate harmful myths, reinforce social hierarchies, and hinder efforts at reconciliation and understanding. As such, it is essential to critically examine and challenge historical revisionism wherever it appears, to promote a more accurate and inclusive understanding of the past and to foster a more just and equitable future.

• • •

CHAPTER IV

Historical Revisionism and The BJP Govt. (INDIA)

The political strategy of the Bharatiya Janata Party (BJP) in India has much benefited from historical revisionism. The BJP has aimed to match India's history with its ideological underpinnings, especially those of Hindutva, a kind of Hindu nationalism, by selectively reading and changing historical accounts. Both under the current leadership of Narendra Modi, who has been in office since 2014, and during the tenure of Atal Bihari Vajpayee, who was Prime Minister from 1998 to 2004, this revisionism is clear-cut. With major consequences for India's social fabric, educational system, and communal relations, the BJP's historical perspective has sought not only to honour Hindu civilisation but also to minimise or reinterpret the contributions of non-Hindu personalities and periods.

Tenure of Atal Bihari Vajpayee: Historical Revisionism

Under Atal Bihari Vajpayee, the BJP started working to change India's past to better represent its ideological bent. Though Vajpayee personally was renowned for his moderate approach in comparison to other BJP leaders, his government started various actions that prepared the stage for more comprehensive historical revisionism under next BJP rule.

1. Educational Reforms and Textbook Revisions : Revision of school textbooks was one of the most important features of historical revisionism under Vajpayee's direction. Under the direction of then-HRD Minister Murli Manohar Joshi, the National Council of Educational Research and Training (NCERT) set out to rewrite history textbooks to more fairly represent the BJP's ideological points of view. These changes included downplaying the

importance of the Mughal period, stressing the ancient and mediaeval Hindu kingdoms, and elevating Hindu warriors as Shivaji, Maharana Pratap, and others. Critics said that these revisions skewed historical events, excluded the contributions made by Muslim leaders, and encouraged a biassed perspective of Indian history among students.

2. Cultural Narratives and the Promotion of Hindutva values: The Vajpayee government also supported cultural narratives consistent with Hindutva values. This includes the support of celebrations and events stressing Hindu religious and cultural legacy while undervaluing the efforts of India's many communities. Particularly Muslims and Christians, the government's focus on India as a primarily Hindu country added to their rising sense of isolation.

Under Vajpayee, the BJP deliberately drew support for its nationalist program by skilfully using historical events and symbols. The party's backing for the Ram Janmabhoomi movement, which aimed to erect a temple at the disputed site in Ayodhya, was a good example of how historical revisionism and the manipulation of historical symbols were used to rally political support and polarize populations.

Historical Revisionism Under Narendra Modi's Leadership

Under Narendra Modi's direction, historical revisionism's trend grew especially more pronounced. Since coming to power in 2014, Modi's government has methodically pursued an ambition to change India's historical narrative in line with the BJP's ideological framework.

1. Aggressive Textbook Revisions: Under Modi's leadership, the modification of history textbooks has been undertaken more actively than during Vajpayee's term. The NCERT has conducted further changes, with a heavier focus on the ancient and medieval Hindu periods, while lowering the emphasis on the achievements of Muslim kings like Akbar, Aurangzeb, and others. Additionally, the contributions of freedom fighters aligned with the BJP's ideology, such as Vinayak Damodar Savarkar and Shyama Prasad Mukherjee,

have been elevated, often at the expense of figures like Jawaharlal Nehru and Mahatma Gandhi, whose ideas of secularism and inclusivity contrast with the BJP's vision.

2. Erasure and Reinterpretation of Historical people and Events: The Modi government has also been accused of erasing or reinterpreting the contributions of historical people who do not accord with the BJP's ideological narrative. This includes minimising the importance of India's first Prime Minister, Jawaharlal Nehru, who is generally portrayed in a bad manner, and reinterpreting the events of India's freedom war to stress the role of Hindutva leaders. For instance, there has been a determined campaign to portray Savarkar, a controversial figure noted for his early embrace of Hindu nationalism, as a crucial liberation warrior, despite his divisive legacy.

3. Renaming Cities and Landmarks: Another prominent component of historical revisionism under Modi has been the renaming of cities, streets, and landmarks to represent Hindu heritage. For example, Allahabad was renamed Prayagraj in 2018, a decision that was perceived as an attempt to whitewash the city's Mughal past and stress its historic Hindu significance. Similarly, Faizabad district was renamed Ayodhya, further underlining the BJP's focus on Hindu religious symbolism.Numerous streets, parks, and public institutions have been renamed around the country to reflect Hindu leaders and figures, typically replacing names connected with Muslim monarchs or colonial characters. For instance, Aurangzeb Road in Delhi was renamed Dr. APJ Abdul Kalam Road in 2015, a decision considered as symptomatic of the BJP's aim to reduce the legacy of one of India's most contentious Mughal kings. These renaming initiatives have spurred concerns over the erasing of India's varied history and the marginalization of Muslim contributions to Indian culture and heritage.

4. Glorification of Hindu Symbols and Leaders: The Modi government has also actively glorified Hindu symbols and leaders, often to the exclusion of others. The Statue of Unity, a colossal statue of Sardar Vallabhbhai Patel, was inaugurated by Modi in

2018. While Patel is widely respected as one of India's founding fathers, the BJP's promotion of his legacy is often seen as an attempt to diminish the influence of Jawaharlal Nehru, who is portrayed by the BJP as being too soft on issues of national unity and security. The statue, which is the tallest in the world, symbolizes the BJP's effort to reclaim nationalist symbols and reinterpret them in line with its ideology.

In the field of historical revisionism, the building of the Ram Temple in Ayodhya marks the most important and symbolic accomplishment of Modi's government. Modi personally set the ground stone in 2020 following the 2019 Supreme Court decision allowing the building of the temple. Considered as the pinnacle of the decades-long Ram Janmabhoomi agitation and a huge triumph for Hindutva philosophy, the temple's construction marks Reinforcing the BJP's narrative of Hindu cultural and religious supremacy, the temple has evolved into a potent emblem of the goal for a Hindu nation.

Under Modi's government, there has also been an increasing trend of suppressing dissenting historical narratives challenging the BJP's interpretation of history. Scholars, authors, and activists who offer different perspectives of India's past—especially those emphasising the contributions of Muslims, Dalits, and other underprivileged groups—have experienced harassment, censorship, and, in some cases violence. This censoring of competing points of view has created a climate whereby only the mainstream, BJP-approved narrative is let to flourish, therefore suppressing critical interaction with history.

- Control Over Historical Institutions: The Modi government has also aimed at managing important historical and cultural establishments including the National Archives and the Indian Council of Historical Research (ICHR). The government has guaranteed that the research and historical narratives supported by these bodies complement its vision by selecting people consistent with its values to run these establishments. This management of historical institutions has strengthened the BJP's capacity to influence public perspective of India's past.

Implications of Historical Revisionism by the BJP

The historical revisionism undertaken by the BJP has profound implications for India's social fabric, education system, and communal relations. By promoting a selective and often distorted version of history, the BJP has contributed to the polarization of Indian society along religious and communal lines. The glorification of Hindu symbols and leaders, coupled with the erasure or marginalization of Muslim contributions, has deepened the sense of alienation and exclusion among India's religious minorities.

In the educational sphere, the revision of history textbooks has created a generation of students with a skewed understanding of India's past. The emphasis on a singular narrative that glorifies Hindu civilization while downplaying or ignoring other contributions risks fostering intolerance and prejudice among young people. This biased portrayal of history undermines the values of pluralism, secularism, and inclusivity that are enshrined in India's Constitution.

Furthermore, the use of historical revisionism as a political tool has heightened communal tensions and conflicts. The renaming of cities, the construction of religious monuments, and the glorification of certain historical figures have all served to inflame communal sentiments and deepen divisions within Indian society. This has led to a rise in communal violence, hate crimes, and social unrest, as different groups vie for recognition and validation of their historical narratives.

The BJP's historical revisionism under both Vajpayee and Modi's leadership represents a significant departure from India's traditionally pluralistic approach to history. By promoting a selective and exclusionary version of history, the BJP has sought to reshape India's national identity in line with its ideological vision of a Hindu nation. However, this approach carries significant risks, as it undermines the principles of inclusivity, diversity, and secularism that are central to India's democratic fabric.

• • •

However, the BJP's historical revisionism is a form of patriotism. Hitler had propagated this ideology in Germany. Mussolini brought back the barbarism of the Middle Ages to Italy. Or that Franco of Spain destroyed Pablo Picasso's studio on the basis of such a theory. The education of the Sangh Parivar reminds one of Hitler's education policy. At that time three types of schools were established in Germany - (1) Adolf Hitler School (2) National Political Institute of Education (3) Order Castles. In the castles of this order was taught the fatal lesson - that the German nation is the only one bearing pure blood. So everything is fine with them. The Jews are the source of all uncleanness. By crushing them, the German nation, the vehicle of pure blood and pure culture, must be established in its own country and throughout the world. Perhaps this is what is called intellectual fascism. The same fascism is being imposed today in the education conference, in the new activities related to education.

Saraswati Vandana and Sanskrit language education need to be considered from this perspective. The thing is, if a dull wise Arya digs his head again and again at Saraswati's doorstep and thinks that education will be complete, let him do it. No objection. Please, don't force that 'goddess' on everyone's neck. To sing her praises, one must first sing of Venus, the goddess of beauty, and of Aphrodite and Apello. Do you agree with me?

The Radhakrishnan Commission was set up in 48-49. It was an important recommendation of the committee. Read not only the life stories of Hinduism or Hindu spiritual leaders, but also of

Buddha-Confucius-Zoroastrian-Socrates-Jesus-Mohammad-Kabir-Nanak and master the radical human vision of religion. It is this vision that can sustain the pluralistic culture of a pluralistic society. Isn't the Sangh Parivar and the central government's education reforms hurting the basic spirit of the commission?

Mudaliar Commission was set up in 1952-53. One of the conclusions of the commission was: "The basic and fundamental pattern of education should be liberal-nationalist-secular-humanist. Otherwise, it will be of no use to the country. " The Kothari Commission is the most well-organised. His recommendation was that in the question of nation-building, education should leave the rigid classical pattern and adopt the modern scientific approach. Is the re-establishment of the Vedas, Upanishads and Sanskrit compatible with the idea of these commissions? The time has come for any reform-free Indian to think about it.

Sanskrit Education

The government of the Sangh Parivar has strongly advocated the teaching of Sanskrit language. In the RSS manifesto, it was clearly stated that Sanskrit is Indian culture. Sanskrit is essential for the development and preservation of Indian culture.

What did Swami Vivekananda feel about this Sanskrit? In a letter written by him to the editor of 'Udbhavana' magazine from America on February 20, 1900 AD, he commented on Sanskrit - "Since our country has had all the knowledge of Sanskrit since ancient times, an immense sea has stood between the learned and the common man. " Is the gairik Sangh Parivar not making the demand for the introduction of Sanskrit even more extravagant? At the end of the letter, Swamiji said, "Look at Sanskrit. When people are alive, they speak. Do you speak the language of the dead? What is he up to? Ten pages long long adjective followed by adjective, ki bahadur samas, ki shansh. It's all signs of death. When the country began to fall, that sign appeared. " "Aren't the Sanskrit people trying to kill the country by imposing that "dead language" ?"

'Sanskrit is the mother of all Indian languages' - this old idea has been destroyed by almost every reformist scientist. Some say, Sanskrit old grandmother, or old grandfather - never mother. The mother tongue is the Prakrit language. It is by resorting to the literary and practical forms of this Prakrit language that literary and worldly distortions have been created and from which every language of the northern path has been born. Nature is the language of the people and the people. Sanskrit, on the other hand, is the official language. It had nothing to do with the people. It is derived from the Vedic language. The grammarian Panini or contributed to the formulation of that language. A rich literature has been created in this language, but Kalidasa-Vasa-Sudraka have taken shelter of Sanskrit as well as literary and secular Prakrit in their plays, poems and epics. You don't need to do much. This is evident when one looks at Kalidasa's 'Abhigyana Shakuntalam' and the Shudra's 'Mrichchakatike'. No one relied solely on Sanskrit: alternative living languages were also adopted. That's why their literature is so rich.

Even if you do not want to accept this information (Truth), it must be admitted that in order to learn Sanskrit, it is necessary to memorize all the languages, especially the southern languages and even the languages of different tribes. Because these languages also play a role in the formation of Indian society and culture. The upper caste Benia Hindus are, of course, the majority. But if minorities from all over India come together, the majority will be reduced to a minority. Therefore, the insistence of those 'majority' representatives, their cultural aggression can not be accepted at all. This is destroying the unity of the country.

If inciting more than 500 communal riots is punishable in the court of morality, then all these education amendments are punishable in equal measure. There are two goals behind all this - we will be the only ones, and everyone will have to put their heads down. The second goal is to take the country to the medieval darkness by completely destroying the scientific rational thinking. This is the nature of our education system. There again the consumerist trend is going to start under the pressure of globalization. Then there will be no more 'spiritualisation' and so-called 'Hindutvaisation'. More and more mosques will be destroyed, communal riots will occur, you can say, the fascist equation is all together. In this equation, today efforts are being made to transform the Indian Council of Historical Research, Social Science Research, Philosophical Research and Indian Institute of Advanced Study. Today Romila Thapar, Irfan Habib have been sacked. Tomorrow maybe Nazrul-Sukanta will be banned, Khudiram-Bhagat Singh will be made Agamarka Hinduveer. Rabindranath is not left out. He should probably be labeled a traitor. Those who are doing this are, in fact, bloodthirsty cowards. They were born in this country. But not in this country. They're the real outsiders.

However, friends, to get rid of all this, you must know the real truth. You really need to be educated. Public opinion has to be created against it. People should be explained not by hot blood, but by cold reason. There is no problem where the general people of the country elect the government. It is the duty of the educated to present the truth to the people.

• • •

CHAPTER V

Rabindranath's Thoughts on Nationalism

Rabindranath Tagore was an outstanding poet, philosopher, playwright, dramatist, composer, social reformer and a talented painter. He completed his higher education in England. In 1913 Tagore became the first non-European and the first lyricist to win the Nobel Prize in Literature.Tagore was known by the sobriquets Gurudeb, Kobiguru, and Biswokobi. A Bengali Brahmin from Calcutta, British India.

To my readers, Now I will try to figure out what Rabindranath Tagore, the most prominent Indian thinker of the 20th century, thought about nationalism.

In the public discourse, it would seem that Rabindranath was strongly obsessed with nationalism. But the authenticity of theory, data and logic presents the opposite reality. However, following the political and cultural nature of the 19th century, he also leaned towards nationalism. His association with the "Hindu Mela" or the "Sanjeevani Sabha" is only a boyish chapter, not a sign of a mature Rabindranath. But yes, he responded to the "Swadeshi" movement. Rabindranath passed 40 then. Padayatra, Rakhi Bandhan - everything is done. Again he stood back from the trend of "Swadeshi" movement. The question is, despite him, why is he not a nationalist?

In fact, Rabindranath's understanding of nationalism was changing at the height of the "Swadeshi" movement. His great proof is the novel 'Ghare Baire' (1916). In this novel, Rabindranath showed how nationalism incites communalism, sows the seeds of division in the name of reconciliation. In another novel "Gora" (1910) written during the period of "Swadeshi" movement, he showed the consequences of staunch patriotism and nationalism. Narrow nationalism engulfs the novel's main character 'Gora' as he searches for the boundaries of self-identity.

But did Rabindranath create a lesson critical of nationalism in himself? Basically, within the first two decades of the 20th century, the scene of local and world politics changed drastically. Communalism, mass discontent, divergent approaches to the search for identity were tearing apart the politics of the Indian subcontinent. The aims and objectives of the Congress and the Muslim League were pushing each other apart. On the other hand, the people of the world had to listen to the gunfire of the world war. The epics of modernity were falling apart. In the post-Renaissance world, it was Europe that created the rhetoric of humanism, modernity, freedom, equality. Once again, Europe's hands are in the hands of the unbearable demand for weapons. Long before the First World War, a new world and India were unfolding before the 'romantic' Rabindranath. Rabindranath showed the crisis of nation and nationalism more clearly during the First World War. Rabindranath's Nationalism was published in 1917 after his speeches in America and Japan were compiled. In three essays of this book, he paints a picture of nationalism developed in the West, Japan and India. Rabindranath says here, Neither the colourless vagueness of cosmopolitanism, nor the fierce self-idolatry of nation-worship, is the goal of human history. And India has been trying to accomplish her task through social regulation of differences, on the one hand, and the spiritual recognition of unity on the other. She (India) has made grave errors in setting up the boundary walls too rigidly between races, in perpetuating in her classifications the results of inferiority; often she has crippled her children's minds and narrowed their lives in order to fit them into her social forms; but for centuries new experiments have been made and adjustments carried out.

Her (India) mission has been like that of a hostess who has to provide proper accommodation for numerous guests, whose habits and requirements are different from one another.This gives rise to infinite complexities whose solution depends not merely upon tactfulness but upon sympathy and true realisation of the unity of man. Towards this realisation have worked, from the early time of the Upanishads up to the present moment, a series of great spiritual teachers, whose one object has been to set at naught all differences of man by the overflow of our consciousness of God. In fact, our history has not been of the rise and fall of kingdoms, of fights for political supremacy. In our country records of these days have been despised and forgotten, for they in no way represent the true history of our people. Our history is that of our social life and attainment of spiritual ideals. But we feel that our task is not yet done. The world-flood has swept over our country,new elements have been introduced, and wider adjustments are waiting to be made. We feel this all the more, because the teaching and example of the West have entirely run counter to what we think was given to India to accomplish. In the West the national machinery of commerce and politics turns out neatly compressed bales of humanity which have their use and high market value; but they are bound in iron hoops, labelled and separated off with scientific care and precision. Obviously God made man to be human; but this modern product has such marvellous square-cut finish, savouring of gigantic manufacture, that the Creator will find it difficult to recognize it as a thing of spirit and a creature made in His own divine image. He said – Take it in whatever spirit you like, here is India, of about fifty centuries at least, who tried to live peacefully and think deeply, the India devoid of all politics, the India of no nations, whose one ambition has been to know this world as of soul, to live here every moment of her life in the meek spirit of adoration, in the glad consciousness of an eternal and personal relationship with it. It was upon this remote portion of humanity, childlike in its manner, with the wisdom of the old, that the Nation of the West burst in.Through all the fights and intrigues and deceptions of her earlier history India had remained aloof. Because her homes, her fields, her temples of worship, her schools, where her teachers and students lived together in the atmosphere of simplicity and devotion and learning, her village self-government with its simple laws and peaceful administration—all these truly belonged to her. But her thrones were not her concern.

They passed over her head like clouds, now tinged with purple gorgeousness, nowblack with the threat of thunder. Often they brought devastations in their wake, but they were like catastrophes of nature whose traces are soon forgotten. But this time it was different. It was not a mere drift over her surface of life,—drift of cavalry and foot soldiers, richly caparisoned elephants, white tents and canopies,strings of patient camels bearing the loads of royalty, bands of kettle-drums and flutes,marble domes of mosques, palaces and tombs, like the bubbles of the foaming wine of extravagance; stories of treachery and loyal devotion, of changes of fortune, of dramatic surprises of fate. This time it was the Nation of the West driving its tentacles of machinery deep down into the soil. Therefore I say to you, it is we who are called as witnesses to give evidence as to what our Nation has been to humanity. We had known the hordes of Mughals and Pathans who invaded India, but we had known them as human races, with their own religions and customs, likes and dislikes,—we had never known them as a nation. We loved and hated them as occasions arose; we fought for them and against them, talked with them in a language which was theirs as well as our own, and guided the destiny of the Empire in which we had our active share. But this time we had to deal, not with kings, not with human races, but with a nation—we, who are no nation ourselves.

He defines 'Nation' as a political and economic unity; Nationalism mobilises the masses to achieve largely mechanical ends. Rabindranath issued a warning that nationalism is an epidemic of cruel evil, harmful to the human world. Rabindranath believed that nationalism was the driving force behind the mechanised civilization of Europe and the West. Its sole purpose is to exploit and empty the subjugated countries. The nationalism of Western civilization is a grave danger to the entire human race and the entire human civilization. Rabindranath wrote with deep sadness and anger in his essay 'Crisis of Civilization' at the end of his life, "It has become impossible to respect the civilization-conceit of the Western nation. It has shown us its strength. It has not been able to show its liberation...

Rabindranath has clearly said this in his essay "Sikshar Milan",That nation is formed by truth but nationalism is not true. According to him, nationalism is a kind of stupidity, where the pride of the country is revealed. This is a repu where there is more tension towards yourself than towards everyone else.

According to Rabindranath Tagore, What is this Nation?

A nation, in the sense of the political and economic union of a people, is that aspect which a whole population assumes when organised for a mechanical purpose. Society as such has no ulterior purpose. It is an end in itself. It is a spontaneous self-expression of man as a social being. It is a natural regulation of human relationships, so that men can develop ideals of life in cooperation with one another. It also has a political side, but this is only for a special purpose. It is for self-preservation. It is merely the side of power, not of human ideals. And in the early days it had its separate place in society,restricted to the professionals. But when with the help of science and the perfecting of organisation this power begins to grow and brings in harvests of wealth, then it crosses its boundaries with amazing rapidity. For then it goads all its neighbouring societies with greed of material prosperity, and consequent mutual jealousy, and by the fear of each other's growth into powerfulness. The time comes when it can stop no longer, for the competition grows keener, organisation grows vaster, and selfishness attains supremacy. Trading upon the greed and fear of man, it occupies more and more space in society, and at last becomes its ruling force. It is just possible that you have lost through habit consciousness that the living bonds of society are breaking up, and giving place to merely mechanical organisation. But you see signs of it everywhere. It is owing to this that war has been declared between man and woman, because the natural thread is snapping which holds them together in harmony; because man is driven to professionalism, producing wealth for himself and others, continually turning the wheel of power for his own sake or for the sake of the universal officialdom, leaving woman alone to wither and to die or to fight her own battle unaided. And thus where cooperation is natural has intruded competition. The very psychology of men and women about their mutual relation is changing and becoming the psychology of the primitive fighting elements, rather than of humanity seeking its completeness through the union based upon mutual self-surrender. For the elements which have lost their living bond of reality have lost the meaning of their existence. Like gaseous particles forced into a too narrow space, they come in continual conflict with each other till they burst the very arrangement which holds them in bondage. Then look at those who call themselves anarchists, who resent the imposition of power, in any form whatever, upon the individual. The only reason for this is that power has become too abstract—it is a scientific product made in the political laboratory of the Nation, through the dissolution of personal humanity. And what is the meaning of these strikes in the economic world, which like the prickly shrubs in a barren soil shoot up with renewed vigour each time they are cut down? What, but that the wealth-producing mechanism is incessantly growing into vast stature, out of proportion to all other needs of society,—and the full reality of man is more and more crushed under its weight? This state of things inevitably gives rise to eternal feuds among the elements freed from the wholeness and wholesomeness of human ideals, and interminable economic war is waged between capital and labour. For greed of wealth and power can never have a limit, and compromise of self-interest can never attain the final spirit of reconciliation. They must go on breeding jealousy and suspicion to the end—the end which only comes through some sudden catastrophe or a spiritual rebirth. When this organisation of politics and commerce, whose other name is the Nation, becomes all-powerful at the cost of the harmony of the higher social life, then it is an evil day for humanity. When a father becomes a gambler and his obligations to his family take the secondary place in his mind, then he is no longer a man, but an automaton led by the power of greed. Then he can do things which, in his normal state of mind, he would be ashamed to do. It is the same thing with society. When it allows itself to be turned into a perfect organisation of power, then there are few crimes which it is unable to perpetrate. Because success is the object and justification of a machine, while goodness only is the end and purpose of man. When this engine of organisation begins to attain a vast size, and those who are mechanics are made into parts of the machine, then the personal man is eliminated to a phantom, everything becomes a revolution of policy carried out by the human parts of the machine, with no twinge of pity or moral responsibility. It may happen that even through this apparatus the moral The nature of man tries to assert itself, but the whole series of ropes and pulleys creak and cry, the forces of the human heart become entangled among the forces of the human automaton, and only with difficulty can the moral purpose transmit itself into some tortured shape of result.

Rabindranath explained nation in purely social and human terms and made the link between individual and community. He gave more importance to society, which was the main basis of his self-help. So the poet can be called a kind of institutionalist (Communitarianism). He could not accept the modern concept of nation. But he has not completely ignored the nation. He said, "I am not against one nation in particular, but against the general idea of all nations."

Rabindranath nation means 'living entity and mental substance' that is, nation is born from human mind and cast from history; It is not the building block of any territory, language or religious unity. Nation is a living entity, united by honouring the memory of the past and preserving its heritage. In other words, the poet wants to convey that the nation is formed when there is a desire and determination to carry the glory and devotion of the past into the present and the future and protect it in a suitable way. If any community tries to live together despite its linguistic, geographical and religious diversity, it is the nation.

Rabindranath said that, The truth is that the spirit of conflict and conquest is at the origin and in the centre of Western nationalism;

its basis is not social co-operation. It has evolved a perfect organisation of power, but not spiritual idealism. It is like the pack of predatory creatures that must have its victims. With all its heart it cannot bear to see its hunting-grounds converted into cultivated fields. In fact, these nations are fighting among themselves for the extension of their victims and their reserve forests. Therefore the Western Nation acts like a dam to check the free flow of Western civilization into the country of the No-Nation. Because this civilization is the civilization of power, therefore it is exclusive, it is naturally unwilling to open its sources of power to those whom it has selected for its purposes of exploitation.

But all the same moral law is the law of humanity, and the exclusive civilization which thrives upon others who are barred from its benefit carries its own death-sentence in its moral limitations. The slavery that it gives rise to unconsciously drains its own love of freedom dry. The helplessness with which it weighs down its world of victims exerts its force of gravitation every moment upon the power that creates it. And the greater part of the world which is being denuded of its self-sustaining life by the Nation will one day becomes the most terrible of all its burdens, ready to drag it down into the bottom of destruction. Whenever Power removes all checks from its path to make its career easy, it triumphantly rides into its ultimate crash of death. Its moral brake becomes slacker every day without its knowing it, and its slippery path of ease becomes its path of doom.

Rabindranath deeply understood how blatant the snare of nationalism could be. From Rabindranath's discourse it seems that modernization, modernism, nationalism are inextricably linked. Along with these three contexts we can include two more phenomena - imperialism and colonialism. European nationalism is a friend of both. According to him,'This history has come to a stage when the moral man, the complete man, is more and more giving way, almost without knowing it, to make room for the political and the commercial man, the man of limited purpose. This process, aided by the wonderful progress in science, is assuming gigantic proportion and power, causing the upset of man's moral balance, obscuring his human side under the shadow of soul-less organisation. We have felt its iron grip at the root of our life, and for the sake of humanity we must stand up and give warning to all, that this nationalism is a cruel epidemic of evil that is sweeping over the human world of the present age, and eating into its moral vitality. I have a deep love and a great respect for the British race as human beings. It has produced great-hearted men, thinkers of great thoughts, doers of great deeds. It has given rise to a great literature. I know that these people love justice and freedom, and hate lies. They are clean in their minds, frank in their manners, true in their friendships; in their behaviour they are honest and reliable. The personal experience which I have had of their literary men has roused my admiration not merely for their power of thought or expression but for their chivalrous humanity. We have felt the greatness of these people as we feel the sun; but as for the Nation, it is for us a thick mist of a stifling nature covering the sun itself.'

Rabindranath wrote in the article 'Kalantar' in Bengali 1340, 'Even today in the United States of America the Negro race is humiliated with social indignity, and when such unfortunates are cremated alive, white-skinned women flock to enjoy the barbaric spectacle.' The irony of civilization is that this scene has been staged in recent times in America as well. It means that the idea of racial superiority is still entrenched, radical nationalism is still active in essence. At the end of his life, Rabindranath said in his essay 'Crisis of Civilization' that humanity is in crisis and without a way forward. The British and the Soviets called Russia a state power capable of 'exercising influence over many nations'. After Rabindranath's death, the number of aggressive or dominant nations continued to increase. Even oppressed nations are in conflict with each other.

He declared in an unhesitating voice,"Have you not seen, since the commencement of the existence of the Nation, that the dread of it has been the one goblin-dread with which the whole world has been trembling? Wherever there is a dark corner, there is the suspicion of its secret malevolence; and people live in a perpetual distrust of its back where it has no eyes. Every sound of a footstep, every rustle of movement in the neighbourhood, sends a thrill of terror all around. And this terror is the parent of all that is based in man's nature. It makes one almost openly unashamed of inhumanity. Clever lies become matters of self-congratulation. Solemn pledges become a farce,—laughable for their very solemnity.

The Nation, with all its paraphernalia of power and prosperity, its flags and pioushymns, its blasphemous prayers in the churches, and the literary mock thunders of its patriotic bragging, cannot hide the fact that the Nation is the greatest evil for the Nation, that all its precautions are against it, and any new birth of its fellow in the world is always followed in its mind by the dread of a new peril. It's one wish is to trade on the feebleness of the rest of the world, like some insects that are bred in the paralyzed flesh of victims kept just enough alive to make them toothsome and nutritious. Therefore it is ready to send its poisonous fluid into the vitals of the other living peoples, who, not being nations, are harmless. For this the Nation has had and still has its richest pasture in Asia. Great China, rich with her ancient wisdom and social ethics, her discipline of industry and self-control, is like a whale awakening the lust of spoil in the heart of the Nation. She is already carrying in her quivering flesh harpoons sent by the unerring aim of the Nation, the creature of science and selfishness. Her pitiful attempt to shake off her traditions of humanity, her social ideals, and spend her last exhausted resources in drilling herself into modern efficiency, is thwarted at every step by the Nation. It is tightening its financial ropes round her, trying to drag her up on the shore and cut her into pieces, and then go and offer public thanksgiving to God for supporting the one existing evil and shattering the possibility of a new one. And for all this the Nation has been claiming the gratitude of history, and all eternity for its exploitation; ordering its band of praise to be struck up from end to end of the world, declaring itself to be the salt of the earth, the flower of humanity, the blessing of

God hurled with all His force upon the naked skulls of the world of No-Nations."

Humanist Rabindranath believed that people were bigger than nations. So he strongly opposed Jatipunja (Nation Worship). Rabindranath believed that the alienation created by nationalism led to the degradation of humanity. Nationalist ideas sacrifice the individual. Here the independent development of human creative beings does not take place. Nationalism's passion for national pride, which creates division in people's minds, gradually turns people into monsters. All good thoughts, good consciousness of people are destroyed. Thus, nationalism brings about the crisis of human civilization.

What is the problem with the Indian subcontinent ?

He saw no signs of social cooperation in Western nationalism. On the other hand, the Indian subcontinent is mainly social dependent. Social power is not concentrated here in political power. Therefore, he raised the question whether European nationalism is applicable in Indian civilization and also rejected nationalism. Because the nationalism that arose in Europe is essentially a 'best combination of powers'. Rabindranath paints a grim picture, saying that Western nationalism is a predator that must necessarily have prey; Westerners cannot imagine converting hunting grounds into arable land. Not only that, Western nations are at war with each other; Because they seek to increase their hunting and protected forest land.

What is the problem with the Indian subcontinent? In this context, Rabindranath says, 'Our real problem is not political, but social.' In this case too, Ravi Babu is a strong critic of Europe. He thinks that the politics of Europe has controlled the ideals of Europe; And the Indian subcontinent is imitating him. The monstrous form of 'Nation' or 'Nationalism' can never be desirable in India. India aspires to be a country of universal ideals inspired by the greatest human and spiritual unity. But he did not ask India to remain isolated from the West. He talked about co-existence with them by taking only the best part of the West.

Rabindranath said that,To India has been given her problem from the beginning of history—it is the race problem. Races ethnologically different have in this country come into close contact.This fact has been and still continues to be the most important one in our history. It is our mission to face it and prove our humanity by dealing with it in the fullest truth. Until we fulfil our mission all other benefits will be denied us. There are other peoples in the world who have to overcome obstacles in their physical surroundings, or the menace of their powerful neighbours. They have organised their power till they are not only reasonably free from the tyranny of Nature and human neighbours, but have a surplus of it left in their hands to employ against others. But in India, our difficulties being internal, our history has been the history of continual social adjustment and not that of organised power for defence and aggression.

He said to the countrymen,'Government by the Nation—the Nation which is the organised self-interest of a whole people, where it is least human and least spiritual. Our only intimate experience of the Nation is with the British Nation, and as far as the government by the Nation goes there are reasons to believe that it is one of the best. Then, again, we have to consider that the West is necessary to the East. We are complementary to each other because of our different outlooks on life which have given us different aspects of truth. Therefore if it be true that the spirit of the West has come upon our fields in the in the guise of a storm it is nevertheless scattering living seeds that are immortal. And when in India we become able to assimilate in our life what is permanent in Western civilization we shall be in the position to bring about a reconciliation of these two great worlds. Then will come to an end the one-sided dominance which is galling. What is more, we have to recognize that the history of India does not belong to one particular race but to a process of creation to which various races of the world contributed—the Dravidians and the Aryans, the ancient Greeks and the Persians, the Mohammedans of the West and those of central Asia. Now at last has come the turn of the English to become true to this history and bring to it the tribute of their life, and we neither have the right nor the power to exclude these people from the building of the destiny of India. Therefore what I say about the Nation has more to do with the history of Man than specially with that of India.'

He declared in an unmistakable voice, When the humanity of India was not under the government of the Organization, the the elasticity of change was great enough to encourage men of power and spirit to feel that they had their destinies in their own hands. The hope of the unexpected was never absent, and a freer play of imagination, on the part both of the governor and the governed, had its effect in the making of history. We were not confronted with a future, which was a dead white wall of granite blocks eternally guarding against the expression and extension of our own powers, the hopelessness of which lies in the reason that these powers are becoming atrophied at their very roots by the scientific process of paralysis. For every single individual in the country of the No-Nation is completely in the grip of a whole nation,—whose tireless vigilance, being the vigilance of a machine, has not the human power to overlook or to discriminate. At the least pressing of its button the monster organisation becomes all eyes, whose ugly stare of inquisitiveness cannot be avoided by a single person amongst the immense multitude of the ruled. At the least turn of its screw, by the fraction of an inch, the grip is tightened to the point of suffocation around every man, woman and child of a vast population, for whom no escape is imaginable in their own country, or even in any country outside their own. It is the continual and stupendous dead pressure of this inhuman upon the living human under which the modern world is groaning. Not merely the subject races, but you who live under the delusion that you are free, are every day sacrificing your freedom and humanity to this fetich of nationalism, living in the dense poisonous atmosphere of world-wide suspicion and greed and panic.

According to Rabindranath the concept of nation is western and completely modern. He also explained it as mechanical and political. The main purpose of the nation is self-determination within the society for political and economic interests and attempts to impose force on others to prove one's superiority. The poet said that when a society becomes powerful by proving its superiority and starts imposing force on others, it is very harmful to mankind. Because then people started to give priority to power and became completely mechanised by the extreme addiction of being modern. By this, the human aspect of the society is gradually disappearing. According to the poet, in the modern and mechanical rationality of the nation, people are sacrificing their freedom and humanity every day and are becoming the machine of the nation.

Rabindranath in his Nationalism in Europe said,"And the idea of the Nation is one of the most powerful anaesthetics that man has invented. Under the influence of its fumes the whole people can carry out its systematic programme of the most virulent self-seeking without being in the least aware of its moral perversion,—in fact feeling dangerously resentful if it is pointed out. But can this go on indefinitely? continually producing barrenness of moral insensibility upon a large tract of our living nature? Can it escape its nemesis forever? Has this giant power of mechanical organisation no limit in this world against which it may shatter itself all the more completely because of its terrible strength and velocity? Do you believe that evil can be permanently kept in check by competition with evil, and that conference of prudence can keep the devil chained in its makeshift cage of mutual agreement?

This European war of Nations is the war of retribution. Man, the person, must protest for his very life against the heaping up of things where there should be the heart, and systems and policies where there should flow living human relationships. The time has come when, for the sake of the whole outraged world, Europe should fully know in her own person the terrible absurdity of the thing called the Nation.

The Nation has thriven long upon mutilated humanity. Men, the fairest creations of God, came out of the National manufactory in huge numbers as war-making and money-making puppets, ludicrously vain of their pitiful perfection of mechanism. Human society grew more and more into a marionette show of politicians, soldiers, manufacturers and bureaucrats, pulled by wire arrangements of wonderful efficiency.But the apotheosis of selfishness can never make its interminable breed of hatred and greed, fear and hypocrisy, suspicion and tyranny, an end in themselves. These monsters grow into huge shapes but never into harmony. And this Nation may grow on to an unimaginable corpulence, not of a living body, but of steel and steam and office buildings, till it's deformity can contain no longer its ugly voluminousness,—till it begins to crack and gape, breathe gas and fire in gasps, and its death-rattles sound in cannon roars. In this war the death-throes of the Nation have commenced. Suddenly, all its mechanisms going mad, it has begun the dance of the Furies, shattering its own limbs, scattering them into the dust. It is the fifth act of the tragedy of the unreal.

Those who have any faith in Man cannot but fervently hope that the tyranny of the Nation will not be restored to all its former teeth and claws, to its far-reaching iron arms and its immense inner cavity, all stomach and no heart; that man will have his new birth, in the freedom of his individuality, from the enveloping vagueness of abstraction. The veil has been raised, and in this frightful war the West has stood face to face with her own creation, to which she had offered her soul. She must know what it truly is. She had never let herself suspect what slow decay and decomposition were secretly going on in her moral nature, which often broke out in doctrines of scepticism, but still oftener and in still more dangerously subtle manner showed itself in her unconsciousness of the mutilation and insult that she had been inflicting upon a vast part of the world. Now she must know the truth nearer home. And then there will come from her own children those who will break themselves free from the slavery of this illusion, this perversion of brotherhood founded upon self-seeking, those who will own themselves as God's children and as no bond-slaves of machinery, which turns souls into commodities and life into compartments, which, with its iron claws, scratches out the heart of the world and knows not what it has done. And we of no nations of the world, whose heads have been bowed to the dust, will know that this dust is more sacred than the bricks which build the pride of power. For this dust is fertile of life, and of beauty and worship. We shall thank God that we were made to wait in silence through the night of despair, had to bear the insult of the proud and the strong man's burden, yet all through it, though our hearts quaked with doubt and fear, never could we blindly believe in the salvation which machinery offered to man, but we held fast to our trust in God and the truth of the human soul. And we can still cherish the hope that, when power becomes ashamed to occupy its throne and is ready to make way for love, when the morning comes for cleansing the blood-stained steps of the Nation along the highroad of humanity, we shall be called upon to bring our own vessel of sacred water—the water of worship—to sweeten the history of man into purity, and with its sprinkling make the trampled dust of the centuries blessed with fruitfulness."

He saw India's struggle as part of a larger global problem, noting that the world was becoming increasingly interconnected through advances in science and communication. Tagore argued that the solution to this new global challenge could not be found in political unity alone but required a deeper, moral unity. He believed that India's experience in attempting to reconcile racial differences could offer valuable lessons to the world, contributing to a broader understanding of humanity.He stressed that humanity's survival depended on solving this problem through higher moral instincts rather than through the brute force of military and economic power. Tagore concluded by stating that India had never truly embraced nationalism in the way the West had. He admitted that while he had been taught to idolise the nation above all else, he had come to believe that such idolatry was misguided. Instead, he argued that the true path for India was not in nationalism, but in upholding the ideals of humanity above the nation. He believed that by rejecting the narrow education that placed the nation above humanity, India could truly gain its freedom and contribute to the greater good of all humanity.

"India has never had a real sense of nationalism. Even though from childhood I had been taught that idolatry of the Nation is almost better than reverence for God and humanity, I believe I have outgrown that teaching, and it is my conviction that my countrymen will truly gain their India by fighting against the education which teaches them that a country is greater than the ideals of humanity." - Rabindranath Tagore

Evaluation:

Rabindranath's various writings and thoughts reveal that he was a realist. He believed that racist thought contained the seeds of power, domination and struggle, which created disparity in mankind and social order and injured individual freedom. So he was strongly opposed to Western radical nationalism. The main features of such nationalism are politics and commerce, which may empower mankind, but block the spontaneous self-expression of man as a social being. Man becomes a machine driven by greed and power. As a result, morals, ideals, mutual cooperation between people and sense of humanity within the society disappeared. In the poet's view, nationalism is a collective form of self-interested people, which is never human, never spiritual. Nationalism is an intimidation of humanity and trampling on human morals, sentiments and sense of unity. Your country, your nation is big and all other countries, all other nations are small and low! This idea of nationalism, which sows the seeds of division, eventually leads to colonialism and imperialism. Ultimately it seeks to dominate the world while devouring weaker states. That's why Rabindranath called Western nationalism hegemony or lordship. In 1916-17 AD, his book 'Nationalism' was published based on the lectures he gave during his travels in Japan and USA. In the book 'Nationalism', Rabindranath expressed that nationalism only creates hatred, hatred, discord and division. This nationalism is not based on religion, humanism, ethics and values. On the other hand,

Rabindranath's nationalism is based on spiritual unity and social, spiritual and moral principles. He extolled international human love and spoke of the union of East and West, vehemently condemning the workings of radical patriotism for mechanical interests.

At a turbulent time in India's history, nationalist ideals and programs brought common people out of their homes and initiated them. Rabindranath, the great personality of such a period of Indian history, sometimes tied the thread of unity between Hindus and Muslims by opposing Lord Curzon's declaration of partition of Bengal, and sometimes he vehemently condemned the divisive narrow nationalist ideals and sang the praises of universal humanity and international unity. He gave sole priority to society and social unity rather than 'Nation'.

But whatever Rabindranath thought, nationalism developed in a colonial context. Again there was a long-term conflict around nationalism. The cash result of which has been suffered by the people of the Indian subcontinent in various ways. In fact, national consciousness and nationalism are divided. Doubts about the elements of nation building have turned into controversies. From such nationalism, Rabindranath brought out examples of many contradictions - state and individual, labour and capital, man and woman, material greed and spiritual life, monstrous organisation of business and the state, human instinct towards simplicity and beauty and state, simplicity and beauty. Fulfilment of human natural expectations and leisure. According to him, these conflicts must be reconciled in a way that may not have been dreamed of.

As Rabindranath felt that nationalism fostered secession in the name of fierce patriotism, the poet never placed patriotism first. He said patriotism does not come above humanity. He called for internationalism instead of petty patriotism. Nikhilesh, the best character in his novel "Ghare Baire", did not want to put the country above everyone else. Rabindranath said in a letter to his friend A.M.Bose, "Patriotism cannot be our final spiritual shelter. I will not buy glass for the price of diamonds and I will never allow patriotism to triumph over humanity as long as I live" (Andrew), he was more of a humanitarian than a patriot. As a humanist, he took up the pen against capitalism, mechanised civilization and radical nationalism. The form of imperialism that the poet saw in his time may no longer exist in the 21st century world. But after the Cold War, world politics and economics have come into constant competition and pitched battles with each other under the banner of globalisation. The exploitation and control that existed in the imperialist era continues in modern world politics, but in a different form. It is true that political ideology and politics have triumphed over time, but no one has sung the praises of collective humanity and human love.

Currently, many countries of the world are doing public welfare work. In the era of democracy, the responsibility of governing the state is not only in the hands of the ruler, it is in the hands of the people. The people now elect the rulers. However, in the present time, capitalism has occupied the terrible place of exploiting the common people. They are the ones who are directing and controlling the modern age dictatorship. Even in today's world, we see nationalism in many forms. Nationalism, rooted in the question of politics, religion, sports or the spread of authority, became aggressive sometimes in Russia, Japan, India, Pakistan, sometimes even in Bangladesh. Where the supremacy of nationalism denigrates the culture and identity of other nations and seeks to eradicate diversity, will this hegemonic organisation of power liberate people? In this era of science and technology, we have to wonder where the world is going. Why are there humanitarian disasters in countries? When and who will be the victims of nationalism?

• • •

CHAPTER VI

What Factors Can Contribute To The Establishment Of A Dictatorship?

A dictatorship is an autocratic form of government (Autocracy is a system of government in which absolute power is held by the ruler, known as an autocrat) which is characterised by a leader, or a group of leaders, who hold governmental powers with few to no limitations. Politics in a dictatorship are controlled by a dictator, and they are facilitated through an inner circle of elites that includes advisers, generals, and other high-ranking officials. The dictator maintains control by influencing and appeasing the inner circle and repressing any opposition, which may include rival political parties, armed resistance, or disloyal members of the dictator's inner circle. Dictatorships can be formed by a military coup that overthrows the previous government through force or they can be formed by a self-coup in which elected leaders make their rule permanent. Dictatorships are authoritarian or totalitarian. There are three types of dictatorships. Military dictatorships are controlled by military officers, one-party dictatorships are controlled by the leadership of a political party, and personalist dictatorships are controlled by a single individual. In some circumstances, monarchies are also considered dictatorships if the monarchs hold a significant amount of political power. Hybrid dictatorships are regimes that have a combination of these classifications.

Modern dictatorships first developed in the 19th century, which included Bonapartism in Europe and caudillos in Latin America. The 20th century saw the rise of fascist and communist dictatorships in Europe; fascism was largely eradicated in the aftermath of World War II in 1945, while communism spread to other continents, maintaining prominence until the end of the Cold War in 1991. The 20th century also saw the rise of personalist dictatorships in Africa and military dictatorships in Latin America, both of which became prominent in the 1960s and 1970s. The period following the collapse of the Soviet Union witnessed a sporadic rise in democracies around the world, despite several dictatorships persisting into the 21st century, particularly in Africa and Asia. During the early 21st century, democratic governments came to outnumber authoritarian states by 98 to 80. The second decade was marked by a democratic recession, following the 2008 global financial crisis which drastically reduced the appeal of the Western model around the world. By 2019, the number of authoritarian governments had again surmounted that of democracies by 92 to 87.

The dictator exercises most or total power over the government and society, but sometimes elites are necessary to carry out the dictator's rule. They form an inner circle, making up a class of elites that hold a degree of power within the dictatorship and receive benefits in exchange for their support. They may be military officers, party members, or friends or family of the dictator. Elites are also the primary political threats of a dictator, as they can leverage their power to influence or overthrow the dictatorship. The inner circle's support is necessary for a dictator's orders to be carried out, causing elites to serve as a check on the dictator's power. To enact policy, a dictator must either appease the regime's elites or attempt to replace them. Elites must also compete to wield more power than one another, but the amount of power held by elites also depends on their unity. Factions or divisions among the elites will mitigate their ability to bargain with the dictator, resulting in the dictator having more unrestrained power. A unified inner circle has the capacity to overthrow a dictator, and the dictator must make greater concessions to the inner circle to stay in power. This is particularly true when the inner circle is made up of military officers that have the resources to carry out a military coup.

Most dictatorships are formed through military means or through a political party. Nearly half of dictatorships start as a military coup, though others have been started by foreign intervention, elected officials ending competitive elections, insurgent takeovers, popular uprisings by citizens, or legal manoeuvring by autocratic elites to take power within their government. Between 1946 and 2010, 42% of dictatorships began by overthrowing a different dictatorship, and 26% began after achieving independence from a foreign government. Many others developed following a period of warlordism.

Radical nationalism is a powerful force that can be used to establish and maintain dictatorial regimes. It operates through a combination of ideological manipulation, populist rhetoric, the exploitation of social divisions, the centralization of power, and the suppression of dissent. Apart from extreme nationalism, several other factors and conditions can contribute to the establishment of a dictatorship in a country. These factors often involve a combination of political, social, economic, and cultural dynamics that create an environment where democratic norms and institutions are eroded or overthrown. Dear Friends In this chapter we will try to understand how and what factors can help to establish a dictatorial government.

How Radical Nationalism Helps Establish Dictatorships

Radical nationalism is a potent ideological force that has played a significant role in the establishment of dictatorial regimes throughout history. It involves the promotion of a strong sense of national identity, often coupled with the exclusion or demonization of certain groups considered as "others." This ideology taps into the deep-seated emotions of pride, fear, and loyalty, and can be used by ambitious leaders to consolidate power and suppress dissent. When radical nationalism is coupled with charismatic leadership and populist rhetoric, it can create a fertile ground for authoritarianism to take root.

Radical nationalism has been a driving force behind many of the most oppressive regimes in history. It typically emerges in times of social, economic, or political upheaval, when traditional institutions are perceived as weak or corrupt. In such periods, radical nationalists offer a vision of national renewal, often characterised by a return to "true" or "pure" national values, which they claim have been eroded by internal and external enemies.

One of the most notorious examples of radical nationalism leading to dictatorship is Adolf Hitler's rise to power in Germany. The Nazi party's ideology was deeply rooted in a radical form of nationalism that emphasised the superiority of the "Aryan" race and the need for Lebensraum (living space) for the German people. This ideology justified the exclusion, persecution, and ultimately the extermination of Jews, Romani people, and other minorities. Hitler's nationalist rhetoric resonated with a population traumatised by the Treaty of Versailles and the economic hardships of the Weimar Republic, allowing him to dismantle democratic institutions and establish a totalitarian regime.

Similarly, Benito Mussolini's fascist regime in Italy was built on radical nationalism. Mussolini exploited the disillusionment of Italians after World War I, promising to restore Italy to its former glory by reviving the Roman Empire. His nationalist propaganda emphasised the need for a strong, centralised state to achieve this goal, and he used this narrative to justify the suppression of political opponents and the establishment of a dictatorship.

In both cases, radical nationalism served as a unifying force, rallying the population behind a common cause while simultaneously creating a climate of fear and hatred towards those deemed as threats to the nation. This dual strategy of inclusion and exclusion is a hallmark of radical nationalist movements and is key to understanding how they can lead to the establishment of dictatorships.

The Mechanisms of Radical Nationalism in Establishing Dictatorships

Radical nationalism operates through a combination of ideological manipulation, populist rhetoric, and the exploitation of social divisions. These mechanisms work together to create an environment where democratic institutions can be eroded, and power can be centralised in the hands of a single leader or ruling party.

1. At the core of radical nationalism is the construction of a national identity that is defined in opposition to certain groups or ideologies. This often involves the use of historical narratives, cultural symbols, and myths that emphasise the uniqueness and superiority of the nation. These narratives are selectively constructed to promote a sense of victimhood or a belief that the nation is under threat from external enemies or internal traitors. This ideological manipulation creates a binary worldview where individuals are either loyal to the nation or are seen as enemies. This dichotomy allows for the justification of extreme measures, such as the suppression of dissent, the erosion of civil liberties, and the use of violence against perceived enemies. By framing these actions as necessary for the survival of the nation, radical nationalists can gain popular support for policies that would otherwise be seen as authoritarian or undemocratic.

2. Radical nationalists often use populist rhetoric to mobilise support and legitimise their authority. This rhetoric typically appeals to "the people" as a homogenous, virtuous group who are opposed by corrupt elites and dangerous outsiders. The leader positions themselves as the true representative of the people's will, promising to restore the nation to greatness by defeating these enemies. Populist rhetoric is highly effective in creating a direct, emotional connection between the leader and the populace. It bypasses traditional democratic institutions, such as parliaments and courts, which are often portrayed as corrupt or ineffective. This allows the leader to present themselves as a saviour who is

unburdened by the constraints of democracy and is therefore uniquely capable of solving the nation's problems.

3. Radical nationalism thrives in societies that are already divided along ethnic, religious, or cultural lines. These divisions can be exacerbated by economic inequality, social unrest, or external threats. Radical nationalists exploit these divisions by scapegoating certain groups, portraying them as the cause of the nation's problems, and rallying the majority population against them. This strategy of divide and rule is central to the establishment of dictatorial regimes. By creating a sense of unity among the majority population, radical nationalists can marginalise and silence opposition groups. At the same time, the fear of being labelled as a traitor or enemy of the nation discourages dissent and fosters a culture of conformity and obedience.

Real-Life Examples of Radical Nationalism Leading to Dictatorship

To understand how these mechanisms play out in practice, it is useful to examine specific cases where radical nationalism has contributed to the rise of dictatorial regimes. In addition to the historical examples of Nazi Germany and Fascist Italy, we can look at more contemporary instances, including the leadership of Narendra Modi in India.

1. Adolf Hitler and Nazi Germany

As mentioned earlier, Adolf Hitler's rise to power in Germany is one of the most well-known examples of radical nationalism leading to dictatorship. The Nazi party's ideology was built on the concept of Aryan racial superiority and the belief that Germany had been betrayed by Jews, communists, and other "undesirable" elements. Hitler used this ideology to rally support among the German population, who were suffering from the economic hardships of the Great Depression and the humiliation of the Treaty of Versailles.

Through a combination of propaganda, violence, and political manoeuvring, Hitler was able to dismantle the Weimar Republic's democratic institutions and establish a totalitarian regime. The Reichstag Fire of 1933, which the Nazis blamed on communists, provided the pretext for the Enabling Act, which gave Hitler dictatorial powers. The Nazi regime then embarked on a campaign of terror, targeting Jews, political opponents, and other minorities, leading to the horrors of the Holocaust.

Hitler's use of radical nationalism to create a sense of unity among the German people, while simultaneously demonising and persecuting those deemed as enemies, is a textbook example of how this ideology can be used to establish a dictatorship.

2. Benito Mussolini and Fascist Italy

Benito Mussolini's rise to power in Italy followed a similar trajectory. After World War I, Italy was plagued by economic instability, social unrest, and a sense of national decline. Mussolini capitalised on this discontent by promoting a radical nationalist ideology that emphasised the need for a strong, centralised state to restore Italy to its former glory.

Mussolini's fascist movement used a combination of propaganda, violence, and political alliances to undermine Italy's democratic institutions. In 1922, Mussolini led the "March on Rome," which resulted in King Victor Emmanuel III appointing him as Prime Minister. Once in power, Mussolini moved quickly to consolidate his authority, using the Fascist Party's paramilitary wing, the Blackshirts, to intimidate and eliminate political opponents.

By 1925, Mussolini had established a dictatorship, ruling Italy as "Il Duce" (The Leader). His regime was characterised by the suppression of political freedoms, the persecution of minorities, and aggressive nationalist policies that ultimately led to Italy's involvement in World War II. Mussolini's use of radical nationalism to rally support for his authoritarian regime, while suppressing dissent and promoting a cult of personality, provides another clear example of how this ideology can pave the way for dictatorship.

3. Narendra Modi and India (Within a democratic framework)

The case of Narendra Modi in India offers a more contemporary example of how radical nationalism can be used to establish authoritarian tendencies, even within a democratic framework. Modi's rise to power and his tenure as Prime Minister have been marked by a strong emphasis on Hindu nationalism, which has been used to consolidate his authority and marginalised opposition.

Modi's political career began in the Rashtriya Swayamsevak Sangh (RSS), a right-wing Hindu nationalist organisation that advocates for the idea of India as a Hindu Rashtra (Hindu Nation). The RSS has a long history of promoting a radical nationalist ideology that seeks to establish Hindu cultural and religious dominance in India, often at the expense of minority communities, particularly Muslims. Modi first came to national prominence as the Chief Minister of Gujarat, where he was accused of turning a blind eye, or even tacitly supporting, the 2002 Gujarat riots, in which over a thousand people, mostly Muslims, were killed. The riots solidified Modi's image as a strong leader who was willing to take a hard line against perceived enemies of the nation, an image that resonated with many Hindu nationalists.

In 2014, Modi led the Bharatiya Janata Party (BJP) to a landslide victory in the general elections, becoming the Prime Minister of India. His campaign was marked by a strong nationalist rhetoric, promising to make India a global power and restore its ancient glory. Modi's leadership has since been characterised by a centralization of power, the promotion of Hindu nationalist policies, and the marginalisation of minority communities. One of the most controversial policies of Modi's government has been the Citizenship Amendment Act (CAA) of 2019, which provides a path to citizenship for non-Muslim refugees from neighbouring countries. Critics argue that the CAA, combined with the proposed National Register of Citizens (NRC), is part of a broader strategy to disenfranchise Muslim citizens and reshape India as a Hindu nation.

Modi's government has also been accused of using state institutions to target political opponents, suppress dissent, and control the media. Journalists, activists, and academics who criticise the government have faced harassment, arrests, and violence. The independence of the judiciary has been called into question, and there have been concerns about the erosion of democratic norms and civil liberties. Despite these authoritarian tendencies, Modi remains highly popular among large segments of the Indian population. His nationalist rhetoric, combined with his image as a decisive leader, has allowed him to maintain a strong grip on power, even as his government faces increasing criticism both domestically and internationally. Modi's use of radical nationalism to consolidate his authority, marginalise opposition, and promote a vision of India as a Hindu nation provides a contemporary example of how this ideology can be used to establish authoritarian tendencies within a democratic framework.

Dear Readers So we understand that Radical nationalism is a powerful force that can be used to establish and maintain dictatorial regimes. It operates through a combination of ideological manipulation, populist rhetoric, the exploitation of social divisions, the centralization of power, and the suppression of dissent. By creating a sense of unity among the majority population while excluding and demonising certain groups, radical nationalists can rally support for authoritarian measures and erode democratic institutions. And The leadership of Narendra Modi in India provides a contemporary example of how radical nationalism can be used to consolidate power and promote authoritarian tendencies within a democratic framework. Modi's emphasis on Hindu nationalism, his centralization of authority, his use of populist rhetoric, and his cultivation of a cult of personality have all contributed to the erosion of democratic norms and the marginalisation of minority communities. As history has shown, the rise of radical nationalism and the establishment of dictatorial regimes can have devastating consequences for both the nation and the international community. It is essential to recognize the warning signs and take action to protect democratic institutions, civil liberties, and the rights of all people. Only by doing so can we prevent the emergence of authoritarianism and ensure that the values of democracy, tolerance, and human rights are upheld.

• • •

Several Other Factors and Conditions by Which A Dictatorship Can Be Established

Apart from extreme nationalism, several other factors and conditions can contribute to the establishment of a dictatorship in a country. These factors often involve a combination of political, social, economic, and cultural dynamics that create an environment where democratic norms and institutions are eroded or overthrown. Here are some key mechanisms by which a dictatorship can be established:

1. Military Coup

A military coup is one of the most direct and forceful ways to establish a dictatorship. In this scenario, the military, often dissatisfied with the current government, takes control of the state by force, suspending the constitution, dissolving democratic institutions, and imposing martial law. Military leaders may justify their actions by claiming they are restoring order, combating corruption, or protecting national security. Examples include the coups in Egypt in 2013 and Chile in 1973.

2. Erosion of Democratic Institutions

A dictatorship can gradually emerge through the systematic erosion of democratic institutions from within. Leaders may undermine the independence of the judiciary, weaken the legislature, suppress the media, and centralise power in the executive branch. This process often happens under the guise of legal reforms, security measures, or anti-corruption campaigns. Leaders may exploit crises (real or manufactured) to justify these actions, as seen in the rise of authoritarian regimes in countries like Hungary and Turkey.

3. Manipulation of Electoral Processes

Dictatorships can also be established through the manipulation of electoral processes. This can involve rigging elections, manipulating electoral laws, disenfranchising opposition supporters, and using state resources to ensure the ruling party's victory. By controlling the electoral process, a leader or party can maintain the facade of democracy while effectively eliminating any real political competition. Venezuela under Hugo Chávez and Nicolás Maduro is an example of this approach.

4. Control of the Media and Information

Controlling the flow of information is a critical tool for establishing and maintaining a dictatorship. Governments may censor or shut down independent media, spread propaganda, and control the narrative through state-run media outlets. By monopolising information, dictatorships can shape public perception, suppress dissent, and create an environment where opposition voices are marginalised or silenced. The state-controlled media in North Korea and the censorship practices in China are notable examples.

5. Exploitation of Economic Crises

Economic crises can create fertile ground for the rise of dictatorships. When people are facing severe economic hardships, they may become disillusioned with democratic governance and open to authoritarian solutions that promise stability, order, and economic recovery. Dictators may use economic hardship to justify the concentration of power, the suspension of civil liberties, and the suppression of political opposition. The rise of fascism in Europe during the Great Depression, particularly in Germany and Italy, illustrates how economic crises can lead to dictatorship.

6. Charismatic Leadership and Cult of Personality

A charismatic leader can play a significant role in the establishment of a dictatorship. Such leaders often present themselves as saviours of the nation, capable of solving the country's problems single-handedly. They may build a cult of personality around themselves, where they are portrayed as infallible, wise, and indispensable. This cult of personality can be used to justify the centralization of power, the suppression of dissent, and the dismantling of democratic institutions. Leaders like Joseph Stalin in the Soviet Union and Kim Il-sung in North Korea used this approach to establish and maintain dictatorial regimes.

7. Legal Manipulation and Constitutional Changes

Dictatorships can also be established through legal manipulation and constitutional changes. Leaders may amend or rewrite the constitution to grant themselves extended powers, eliminate term limits, or weaken checks and balances. These changes may be presented as necessary for stability or reform but ultimately serve to entrench the leader's authority and eliminate democratic safeguards. The transition of Russia under Vladimir Putin, who has extended his rule through constitutional amendments, is an example of this strategy.

8. Suppression of Civil Society and Opposition

The suppression of civil society and political opposition is a common method used to establish and maintain a dictatorship. This can include the harassment, imprisonment, or assassination of opposition leaders, the banning of political parties, and the restriction of non-governmental organisations (NGOs) and civil society groups. By eliminating organised opposition, a dictator can prevent challenges to their rule and create an atmosphere of fear and repression. The authoritarian regime in Belarus under Alexander Lukashenko has employed these tactics to maintain control.

9. Use of Fear, Intimidation, and Violence

Fear, intimidation, and violence are often used to establish and sustain a dictatorship. Secret police, paramilitary groups, and surveillance are tools used to monitor and suppress dissent. The threat or use of violence against political opponents, activists, journalists, and ordinary citizens creates an environment where people are too afraid to challenge the regime. The reign of terror in Nazi Germany and the purges in Stalinist Russia are extreme examples of how fear and violence can be used to consolidate dictatorial power.

10. Exploitation of Social Divisions

Dictatorships can also arise by exploiting social divisions, such as ethnic, religious, or class tensions. Leaders may use these divisions to rally support among certain groups while demonising others as enemies of the state. By stoking fears and hatred, dictators can justify repressive measures and the centralization of power. The apartheid regime in South Africa and the ethnic conflicts manipulated by leaders like Slobodan Milošević in the former Yugoslavia illustrate how social divisions can be exploited to establish authoritarian rule.

11. Emergency Powers and States of Exception

Declaring a state of emergency or invoking emergency powers can be a pathway to dictatorship. During crises such as war, terrorism, or natural disasters, leaders may claim the need for extraordinary powers to protect the nation. While such powers are sometimes necessary, they can also be abused to bypass democratic processes, suppress opposition, and concentrate power in the hands of a single leader or party. Once emergency powers are in place, they can be difficult to reverse, as seen in the prolonged state of emergency in Egypt under Hosni Mubarak.

12. Weakness of Democratic Institutions

The establishment of a dictatorship is often facilitated by the weakness or fragility of democratic institutions. In countries where democratic norms are not deeply entrenched, or where institutions like the judiciary, legislature, and civil society are weak, it is easier for authoritarian leaders to seize power. In such contexts, leaders can manipulate or bypass institutions without facing significant resistance. Countries transitioning from colonial rule or those with a history of political instability are particularly vulnerable to this dynamic.

13. International Support and Geopolitical Context

The establishment of a dictatorship can also be influenced by international support and the broader geopolitical context. In some cases, foreign powers may support or tolerate a dictatorship if it aligns with their strategic interests. This support can come in the form of military aid, economic assistance, or diplomatic backing. During the Cold War, for example, both the United States and the Soviet Union supported dictatorships in various parts of the world as part of their geopolitical rivalry.

14. Populism and the Erosion of Liberal Values

Populism, characterised by the appeal to "the people" against a perceived corrupt elite, can be a precursor to dictatorship. Populist leaders often promise to restore the will of the people by dismantling established institutions, undermining checks and balances, and concentrating power in their hands. By exploiting public discontent with the status quo, populists can erode liberal values, such as the rule of law, individual rights, and minority protections, paving the way for authoritarian rule. The rise of populist leaders in various parts of the world, including in Latin America and Europe, demonstrates this danger.

15. Weak or Non-existent Civil Liberties

In societies where civil liberties are already weak or non-existent, the transition to a dictatorship can occur with little resistance. When people lack the freedom to speak out, organise, or protest, it becomes much easier for authoritarian leaders to consolidate power. In such environments, the absence of a vibrant civil society and independent media allows dictatorships to take root without significant opposition. This is often seen in countries with a history of authoritarianism or where state control over society is deeply entrenched.

Setting up a dictatorship is a complicated process that can happen in many ways, often by combining factors from inside and outside the country. To spot the early signs of authoritarianism and protect democratic institutions and values, it is important to understand how these things work.

• • •

CHAPTER VII

An Analysis of Fascism

Fascism is a far-right form of government in which most of the country's power is held by one ruler or a small group, under a single party. The history of fascist ideology is long and it draws on many sources. Fascists took inspiration from sources as ancient as the Spartans (Ancient Greece) for their focus on racial purity and their emphasis on rule by an elite minority. The Spartans were emulated by the quasi-fascist regime of Ioannis Metaxas who called for Greeks to wholly commit themselves to the nation with self-control as the Spartans had done. The Greek philosopher Plato supported many similar political positions to fascism. Plato believed the ideal state would be ruled by an elite class of rulers known as "Guardians" and rejected the idea of social equality. Plato believed in an authoritarian state. Plato held Athenian democracy in contempt by saying: "The laws of democracy remain a dead letter, its freedom is anarchy, its equality the equality of unequals".

Fascism styled itself as the ideological successor to Rome, particularly the Roman Empire. Georg Wilhelm Friedrich Hegel's view on the absolute authority of the state also strongly influenced fascist thinking. There were a number of influences on fascism from the Renaissance era in Europe. Niccolò Machiavelli is known to have influenced Italian Fascism, particularly through his promotion of the absolute authority of the state. Machiavelli rejected all existing traditional and metaphysical assumptions of the time—especially those associated with the Middle Ages. During the Enlightenment, a number of ideological influences arose that would shape the development of fascism. The development of the study of universal histories by Johann Gottfried Herder resulted in Herder's analysis of the development of nations. Herder developed the term Nationalismus ("nationalism") to describe this cultural phenomenon. At this time nationalism did not refer to the political ideology of nationalism that was later developed during the French Revolution.

The French Revolution was a major influence insofar as the Nazis saw themselves as fighting back against many of the ideas which it brought to prominence, especially liberalism, liberal democracy and racial equality, whereas on the other hand, fascism drew heavily on the revolutionary ideal of nationalism. The prejudice of a "high and noble" Aryan culture as opposed to a "parasitic" Semitic culture was core to Nazi racial views, while other early forms of fascism concerned themselves with non-racialized conceptions of the nation.

However, Maurice Barrès, a French politician of the late 19th and early 20th centuries who influenced the fascist movement, claimed that true democracy was authoritarian democracy while rejecting liberal democracy as a fraud. Barrès claimed that authoritarian democracy involved a spiritual connection between a leader of a nation and the nation's people, and that true freedom did not arise from individual rights nor parliamentary restraints, but through "heroic leadership" and "national power". He emphasised the need for hero worship and charismatic leadership in national society. Later in life he returned to cultural traditionalism and parliamentary conservatism, but his ideas contributed to the development of an extremist form of nationalism in pre-1914 France.

Fascism's relationship with other ideologies of its day has been complex. It frequently considered those ideologies its adversaries, but at the same time it was also focused on co-opting their more popular aspects. Fascism supported private property rights – except for the groups which it persecuted – and the profit motive of capitalism, but it sought to eliminate the autonomy of large-scale capitalism from the state. Fascists shared many of the goals of the conservatives of their day and they often allied themselves with them by drawing recruits from disaffected conservative ranks, but they presented themselves as holding a more modern ideology, with less focus on things like traditional religion, and sought to radically reshape society through revolutionary action rather than preserve the status quo. Fascism opposed class conflict and the egalitarian and international character of socialism. It strongly opposed liberalism, communism, anarchism, and democratic socialism. According to *Waxman, Olivia B. (March 22, 2019). "What to Know About the Origins of Fascism's Brutal Ideology" - *One of the reasons fascism spread in the early 20th century was because the Russian Revolution had just happened and people were afraid of communism. Sometimes landowners and business owners would support fascists because they were afraid of what would happen if the country became communist instead.* Mussolini saw fascism as opposing socialism and other left-wing ideologies, writing in The Doctrine of Fascism: "If it is admitted that the nineteenth century has been the century of Socialism, Liberalism and Democracy, it does not follow that the twentieth must also be the century of Liberalism, Socialism and Democracy. Political doctrines pass; people remain. It is to be expected that this century may be that of authority, a century of the 'Right,' a Fascist century."

Dear Readers, Common themes among fascist movements include: authoritarianism, nationalism (including racial nationalism and religious nationalism), hierarchy and elitism, and militarism. Other aspects of fascism such as perception of decadence, anti-egalitarianism and totalitarianism can be seen to originate from these ideas. Roger Griffin has proposed that fascism is a synthesis of totalitarianism and ultranationalism sacralized through a myth of national rebirth and regeneration, which he terms "Palingenetic ultranationalism".

Fascism had a complex relationship with capitalism, both supporting and opposing different aspects of it at different times and in different countries. In general, fascists held an instrumental view of capitalism, regarding it as a tool that may be useful or not, depending on circumstances. Fascists aimed to promote what they considered the national interests of their countries; they supported the right to own private property and the profit motive. The economic policies of fascist governments, meanwhile, were generally not based on ideological commitment instead being dictated by pragmatic concerns.

Exactly what constitutes fascism is still debated today. Who oppresses, suppresses the voice of others, robs democratic rights, imposes his will on others - is this fascism? Does a party become fascist or does a system become fascist? Can fascism remain unidimensional, is it possible? Or fascism combined with other aggressive ideologies. Some say imperialism—neocolonialism—may exist but the emergence and re-establishment of fascism is impossible. A resurgence of fascism in the modern world today is a far-fetched fantasy. Some thinkers, practitioners of applied politics and sociology have a clear answer - no matter how much science and technology advances, as long as there is capitalism and imperialism in a class society, fascism will emerge in different forms and tones. He does not die even if he dies repeatedly. The matter is like this - 'The King is dead but long live the King'.

Surely there is a reason for this. According to the socio-politicians, fascism does not only shelter the economy or political administrative structure, it breaks down society and human-psychology, philosophy-culture-history-tradition. Rooted in people's way of thinking, social habits. It not only changes colour but also transforms. In each episode of history, fascism manifests itself in each form. If it can be called a poison tree, then its roots spread deep into the ground. Even if it is pruned from the top, it comes up again in a favourable condition. The poison tree will bear poison, the poison of fascism. Its response is overwhelmingly totalitarian. It is really difficult to get rid of it. Political leaders of different countries of the world, thinkers have thought of different ways to end this problem. Sometimes a sharp intellectual political movement, sometimes a cultural activity with a vibrant alternative agenda.

In 2003, Laurence W. Britt wrote "14 Defining Characteristics of Fascism":

1. Powerful and continuing expressions of nationalism.
2. Disdain for the importance of human rights.

3. Identification of enemies/scapegoats as a unifying cause.

4. The supremacy of the military/avid militarism.

5. Rampant sexism.

6. A controlled mass media.

7. Obsession with national security.

8. Religion and the ruling elite tied together.

9. Power of corporations is protected.

10. Power of labour suppressed or eliminated.

11. Disdain and suppression of intellectuals and the arts.

12. Obsession with crime and punishment.

13. Rampant cronyism and corruption.

14. Fraudulent elections.

What is the classical concept of fascism?

A general definition of fascism was given in the program of the Sixth Congress of the Communist International (1928).

"Capitalism adopted fascist principles in its reactionary development due to certain historical mechanisms and reasons."

At the Seventh Congress Georgi Dimitrov wrote in his famous United Front thesis:

"Fascism is the attack of investment capital on oppressed people. Narrow nationalism and the war of aggression it provokes. The most conservative narrow reaction and counter-revolution."

Some specific ideas about fascism stem from Dimitrov's statement:

(1) Fascism is the naked attack of capital on the oppressed people.

(2) Fascism is narrow nationalism and the aggressive wars it promotes.

(3) Fascism is the most conservative narrow reaction and counter-revolution.

(4) Fascism is the number one enemy of the working class and oppressed people.

Rajani Pam Dutta, a controversial figure in the Indian communist movement, in his book 'Fascism and Social Revolution' while clarifying the concept of fascism has said - 'Fascism is not really a novel independent philosophy against the current capitalist society. Exactly the opposite. The most complete and consistent program of the most known principles and trends of modern capitalism in a certain situation of final decline. " Fascism has its own style, its own culture, without which it cannot survive. or unable to move the wings.

What culture is this?

A culture of violence and bloodshed. This culture has a peculiar pattern. That pattern can be broken into layers in this way.

(1) To inflame the passions of the majority of the ignorant people, to incite them against the minority people.

(2) Creating a rumour at one end and spreading it like wildfire through the propaganda machine.

(3) The propaganda machine never mixes the whole truth, not the whole lie, but the truth with the lie. Because a half-truth is worse than a full-blown lie.

4) Not just eliminating opponents. Creating an atmosphere of fear of murder and terror before subduing him. And for that, to torture innocent non-political people mentally and physically. Endless harassment, endless fear are trying to fight with these two powerful weapons.

5) Attacks on the human mind. Removing the thought. To force the practice of unification rather than diversification of thought. Removing the question of mind.

(6) Youth are also targets of fascist-attacks.Sometimes it awakens in the youth a semi-anarchistic licentiousness that turns him into a murderer.

The most brutal and aggressive form of fascism the world has ever seen is German fascism, led by Hitler. In his book Mein Camp (which can be called the Gita of Fascism, Nazism), he explains the aims and objectives of fascism and writes:

(1) The goal is to restore the dignity of the humiliated Germany.

(2) The way of life of the Jews and other nations is not only degraded. They're all nonsense. He has no passion, no energy. The whole of Europe, especially Germany, is tainted by the shadow of that decadent civilization. It is a sacred duty to remove that shadow by force. By their forcible removal, to establish the highly cultured German nation;

(3) The culture of the German nation is ancient. The progress of any country, nation and people in accepting its willful domination.

(4) showing discipline, obedience to a powerful leader, not disorderliness or unrestrained freedom;

(5) Women's work with patience and dedication. A woman's duty is to her husband, to her children, etc. He must inculcate this teaching in his child so that he becomes obedient to the head of the family. There is respect for the state and the supreme leadership.

Hitler based his rabid Nazism on this terrible idea.

Hitler wrote, "You want arms. Everything Must Be Placed at the Service of the Great Mission. " What's that mission? Serving the fascist fighters. Artists and writers have to serve the fascists compulsorily. Otherwise, torture, humiliation and death are inevitable. Art should not be done in another tone, I or we will talk in that tone, we have to talk in that tone. Hitler said this when he inaugurated the House of German Art in Munich in 1937. This is a terrible menace. And that's the horror of fascism.

Fascism came to Europe by harbouring perverted capitalism, radical nationalism and aggressive imperialism. Fascism was defeated in World War II but not dead. Again in the mid-50s and mid-60s. The reason for this is said to be the support of US imperialism.

Philosopher Jason Stanley of Yale University says it is "a cult of the leader who promises national restoration in the face of humiliation brought on by supposed communists, Marxists and minorities and immigrants who are supposedly posing a threat to the character and the history of a nation." That is, fascism focuses on one person as leader, fascism says communism is bad, and fascism says that at least one group of people is bad and has caused the nation's problems. This group could be people from other countries or groups of people within the country. Under Hitler's fascist Germany, the government blamed Jews, communists, homosexuals, the disabled, Roma and other people for Germany's problems, arrested those people, and took them to camps to be killed.

How A Fascist Government Is Established

Usually, a fascist government is set up after a long and complicated process that includes taking advantage of weak spots in society, messing with the political system, and using different types of ideological control. Authoritarian nationalism is a trait of fascism. It tries to concentrate power in one person or the ruling party, often at the expense of individual rights and democratic principles. To fully understand how a fascist government starts to take hold, we need to look at a few key areas: taking advantage of crises, weakening democratic institutions, controlling the media and spreading propaganda, using violence and fear, spreading a nationalist myth, and putting down any opposition. These things work together to make a place where fascism can grow, which will eventually lead to the establishment of a fascist government.

When there is a crisis in the economy, society, or government, fascist movements often gain steam. Crises make a lot of people afraid, uncertain, and disappointed, which is a good environment for extremist ideas to grow. Unstable economies, like those with high unemployment, hyperinflation, or deep recession, can make people less trusting of democratic institutions and leaders, which can make people more open to radical alternatives. As an example, the Great Depression in the 1930s caused a lot of economic problems that helped fascism grow in Europe, especially in Germany and Italy.

A big part is also played by social crises like cultural breakdown or a sense of moral decline. Fascist leaders often present themselves as protectors of traditional values and promise to bring back order and morality to a society they say is in danger from enemies inside or outside the country. People who feel alone or threatened by fast social changes, like moving to cities, immigration, or changes in gender roles, will like this kind of speech. When governments are corrupt, leaders aren't doing their jobs, or coalition governments fall apart, it makes democratic institutions even weaker, which fascist movements can take advantage of.

When this happens, fascist leaders act like they are the only ones who can save the day by giving clear, simple answers to hard problems. They often blame minority groups for the problems facing the country and say they will get rid of these "threats" to society. Many people who feel left behind or betrayed by the current system are drawn to this call to a mythical past and the promise of national rejuvenation.

Once a fascist movement gets going, it works to weaken democratic institutions so it can keep its power. Weaker checks and balances that are meant to stop people from abusing power are often the first step in this process. Fascists attack free press, independent courts, and legislative bodies, making it harder for them to check the power of the executive. The courts, for instance, could be weakened by putting in place loyalists who are ready to interpret the law in ways that help the regime. Legal changes could be made to limit the courts' freedom, which would make it easier for the government to get around laws that limit what it can do. Sometimes, new laws are made or old ones are changed to make it illegal to disagree or fight back. This turns the legal system into a tool for repression. Legislative bodies are often ignored or taken over by other groups. Fascist regimes may start out by forming alliances with other political parties, but once they have enough power, they break up these alliances. Parliaments could be reduced to little more than rubber stamps that agree with the executive's choices without question or debate. In the worst situations, the legislature might not exist at all, and the fascist leader would rule by decree.

Another important target is the free press. Fascist movements depend on controlling the flow of information to change how people think and get rid of those who disagree with them. There is a chance that independent media outlets will be threatened, censored, or even shut down. Instead, media outlets that are controlled by the government or that support it spread propaganda that makes the regime look good and makes its enemies look bad. With this kind of power over the media, fascists can make a different reality where the regime's story is the only true one. Propaganda is one of the most important tools that fascists use to control the people and change public opinion. Fascist governments are very good at telling stories that make people feel strong emotions instead of using logic. This story is often about national rebirth, racial or cultural superiority, and making enemies, both inside and outside the country, look bad. The way the media is skewed helps to support this story. As fascists, they know how powerful symbols, slogans, and pictures can be in changing people's minds. They often use sophisticated forms of propaganda to get their message out, like rallies, speeches, posters, movies, and radio shows. People are supposed to feel like they have a common goal and purpose, while those who don't follow the regime's rules are to be shunned and isolated.

A big part of making the regime's actions seem okay is also propaganda. Fascists say that their authoritarian rules are necessary for the survival and prosperity of the state because they see the government as the embodiment of the nation's will and destiny. Any opposition is seen as treasonous or subversive, which makes it even harder to disagree. Fascist regimes are good at using both old and new ways of talking to their people, not just traditional media. These days, this includes the planned use of social media to spread false information, make "echo chambers," and get people to support a cause. Fascists make sure that their story dominates public discourse by controlling both the message and the medium. This leaves little room for other points of view.

In order to set up a fascist government, violence and fear are necessary. People who support fascist movements often have paramilitary wings or form organised groups that are ready to use force to get what they want. People who disagree with them politically, people of colour, and other marginalised groups are beaten up, scared, and bothered in public by these groups. Violence is used for more than one reason. First, it makes people afraid and uneasy, which stops people from speaking out against the government and shuts down critics. Threats of physical harm keep people and groups from fighting back against the fascist movement when they might otherwise. For the second reason, violence helps to keep people in line because those who don't follow the rules are punished or shunned. Third, violence is used to get rid of political opponents and strengthen fascist power within the movement itself.

When fascist regimes use violence, they often make it hard to tell the difference between state and non-state people. Paramilitary groups may work with the state's knowledge or direct support, which lets the government keep up a plausible deniability while taking advantage of the effects of fear and intimidation. In some cases, these groups become part of the official state security forces later on, which makes violence an even more normal part of government. The government can also use its own security forces to silence opposition. Police, the military, and intelligence agencies are often cleaned out of disloyal people and filled with people who support the regime. Then, these groups are used to silence dissenters by spying on them, arresting them, torturing them, and killing them without a trial. The rule of force takes the place of the rule of law, and the regime uses violence that is approved by the government to keep its power.

Creating and spreading a nationalist myth is an important part of fascist ideology because it brings people together around a common identity and goal. A common theme in this myth is the idea of a country that was once great but has been hurt or betrayed by enemies inside and outside the country. Fascist leaders see themselves as the ones who can bring the country back to its former glory and protect it from what they see as threats. The nationalist myth is often based on picking and choosing which events or people to focus on in history while ignoring or downplaying others. People use revisionist history to tell a story of decline and resurgence, where the country is seen as rising from the ashes of its past to take back its rightful place in the world. There is a sense of destiny in this story, as if the country has a special mission or role to play on the world stage.

Nationalist myths often centre around the idea that one group is better than another based on race or culture. Fascist governments believe that the country's main ethnic or cultural group is naturally better than others and that protecting the purity of this group is important for the country's survival. This sense of superiority makes it okay to keep people out, hurt them, or even kill them if they are seen as threats to the country's integrity. To grow a nationalist myth, you also need to build a cult of personality around the fascist leader. People see the leader as the personification of the nation's spirit and destiny, the only person who can bring the country to greatness. This cult of personality is strengthened by propaganda, rituals, and public displays of loyalty. This creates a personal devotion to the leader that goes beyond normal political loyalty.

It is necessary to suppress all forms of opposition in order to set up a fascist government. Not only does this mean killing political opponents physically, but it also means destroying civil society and getting rid of free thought. Fascist governments want to make society uniform so that people can't disagree with the government. A lot of the time, the first target is political opposition. Fascist movements may start by putting opposition parties on the outside or gaining control over them, using legal and illegal methods to do so. Once the regime is in charge, it can shut down any groups that are connected to the opposition, arrest their leaders, and ban the opposition parties altogether. People who are against the government are sometimes put through show trials, jail time, or even execution.

It also takes apart civil society, which includes labour unions, professional associations, religious groups, and non-governmental organisations. These groups are seen as possible resistance sources, so the regime either takes them over or destroys them. For example, independent labour unions could be swapped out for ones that are run by the government and work for the regime. It is possible for the government to take over religious groups or force them to follow the regime's ideas. Non-governmental groups that fight for social justice or human rights are often shut down or forced to hide. The regime also has control over culture and education. Fascist governments try to take over people's minds and teach them their ideas, especially young people. It does this by changing the lessons in schools to teach fascist ideas and by blocking books, art, and music that don't fit with the government's beliefs. Intellectuals and artists who don't agree with this cultural conformity are often shut down or punished. Even in private, people who are against the government are being shut down. People who live in fascist countries are encouraged to spy on each other, which creates an atmosphere of fear and distrust. People often have to choose between being loyal to the regime and being loyal to their loved ones, which can cause problems in their personal relationships, even within families.

To the Readers, Fascist governments are built slowly and covertly over time. They do this by taking advantage of crises, weakening democratic institutions, controlling the media and spreading propaganda, using violence and fear, spreading a nationalist myth, and putting down any opposition. It's hard to break out of this cycle of authoritarianism because each of these parts makes the others stronger. Once they are in charge, fascist regimes are brutal, intolerable, and always trying to take complete control. This often causes a lot of suffering and damage both inside and outside of the country.

Fascism: The Magic of Survival

There are many studies in the circles of thinkers and researchers about how fascism survives, does not die, and raises its head again and again. I don't know if any recent microbiologist, genetic engineer, parapsychologist or sociopsychologist, who digs into human nature or DNA-RNA, finds a patch of fascism in human nature. However, there is a consensus on the question of whether fascism survives in four respects. What are these four things?

1) Strict organizational discipline and blind loyalty. (We've talked about this before.)

2) To instill fear or terror.

Let me explain how...
"They are taking away your bread, chase them away." OR, "Hindu khatre mein hai"/ "hindutv khatre mein hai"/ "Hindustan khatre mein hai"

Creating an atmosphere of constant fear among people. Convince people that you are in danger.

We've already known, Fascist terrorism has a peculiar pattern. This pattern can be broken down into:

a) To inflame the passions of the majority of the ignorant masses, to incite them against the minority masses.

b) It is never the whole truth, not the whole lie, but the truth mixed with the lie. Because a half-truth is worse than a full-blown lie.

c) To attack the human intellect, to eliminate thought. To force the practice of unification rather than diversification of thought. Removing the mindset of asking questions.

3) Touch the most urgent needs and demands of the people.

As George Dimitrov said, "Fascism in many respects attracts the masses. Because he appeals to the most urgent needs and demands of the people. Fascism not only promotes deep-rooted reforms among the people, but also exploits the revolutionary tradition in various ways. " Terrible thing. But it is undeniably true. Hitler or Mussolini harbored the unfulfilled demands of the disillusioned youth and disorganized precarious workers of Germany or Italy and provoked them in such a way that those Communist-Socialist-Jews are depriving you, insulting you, plundering your homeland. So take care of them. They are taking away your bread and dignity, chase them away. What a horrendous equation! But it is a populist ploy. This is what the famous sociologist Gramsci called Fanatic Offensive Populism. The fascists have not yet given up the weapon of that frenzied aggressive populism.

4) Strong ideological attacks, the ideology of which is mixed with myth-tradition history. In simple words, to embody the philosophy of the old elites in a new way in a new body. Many call it intellectual terrorism, an attack on ideology or philosophy.

• • •

CHAPTER VIII

Fascism in India

Hitler's motto was one: "Ekemabaditum". " I am one and unique. Just leave everything and call me. This mantra is mentioned in the Bhagavad Gita. Hitler and Mussolini's mentor, the German philosopher Nietzsche, said the same thing. That's what? The ultimate recognition of the concept of absolute, spiritual, prophetic and outwardly sovereign single dominion in its essence. Geeta and Nietzsche do not match in the sense of the word. But these two were mixed up by the fascists and the great leaders of the RSS. So Garrick and Gestapo, Hanuman and Goebbels become one. Fascists have come again and again - sometimes in Germany, sometimes in Italy, sometimes in Spain - and now in India. They manifest themselves in new forms, such as garik jhanda, trident and lotus in this country. Even then, they were the enemies of humanity, the worst enemies of civilization, and they still retain that character. However, their numbers are increasing day by day. Today's fascism does not burn the Reichstag. Instead, he joined hands with Ram for votes. Emotions mixed with lies. It confuses people. Terrorist infiltrators enter the country, seek opportunities to create war with the neighbor by removing the smoke of that infiltration, impose the dress of riots on the common people, Christian-Dalit sticks, the eyes of artists-intellectuals-artisans. This is their ploy. This is their great work. They have spread this trap all over India, no one is free from it. This is the greatest curse of the century. Therefore, an attempt is being made to write a new history in the light of myth and Hindutva by dissolving the Council of History. These were not random. One is connected to the other. All together is a complex fascist circle.

- Dear readers, here are a few quotes to support my point.

Quote: 1

"Fascist ideologies and organizations can unite and consolidate the future Indian state and society, especially Hindutva India. Therefore, an organization on the lines of Italian fascist organization should be formed among Indian Hindus. " (RSS leader Hedgewar's advisor BS Munj)

Quote: 2

''If Nazi Germany wins the war, the Hindutva people of India hope to build such a state in the country by joining hands with their swastika symbol. This is how Indian Hindus can regain their past glory. " (Quote by Veer Savarkar)

Quote: 3

"It is not enough just to compile the facts of history. History has to be shaped in such a way that our thousand-year-old Hindu sentiment is preserved and the new generation can think that they are the children of that great tradition. " (Quote by Murli Manohar Joshi, former Minister of Human Resource Development, Government of India)

Quote: 4

"Over the years, in the name of writing objective history, the so-called secular intellectuals have been projecting forces whose ideological allegiance was to non-Indian forces and philosophies. This power is trying to capture the field of history-practice. We need to take history out of their hands. " (Editorial by RSS mouthpiece Organiser)

These quotes seem to be very relevant today at a time when history is in the hands of fanatical forces. They are taking away the history of freedom, the freedom of history.

Reading Quote: 3 and Quote: 4 makes the point clear. "" "Defending Hindu sentiments of thousands of years" "or" "liberating history from the clutches of secular intellectuals" "- these are two great duties, of course." Let's live. Say what it says. History needs to be corrected. That's what Mussolini and Hitler did. First distort history to brainwash the entire nation. Press one ideology, one particular community as the greatest. Hitler wanted to put the German nation above everyone else. And they, the Sangh Parivar, they want to run Hindutva as Indianness.

They are the real Indians and all the outsiders - this equation is terrible. Hitler threw the entire Jewish nation into a gas chamber. The Sangh Parivar and its political affiliates have taken away the right to practise rational history and are following the same Hitlerian path. The Sangh Parivar is not afraid of weapons, it is afraid of the independent intellect of rational intellectuals. Because that talent doesn't belong to anyone. After the demolition of the Babri Masjid, we saw the Medhajivis standing up. For example, Amartya Sen's booklet published in 1993 - 'India at Risk', written by Sumit Sarkar and Tanika Sarkar, 'Khaki Shorts and Saffron Flags' printed in 93. Apart from this, eminent historian Irfan Habib also started some basic work.

Today, India really needs the independent intellect of rational intellectuals. That intelligence will convince the common people - "Narendra Damodardas Modi is not God, he is a wise man. It is completely false to claim Himself to be divine. Who is cheating the people of India, with whom some industrialists are in close touch, who is handing over the control of the country to Adani-Ambani."

In fact, fascism has taken the same path as a spider draws a tiny insect into its web. This poison has been spreading for a long time. The idea of doubt and hatred has been implanted in the minds of the majority of people.

What's that idea?

They're minorities, they're outsiders, they're foreigners, sometimes they're favored by the white race, sometimes they're fed by the Islamic culture of Central Asia. They never matched the great Indian tradition. Indian religion has tarnished the culture, cast a web of caste-hybridism and caused ritualistic bloodshed. Either throw them out, or throw them into a corner of society.

What an equation!

This is what Hitler and Goebbels of Nazi Germany, the apartheid rulers of South Africa, Enoch Powell of Britain and the Kru-Klux Knera of the United States did one day. Actually, there's a story behind it. What is that thread? Arrange everything according to the power equation and power balance. The main components are the numbers. Everything is arranged by them. The minority is outside the circle, not the main axis power. They are in Bengal. Throw them away. And if you want to keep it, make a number. If they have a distinct religion, language and culture, uproot them and join them to the majority tradition.

It is needless to say today that Aryan culture, Brahmanism has not only made the society and the state rapacious and tyrannical, but has also created caste, creed, community and hatred. The aggressive garb of Hindutva has been imposed from above.

Now, I am talking about the world-famous Indian scholar Rabindranath. Rabindranath Tagore wrote:
"Unity in diversity is India's religion. It accepts all ways, and sees the greatness of all in his own place. "

Prophets look at history from a particular point of view. That's a great perspective. This view denies the contradictory complex patterns of history. Imposes the concept of pure goodness. The same happened with Rabindranath Tagore. He says these things guided by a good desire. It would be good if this wish comes true. But that hasn't happened so far. The chauvinistic Hindu culture did not allow this. Rather, it has broken all the good efforts of voluntary union. Isn't this Hindutva, supported by foreign Aryan invaders, flying into this country?

This Brahmanical chauvinism was not united only with the authoritarian state power. A counter-combination process has been forced from above. In the context of the Gnosticism of the Upanishads, the theory of absolute unity, the combinatorial philosophy of the Gita and the theory of 'Ekamavadvatyam', the non-dualism of Shankara, the Samkhya of Kapila, the Yoga of Patanjali, the Smriti-Samhita of Manu-Raghunandan - all these combined to create a field of terrible intellectual and practical aggression. At that point, the process of integration begins. Rabindranath used to say, 'A python swallows a snake'. To be alone by sacrificing self-determination - in fact, the policy of strangling the python serpent that imperialism operates. This leads to more isolation. That's what happened in India. The disintegration of unity from the top to the bottom of the rabid Brahmanical Hindutva is a continual distortion.

We know that during the Gupta period, throughout the northern route, in Aryavarta, under the influence of radical Brahmanism, numerous people of the grassroots were converted. Some are Hindu, some are Sikh, some are Buddhist. During the Pala dynasty, Buddhism was recognized by the royal power, but abandoned by the Brahmanical nobles. In the Sena era, the wheel turns. The state power is in alliance with Brahmanism. The exploitation of upper castes took a terrible form. Communism is institutionalized. The oppression of the poor working people begins. There is only one alternative - escape in a hurry and embrace Buddhism. Dr. Nihar Roy's' History of Bengal 'or Dr. Dinesh Sen's' Bengali Language and Literature 'show how the Hindu-Buddhist conflict intensified. It's not a conflict, it's a conversion. Dear readers, 'Charyapada' is the first example of Bengali literature, but it is not the result of Hindu Brahmanism. This is the tradition of the Buddhist community. It is not the upper-caste majority, but the innumerable lower-caste toilers - from the Tattvabaya to the boatmen, the Dom-Chandal-Shabra - who have taken centre stage. All of them are the poorest marginal power, Sahajya Buddhists.

They had a deep hatred for the elite Hindu Brahmanism. In one verse it is said about the Brahmins - "Nagar bahire re dombi toh hori kudiya. Chhoi chho gayi brahm nadiya"

It means - "Bald-headed Brahmin is going to say "Don't touch me-Don't touch me" but the eyes (brahmin) are on the juicy body of the young Dom.

Hindu fundamentalist historians have time and again tried to show that in the medieval period, the Muslims committed great atrocities on the Hindus of this country. Their culture and tradition are shattered. That's partly true. Partly not true. True, the Islamic state was at one stage aggressive, and under its shadow, a group of infidels, hoping for rapid advancement, invaded the country to curry favour with the royal power. But the assault didn't last long. Again, when the text books are opened, the educational presentations on WhatsApp-Facebook-YouTube show how dangerous Aurangzeb was in history. How cruel he was! I don't need to prove that he is a Muslim. But it is necessary to see what those who have done in-depth research about it want to say. I don't need to tell you what they mean. Instead, you should do some research on the subject. But I want to say, how many more times will an Aurangzeb be highlighted?

• • •

The force wearing the saffron jersey of the Rashtriya Swayamsevak Sangh has united two currents -

The organizational discipline of German-Italian Fascism with Aryan Fascist Absolute Piety and Loyalism. You can say, a hybrid species, duck philosophy. Perhaps that's why this new fascism is even more dangerous.

It is not a farce of civilisation but a tragedy of civilisation. It is not that the tragedy will stop overnight. But if we don't, we are not free. If I think I'll survive with my face in the sand like an ostrich, that's also futile. Because if you are blind, is it blind? Blind man, having eyes, is as much a curse of human culture as the dark ages.

There is no dacoity. There is not a question. Accepting the one and supreme authority. Naji was once a great hero or his' prophet '. He took a step towards the Guru and threw this message in the main camp - 'We want arms more'. .. Everything Beginning with the Child's Primer Down to the Last Newspaper, Every Theater and Every Movie, Every Billboard and Every Bearboard Must Be Placed at the Service of This Great Mission. " What is this great mission or great purpose? Serving the fascist fighters unconditionally. They are killing thousands of Jewish children and old people by putting them in gas chambers, they have to serve them. They are raping thousands of women, maiming young men forever, turning one country after another into a prison. Nevertheless, they must be served and glorified. This is a terrible, unimaginable tragedy for humanity. The Fascists have repeatedly sought to impose that curse on defenseless mankind. He is still not there. The same is happening in India. Hitler was Mussolini at the time. Today, his avowed half-Hanuman is half-human Garik Fascism. When will this farce end? Is there an answer to this in history?

Although the inspiration for this answer could be found from the depths of Indian history, nothing else can be found in the future. There are three eras of history - the ancient, the middle, the modern; the middle ages have 20% and the modern era is in shambles.

Above all -

In the books of history and sociology, Hindu pride has been and is being inflated in the sky. Muslims, on the other hand, have been and are being branded as the devil. History is being distorted. There's a university! Also, it would be my fault if I didn't mention it.

The economic theory that was formulated against a particular community 35 years ago has not been fully applied today, but the mentality to apply it has not died yet. The year was 1984.

The Vishwa Hindu Parishad (VHP) published a handbill or pamphlet in 1984. It was widely circulated on behalf of the Vishwa

Hindu Parishad, even then Godhra did not happen. The title of the pamphlet was - "Get up, think, get organized, get armed, save the country, save religion." The ten commandments of the Sangh Parivar are an indication of how terrible it can be. The purpose of mentioning this old thing today in this article is only one - to understand their mentality.

Here's the ' points of the pamphlet':

1. From now on, you will not buy anything from a Muslim shopkeeper.
2. From now on, you will not sell any goods from your shop to Muslims.
3. From now on you / any of you will not use their hotels and garages.
4. Keep the car in the garage of only Hindus. Don't buy or sell gold to Muslims.
5. Collectively boycott all the films in which Muslim heroes and heroines have acted, label them anti-national.
6. No one will work in the offices of Muslims or allow them to enter their workplaces.
7. Don't buy their property. Don't sell your property. Do not allow them to enter your area, housing complex.
8. From now on, they will vote for those who will protect the interests of Hindus.
9. Be careful that none of your daughters fall in love with any of their sons, do not mix with them in educational institutions.
10. Don't study with any Muslim teacher or take any training from them.

This is what is called economic terrorism. At the root of the terror was a pernicious intellectual and philosophical hatred. A lot of people talk about death. This pamphlet is the poison in which all the elements of the Gujarat genocide were hidden. Now, instead of talking about the Sangh Parivar, the Indian Goebbels, the Indian Hitler, it should be said that the Goebbels-Hitlers and the neo-fascists of Europe can fully learn from the Sangh Shakti who distributed this pamphlet. The Indian goebbels is now the international intellectual centre of communal fascism.

Today, this neo-fascism is spreading across the country, at the level of society. From media to myths, from politics to social media, from cricket to the film world, and sometimes in the film world, Kashmir files, Kerala story or Veer Savarkar or 'Shyam' movie! It's like a documentary film, but it's all drama! But how do people know this is not true? Caught in the open is a far-fetched desire to enchant and conquer the sensitive youth. Fascism-Nazism took the same path. From the beginning to the end, the head hurts. There is not even a drop of land under the feet, but above the head the murky sky of fundamentalism keeps opening up. Sometimes we wonder where we're going. Maybe not in the fullness of innocence, but in the fullness of homicidal demagoguery. The matter didn't end here. The chariot of fundamentalism has sometimes touched the Christians and the Dalits, flooded them with blood, sometimes washed away the foreigners and tried to convert the civilized democratic law of citizenship into a Dalit one. Nothing is isolated, not the madness of the mad king Muhammad bin Tughlaq. Even if it seems crazy, there is a well-planned devil behind it. And these efforts together mark a coherent aggressive culture and ideology. The essence of that ideology is to force the superiority of one opinion by denying the harmonious relationship of many ways to many ways.

Inhuman culture is necessary to establish the superiority of an opinion by force.
And the appearance of this inhuman culture can not be formulated in a straight line. It is multifaceted. Such as -

(1) Organized preaching in mouthpieces.

(2) The same level of publicity throughout the country through the media.

(3) To make sports-culture especially cricket-culture militant-jihadist.

(4) Disciplining the opposition by picking up the dust of ISI char (Agent), perhaps it is called rumour-culture.

Goebbels, Hitler's propaganda secretary, used to say, "Don't tell the whole truth, and you don't have to lie." " Instead, mix the truth with lies. Because half-truths are worse than lies". Through the media, the war-mongering government has taken the traitorous route - the culture of propagating half-truths.

Let's talk about sports culture in point 3.

We know that sport is not just physical exercise. Sport is a growing industry. It forms the thread of harmony even in the midst of fierce competition. As the saying goes, if you don't go to the playground, your heart won't grow. Those who sing, paint, write poetry, are involved in theater are friendly and sensitive, as are people in the field of sports. Along with writers, artists and intellectuals, they also came forward spontaneously in the anti-war struggle in the country. But today, what is the fate of that culture in the hands of Grecian warlords!

Whenever any side has played against Pakistan, the support has been directed towards that side. As Indians, we can be happy the day Pakistan loses to India. But the media took that joy to the peak of madness. Sports-madness seems to have erased war-madness as well. There is a natural support from the Asian audience for the Asian teams. I remember the match between Pakistan and Australia. On that day, the circle of normalcy was torn and support went out to the white Australians, not because they played well, but because they were beating Pakistan miserably. This is a prehistoric predator. On that day, not only did the lotus climb on the back of the kangaroo, but on that day the lotus also tarnished the liberal atmosphere of kangaroo sports and culture. It is a crime to mix religion with politics. But isn't it more dangerous to mix cricket with religious politics? This is a manifestation of the culture of war. This culture of cricket is less dangerous than the culture of war. I don't think Hitler had a culture like that!

This time, let's talk about the rumor-culture in point 4.

That's right, the Pakistani intelligence agency ISI is not sitting idle. Behind them are the petrodollar-backed Oil-Kuber pan-Islamic clique and various religious terrorist activities in Pakistan. It will be easier for them to negotiate with different ruling circles if they exploit the anger of the people and maintain instability in the subcontinent. But on this pretext, the search for the ISI among the opposing views is a serious trend. That's what Hitler did - to brand the Christian-democratic-socialist as the enemy's stooge. It's all rumour-culture.

So far, thousands of people have been arrested on suspicion of ISIS in different parts of the country. There is no way to know if they are really ISIS. One thing to note is that 99% of the population is Muslim. One cannot imagine how easily the arrow of suspicion was turned towards this community. The calculation is clear -- ISI. Kill the goats. I am reminded of a sad chapter in history. The trial of Oswald Pohl, one of the leaders of Hitler's stormtroopers, took place at the Nuremberg trials in June 1946. Paul suddenly spoke of the Final Solution. What's that again? "Paul replied," "The only solution is to exterminate all the Jews and purify the German nation."

Even if you do not remember, Savarkar ji's message is recorded in history, "At this moment, the British can stay. Muslims are the enemy. " Savarkar's statement encouraged the Gandhi-killer RSS leaders and Hindu fundamentalists like Patel who were hiding in the Congress. Their ghosts, their tainted legacy is being carried by today's rioters-warriors-nationalists. This is the painful experience of blue history. Those who want to remove this pain, those who are responsible for the human conscience, must become more and more familiar with this historical experience. The question is not one of liquid emotion, not of idle dreaming; the question is one of consciousness, philosophy, and ideology. Remember, this chauvinistic fascism will dissolve your consciousness, mind and intellect from within, pitting you against yourself, and robbing you of your humanity. This game is unimaginable. To prevent this, political and diplomatic alliances are not enough, consciousness needs to be awakened and sharpened. It is important to create awareness among people.

Culture can be a reliable catalyst in keeping people's consciousness awake, of course, culture with a democratic tradition with scientific zeal. That distinctive culture will make people forget their differences. That unique culture will make people great in the midst of differences. The unique culture that will unite the minds of all classes of people, such as lower caste Hindus, upper caste Hindus, Muslims, Buddhists, Christians, etc., by awakening the sense of humanity in them. Friends, the prominent culture that we want is the prominent culture, but the sky is not a figment of imagination; history is witness to the practical application of this culture of harmony. History shows that there has been an attempt at reconciliation at the grassroots level.

This is not a new culture in India. India has been witness to an unprecedented experience of voluntary integration. How was that experience? What was the tradition like? My dear readers, if we do not discuss a little bit about this, then only the problem will be discussed, not the solution. So let's take a look at history - the tradition of people-to-people contact in the heart of India -

In his Swadeshi Samaj, Rabindranath says, "Between the Hindu and the Muslim societies there was a junction where the two extremes met; the pro-Nanak and pro-Kabir and the lower-class Vaishnavite societies were examples of this. In our country, the educated community does not keep any news of the breaches that are being created in various places among the common people regarding religion and customs, if they had seen it - still the process of adjustment has not stopped. "

Two conclusions emerge from this statement. First, the reluctance and disdain of the educated classes (who are, of course, the upper class majority) towards the process of voluntary amalgamation. Second: Voluntary fusion was attempted at the initiative of the Nanak-Kabir-Lower Vaishnavites. It was a social movement. In the middle of the Middle Ages, they emerged from historical and social inevitability; they developed a simple devotional movement against the aggression of the upper castes and the majority. The movement was joined by various minorities, lower caste forces, especially those involved in manual labour. This movement challenged the idea of Hindu Brahmanical supremacy in terms of philosophy and ideology.

This movement is manifesting itself in the consciousness. He was never a peddler of the bizarre inconceivable heresy that the Brahmanists of later times, especially the Hekshagosvamin of Vrindavan, blended dualism and esoteric dualism within the framework of Vaishnavism. On the contrary, Caitanya wanted to make a real fusion by standing on the ground through the process of 'Achandale Premacharan', 'Dwija-Chandala Milana', 'Namakirtana-Nagara Sankirtana', etc. This process accelerates the process of social reform. Unfortunately, this process did not last long. It really wasn't allowed to stay. However, the state power never saw this movement in the light.

On the other hand, we have learned from history that Humayun Akbar adopted a liberal approach to strengthen and popularize his rule. Akbar's Deen Elahi, in particular, added a new dimension to the question of harmonizing religion and the plan of worship. Bangladesh can also be considered. Under the rulers of Bangladesh, Hussain Shah, Nusrat Shah, Ruknuddin Barabak Shah, instead of the oppression of Islamism, Hindu-Muslim harmony was observed. All of them patronized the translators of the Ramayana-Mahabharata and the Bhagavata.

Another chapter in history. The court of Chittagong-Arakan was called the Rosang court. There's a different mix. a diverse culture. Most of the kings were Buddhists. The ministers are Muslims. Hindus and Muslims are together. The poets belong to the Sufi community. The literature they created, such as Daulat Kazi's' Lor Chandrani ', Syed Alaol's transcendence of all religious differences, touched the aesthetic yearnings of all communities, Hindu and Muslim Buddhist. This is definitely an unforgettable experience.

Sadly, neither the Chaitanya-influenced folk devotionalism, nor this tradition of voluntary union in the Chittagong Arakan region - we have been able to retain in the modern era, especially in the enlightened nineteenth century. Our renaissance movement was cursed, divided because we could not. The vast Muslim community is far away, and we have not been able to draw even middle-class Muslims into this awakening process. I blame them for their lackadaisical attitude. We never thought we were responsible for it. Because we did not think, the joy of our awakening at the bottom has become weak. The renaissance of the early 19th century was pushed by Hindu revivalist ideas in the latter part of that century. The revival of Hindu Purana-Bhakti-Dharma after the Hindu Mela of 67, the National Theatre of 72, did not only complicate the situation. The renaissance has stalled the movement in the middle. It has also given the new awakened countrymen the smell of radical Hinduism. He is neither Jyotirindranath 's drama nor Bankimchandra' s' Anandamath 'free from odour. The anti-English struggle has finally degenerated into an anti-Yavan mentality. The anti-Bengal partition movement, which is the pride of all of us, is also not free from the guilt of this bigotry.

If we look at Rabindranath Tagore's article 'Lokhit', it becomes clear - "The partition of Bengal did not touch our breadbasket, it touched our heart. As far as his heart was concerned, his pain was uncontrollable. The reason why the Muslims of Bengal are not united with us in this pain is that we have never united our hearts with them. " Rabindranath criticized Hindu swadeshi in more harsh words and said, "Swadeshiyana's cheap melodrama on the grand stage of sentiment. " It's not a social issue. There is no question of humanity. By cutting the blood-plaque of Kalima, the Hindu compatriots imposed the principle of patriotism on the Muslim tribes. They were not taken to task. This trend will continue in the future. I pay my respect and homage to the revolutionaries of the Agni Yuga, who were also victims of this blind Hindu sentiment. The idols of Maa Kali and the Karmayoga of the Gita (which can not be called secular elements despite thousands of efforts), day after day they clung to them and moved forward in the Swadeshi movement. On the one hand, the minority Muslim community has moved away. That is why the British took full advantage of the situation. It can be said that Hindu-Brahminical sentiments and the British policy of 'share and enjoy' became complementary to each other.

However, many efforts have been made from time to time to bring about Hindu-Muslim unity. Some of such important efforts can be mentioned here. In 1916, the Indian National Congress and the Muslim League were united by the Lucknow Pact. Through this agreement, the Congress and the Muslim League together made several demands to the British government, one of which was the reform of the electoral system. It is considered an important step in Hindu-Muslim unity. Moreover, after World War I, the Ottoman Empire collapsed, and Indian Muslims began to agitate for the protection of their caliph. Mahatma Gandhi supported this movement and united it with the non-cooperation movement. This initiative was an important example of Hindu-Muslim unity. Moreover, many freedom fighters of India like Netaji Subhas Chandra Bose have taken this work forward. If we include the names of all of them here, we will be far away from the main topic. However, friends, even in independent India, the work of many political leaders is in progress to establish this Hindu-Muslim unity.

• • •

CHAPTER IX

An Analysis of Contemporary Capitalism

Capitalism is an economic system where the means of production—factories, land, machinery, and capital—are privately owned, and economic activity is largely driven by the profit motive. The system is underpinned by market competition, where supply and demand determine prices and the allocation of resources. While capitalist economies have proven effective at generating wealth and driving innovation, they have also faced criticism for their tendency to produce economic inequality, environmental degradation, and social stratification. Capitalism corrupts all social relations. It pulls everyone in a reactionary direction. It forces workers to compete against one another. This fosters sexism, racism, nativism and nationalism. It also forces workers, in order to survive, to be situated in opposition to the natural world. This leads to loggers fighting environmentalists, oil drillers and coal miners demanding more jobs even though the effects of this production is to poison all of us and our families. It pits us against our own allies and puts us at war with our own selves. It has countless methods of manipulating and coercing us to serve them, our common enemy, instead. Because they create dependency, like addicts we throw away our long term interests for short-term needs. Capitalists have deliberately, fiendishly, cleverly set up our lives this way. They super exploit some, like immigrants, and workers in the most dominated countries, so workers living in the imperialist centres can't compete. It's similar to the way capitalists dump grain to make small farmers lose their land. They set the price, and divide us from our own livelihoods. We are led to blame the wrong people for this, to create enemies out of fellow victims.

Historically, capitalism emerged out of earlier systems of economic organisation, such as feudalism and mercantilism. Its development was influenced by the rise of industrialization in the

18th and 19th centuries, particularly in Western Europe and North America. The rise of capitalism was driven by the technological advances of the Industrial Revolution, as well as political changes such as the weakening of aristocratic power and the growth of democratic governance. These forces helped establish the foundations of modern capitalism, which, in its various forms, continues to dominate the global economic landscape today. However, while capitalism has spurred unprecedented economic growth, it has also been linked to a number of negative effects. These include the concentration of wealth and power, economic instability, and exploitation of both labour and natural resources.

Key Features of Capitalism —

Private Ownership of the Means of Production:

One of the defining characteristics of capitalism is the private ownership of the means of production. In this system, individuals or corporations own the resources and capital required to produce goods and services. This contrasts with systems such as socialism or communism, where the means of production are owned collectively or by the state. Private ownership allows individuals and businesses to control how resources are used, including decisions related to production, distribution, and investment. This control gives capitalists the ability to accumulate wealth through profits generated by their businesses. While private ownership incentivizes efficiency and innovation, it also contributes to economic inequality, as those who own the means of production are able to capture the excess (surplus) value generated by labour.

Dear friends, we know that Each social formation is defined by its mode of production (the way the society as a whole meets its needs, how it reproduces itself from one day to the next).

Mode of production: the way a social formation is organised to reproduce its own relations of production and productive forces.

There are many variations of several basic types:

• Subsistence-based (includes hunting and foraging, forest gardening, pastoralism).

• Slavery (wealth is obtained by directly forced labour).

• Feudalism (serfs or peasants must turn over a portion of their crops to the landowner).

• Capitalism (profit is gained by selling commodities at a price higher than their production costs).

• Socialism (a transition stage during which production is controlled by the working class, and performed to meet society's needs rather than to accumulate private wealth).

• Communism (production is engaged voluntarily for the collective good).

• Anarchism (production is engaged in, or not, voluntarily, without the transition period of socialism).Forms/stages of capitalism:

• Colonialism (capitalists expand beyond national limits by conquering and directly administering other social formations to extract resources, exploit labour power, and expand markets).

• Imperialism (the internationalisation of monopoly capital; the globalisation of production through the export not only of goods, but of capital itself).

These are extremely brief and limited abstract concepts, theoretical models which are distinct from historically specific realities. No social formation can be a pure form of one type, and each social formation is different.

Market Competition:

Another key feature of capitalism is market competition. In a capitalist system, businesses compete with one another to attract customers, lower costs, and maximise profits. This competition drives innovation, as businesses strive to develop new products and services that meet consumer demands. Competition drives technological development as each capitalist pursues ever-increasing efficiency and speed. They mechanise their factories to minimise the number of workers and to stay ahead of one another. Companies must minimise waste and reduce costs in order to remain competitive. To remain competitive, the capitalists are forced to continuously cut the costs of production. Wages are the largest variable cost in most businesses, so there's tremendous pressure on capitalists to keep them as low as possible. To accomplish this, even during periods of high employment they manipulate the economy to keep the unemployment rate at about 5% or higher, so there are always plenty of desperate people competing for jobs. They move their factories to countries where wages are the lowest they can find, and where repressive governments prevent workers from organising. (If the governments aren't repressive enough, that will be quickly taken care of). Smaller companies that can't keep up are driven out of business or bought up by larger ones, forming monopolies in certain sectors. Four companies control 90% of the world's grain production. Four airlines hold 80% of the market share in the US. eBay controls 90% of the online auction market in the U.S. and Europe. 33% of all laptops in the world are produced by one company (Quanta Computer in Taiwan). A single firm, AB InBev, produces nearly 25% of the world's beer (more than 200 brands). U.S. company Anheuser-Busch was acquired in 2008 by InBev, which was a merger of Interbrew (which was a merger of Belgian companies Artois and Piedboeuf), and AmBev (which was a merger of Brazilian firms Antarctica and Brahma). Along the way, InBev also picked up Labatt (Canada), Fujian Sedrin (third largest brewery in the world's largest beer market), and several Latin American firms. Anhueser-Busch even on its own was infamous for its public threats to lower its prices below any other company that attempted to undercut them. This was a very effective tactic to keep beer prices elevated overall. Market power paves the way for monopolies to employ various means to control prices, to counteract the tendency of the rate of profit to fall. So while the local hardware store is failing, large oil companies (and beer monopolies) are making more money than ever.So we can understand that Businesses may engage in anti-competitive practices, such as forming monopolies or engaging in price-fixing, which can undermine the benefits of competition. Additionally, the focus on profit maximisation can result in the externalisation of costs, such as environmental damage, that are not borne by the businesses themselves but by society as a whole.

The Profit Motive:

The pursuit of profit is the primary driving force in a capitalist economy. Businesses are motivated to maximise their profits by increasing revenues and reducing costs. This profit motive is central to the functioning of the capitalist system, as it incentivizes businesses to innovate, improve efficiency, and expand their operations. Only through expansion can each company gain a competitive edge over all the others. For capitalism as a whole to function in a reasonably stable way, for capital investment (especially in heavy industry) to be worthwhile and for everyone to stay ahead of their interest payments, it must grow at least about 3% annually. So the cycle goes around again, but bigger. In the next turn, they must extract more raw materials, exploit more labour, manufacture more products, generate more waste, make more profits. Growth is not just linear, because each turn of the cycle is on top of a greater quantity than the time before. Therefore, the relentless pursuit of profit leads to negative outcomes, particularly when profit maximisation comes at the expense of workers, consumers, or the environment. Businesses may seek to minimise labour costs by paying low wages, reducing benefits, or outsourcing jobs to lower-cost regions. They also prioritise short-term profits over long-term sustainability, leading to practices that harm the environment or create economic instability. Basically, they're not paying the full production costs for the commodities. Pollution from the production process is discharged into the environment. The numerous and serious consequences of this, never mind the cleanup which never happens, are not paid for by the capitalist who caused the problem, but by us, by society as a whole, and by all the living beings on Earth who are affected. In fact, none—not one—of the world's top 20 industrial sectors would be profitable (at all!) if they didn't externalise costs.

Now we run into one of capitalism's major contradictions. In order to make a profit, capitalists must exploit workers, in other words, pay them less than the value of the commodities that they produce. So, there will always be more total value on the market than what can be paid for (and consumed) by the domestic population. When markets become saturated, this causes what's called the crisis of overproduction. There's too much stuff, and the people will never—can never—be paid enough to buy it all. The goal of each individual capitalist is to maximise profits, in other words, to accumulate as much excess value (surplus value) as possible, to reinvest as new capital. But for the system overall, too much surplus value causes problems. It can't all be absorbed back into the economy. What do they do with it? They can't just leave it lying around to depreciate; they have to put it to work somehow.

A portion of excess value (surplus value) is syphoned off for personal use by capitalists, to furnish extravagant lifestyles with excessive salaries and bonuses.Some surplus value is simply thrown away, eliminated through waste, wars (more than 54% of the US discretionary budget is spent on perpetrating violent imperialist world domination, terrorising and killing millions of people in the process), and so called international "aid" (which is also employed to extend and intensify imperialist domination). The latter two also function as centres for creating even more profit, which they are compelled to pursue, but which also exacerbates the overall problem.They desperately ramp up the level of consumption with infusions of credit, basing the consumer economy on debt. They issue loans like crazy, even while knowing they can't possibly ever all be paid off. Of course this creates bubbles and instability, which grow progressively worse.They must continuously force open and seize control of more markets. This is one of the driving forces for imperialism. When more than one country does this, major inter-imperialist conflicts ensue. This rivalry—not any sort of moral issue—was the cause of the two major inter-imperialist wars (the so-called "world wars") of the 20th Century. So imperialist war both captures markets and destroys excess products—it's capitalist multitasking.

Wage Labour:

In a capitalist economy, most people earn their living by selling their labour to businesses in exchange for wages. This system of wage labour is a fundamental aspect of capitalism, as it allows businesses to access the labour they need to produce goods and services while providing individuals with the income they need to meet their basic needs.

However, wage labour is also associated with exploitation, particularly in cases where workers are paid less than the value they create for their employers. This exploitation is a central concern of Marxist critiques of capitalism, which argue that workers are alienated from the fruits of their labour and that the surplus value they generate is captured by capitalists as profit.

Capital Accumulation:

Capital accumulation refers to the process by which individuals or businesses reinvest profits into their enterprises in order to generate more wealth. This process is central to the functioning of capitalism, as it allows businesses to grow, expand, and innovate over time. Capital accumulation also leads to the concentration of wealth and power, as those who control capital are able to increase their wealth by reinvesting their profits.

However, capital accumulation can also exacerbate economic inequality, as those who already have capital are able to accumulate more wealth, while those who rely on labour for their income may struggle to maintain economic security. This concentration of wealth can lead to social and political power imbalances, as wealthy individuals and corporations use their resources to influence policy and protect their interests.

• • •

The Reality

Capital, having saturated the globe, has expanded beyond physical limits. Increasingly, capitalists have been busting through the over-production problem by bypassing the production process altogether. As industrial production has surpassed the capacity of world markets to purchase and consume its products, the pressure of too much capital to invest has forced governments to relax regulations and allow more fictitious value into their national economies, leading to the current global dominance of the financial/investment sector. There has been increasing conflict within the capitalist class over the character of current and future growth: concrete excess (surplus) value extracted from labour power on the one hand ("working capital"), vs., on the other hand, inflated forms that are increasingly unstable ("fictitious capital"). Money makes more money (but no material value) through debt, deficits, speculation, arbitrage, and by simply printing more of it.This seems to throw production—along with workers and consumers—out of the equation. They don't appear to need us so much any more. This is reflected in our high unemployment rate and falling incomes. Commodity production is still the largest part of the global economy, but finance has risen more rapidly, increasing its proportion relative to industry. In 1978, 2% of global profit came from finance. By 2011 it increased to 42%. By 2021, the global finance sector contributed around 40% to global profits(BCG Global Visual Capitalist). Fintech alone, for example, has been rapidly expanding, with projections for its market size to reach $1.5

trillion by 2030(BCG Global). Given the ongoing trends, it is likely that the finance sector's share of global profits remains substantial and continues to rise, especially with the growth of digital finance and fintech(Fortuny World Bank Open Knowledge).So the rising influence of finance capital on the economy is considerable, and it's destabilising. But producing more commodities is destabilising too. Capital's escape from production and ability to find refuge in the ballooning financial industry is merely relative, partial and temporary. It's not a long-term solution for the crisis of overproduction, but merely prolongs the agony. The massive amounts of money pouring into stocks, commodity markets, bonds, credit, currencies, real estate, and other instruments of speculation (at least not tulips this time) causes great instability as the amount of fictitious value in the economy increases. As investors begin to acknowledge that their holdings are artificially inflated, that there's nothing underpinning them but bad debt and toxic assets, the bubbles inevitably crash. Financial crises occur as these worthless assets are dumped en masse. After prices collapse, the risks once again become attractive and buying begins anew. Each turn of the cycle generates more fear and greed than the one before.Financial collapse has happened many times before, and it will again. It causes chaos and shake ups. Business interests large and small fail, increasing the suffering of the majority of people who are trapped inside and dependent on the economy. The crisis of faith in the financial sector impacts industry too, because the two forms of capital have become so intertwined. When one receives medicine, the other suffers side effects. Industry has come to depend on credit at every step: to capitalise itself, to operate, and to facilitate the consumption of goods. Plus they've become extremely dependent on the inflation of the speculative value of their companies—their stock price. As industrial capital declines relatively in power, and the financial sector experiences ever-more volatile boom-and-crash cycles that reverberate through the global economy, banks have fewer options they can exercise in response, because they've already implemented whatever they can do to facilitate growth (they can't go below 0% interest rates). These current forms of capital are reaching their ultimate limits.

• • •

113

SAJID MOLLAH

facilitate growth (they can't go below 0% interest rates). These current forms of capital are reaching their ultimate limits.

CHAPTER X

The Evils of Capitalism

In the preceding chapter, I conducted a comprehensive examination of the fundamental components of capitalism, including its definition, operation, and the primary characteristics that characterise this economic system. Capitalism has frequently been praised as a catalyst for innovation, growth, and progress; however, its effects are not universally salutary. It is imperative that we now investigate the opposing perspective—the detrimental consequences of capitalism on both society and the economy—as we progress.

In this chapter, I will investigate the darker undercurrents of capitalism, examining how its unbridled pursuit of profit can result in the marginalisation of vulnerable populations, the erosion of social welfare, and the widening of inequality. I will explore the ways in which capitalism, when left unregulated, can exacerbate economic instability, create boom-and-bust cycles, and further the gap between the wealthy and the impoverished.

This chapter endeavours to balance our comprehension of capitalism by highlighting the inherent flaws and challenges that accompany its implementation in the real world, while retaining the analytical lens from the previous chapter. By doing so, we can gain a more comprehensive understanding of the extensive implications of capitalism on our collective well-being and begin to consider the potential for alternative economic models that prioritise human dignity, equity, and sustainability.

-

-

The Negative Effects of Capitalism on the Economy

While capitalism has been lauded for its ability to generate wealth and drive innovation, it has also been criticised for producing significant negative effects on the economy. These effects include economic inequality, instability, and exploitation.

Economic Inequality:

'Inequality is rising day by day. Workers are frustrated, their salaries not matching the cost of living. This is because of the growing gap between rich and poor which curtails any chances of prosperity.'
– Tariq Mobeen Chaudray, Center for Finance for Development, Indus Consortium, Pakistan

Dear friends,One of the most widely recognized negative effects of capitalism is economic inequality. In a capitalist system, wealth tends to concentrate in the hands of those who own capital, such as businesses, land, or financial assets. This concentration of wealth leads to a widening gap between the rich and the poor, as capitalists accumulate more wealth through profits, while workers receive only a fraction of the value they create through wages.

Economic inequality is exacerbated by the fact that capital ownership is often inherited, rather than earned through labour. As a result, wealth tends to be passed down through generations, leading to the perpetuation of economic disparities. This concentration of wealth can have significant negative effects on the economy, as it reduces social mobility and limits opportunities for individuals to improve their economic standing. Inequality also has broader economic consequences. When wealth is concentrated in the hands of a small percentage of the population, overall demand for goods and services can decline, as lower-income individuals have less purchasing power. This reduction in demand can lead to slower economic growth and increased unemployment, as businesses cut back on production in response to lower consumer spending. Additionally, economic inequality can lead to political instability, as disenfranchised individuals become frustrated with their lack of opportunities and begin to demand change.

There is growing evidence that the current levels of extreme inequality far exceed what can be justified by talent, effort and risk-taking. Instead they are more often the product of inheritance, monopoly or crony connections to government. Approximately a third of billionaire wealth is derived from inheritance. Over the next 20 years, 500 of the world's richest people will hand over $2.4 trillion to their heirs – a sum larger than the GDP of India, a country of 1.3 billion people. Monopolies fuel excessive returns to owners and shareholders at the expense of the rest of the economy. The power of monopoly to generate extreme wealth is demonstrated by the fortune of Carlos Slim, the sixth richest man in the world. His fortune derives from an almost complete monopoly he was able to establish over fixed line, mobile and broadband communications services in Mexico. The OECD found that This monopoly has had significant negative effects for consumers and the economy. Monopoly power is compounded by cronyism, the ability of powerful private interests to manipulate public policy to entrench existing monopolies and create new ones. Privatisation deals, natural resources given away below fair value, corrupt public procurement, or tax exemptions and loopholes are all ways in which well-connected private interests can enrich themselves at the expense of the public. In total, Oxfam has calculated that approximately two-thirds of billionaire wealth is the product of inheritance, monopoly and cronyism.

Economic Instability:

Capitalist economies are prone to periods of boom and bust, characterised by rapid economic growth followed by sharp downturns. These cycles of expansion and contraction are driven by a variety of factors, including changes in consumer demand, technological innovation, and financial speculation. While periods of economic growth can generate wealth and create jobs, they are often followed by periods of economic instability, characterised by high levels of unemployment, falling wages, and reduced investment. This instability can have significant negative effects on the economy, as it creates uncertainty and reduces the ability of individuals and businesses to plan for the future. One of the key drivers of economic instability in capitalist economies is financial speculation. In their pursuit of profit, investors may engage in speculative activities, such as buying and selling financial assets in the hopes of making a quick return. While speculation can lead to short-term gains, it can also create asset bubbles, where the price of an asset becomes inflated beyond its true value. When these bubbles burst, they can lead to financial crises, as was the case during the 2008 global financial crisis. Another driver of economic instability is the inherent tendency of capitalism to overproduce goods and services. In their pursuit of profit, businesses may produce more goods than can be sold at profitable prices, leading to excess supply and falling prices. This overproduction can result in economic downturns, as businesses cut back on production and lay off workers in response to declining profits.

Be sure to remember that Continuous growth isn't easy. We see economists and politicians on the news all the time trying to figure out how to keep it going. But as economies become saturated, there's less opportunity for profitable investment. So they have to invent ways to turn more things into profit generators, invading us through privatisation and assigning monetary value to every aspect of our lives, from our emotions to genetic material.

Exploitation of Labor:

A central critique of capitalism is that it relies on the exploitation of labour. In a capitalist system, workers sell their labour to businesses in exchange for wages. However, the value of the goods and services produced by workers often exceeds the wages they are paid. This surplus value is captured by the capitalists as profit, leading to the exploitation of workers, who do not receive the full value of their labour. This exploitation is particularly pronounced in industries where labour costs are minimised in order to maximise profits. For example, in many low-wage industries, such as retail, fast food, and agriculture, workers are paid wages that are insufficient to meet their basic needs, while businesses generate significant profits. This exploitation is further exacerbated by the fact that workers in these industries often lack the bargaining power to negotiate for higher wages or better working conditions. Exploitation can also take the form of precarious employment, where workers are employed on a temporary or part-time basis, with little job security or access to benefits. This form of employment is increasingly common in capitalist economies, as businesses seek to reduce labour costs by hiring workers on flexible contracts that allow them to adjust their workforce in response to changing market conditions. While this flexibility benefits businesses, it often leaves workers in a state of economic insecurity, as they face unpredictable incomes and limited opportunities for advancement.

On the other hand, Economic rewards are increasingly concentrated at the top. While millions of ordinary workers remain on poverty wages, returns for shareholders and senior executives have gone through the roof. In South Africa, the top 10% of society receives half of all wage income, while the bottom 50% of the workforce receives just 12% of all wages. With just slightly more than one day of work, a CEO in the US earns the same as an ordinary worker makes during the whole year. Men are consistently the majority of the best-paid employees. On average, it takes just over four days for a CEO from the top five companies in the garment sector to earn what an ordinary Bangladeshi woman worker earns in her whole lifetime. Very often, ever-increasing amounts are being returned to wealthy shareholders, fuelling a relentless squeeze on workers. It would cost $2.2bn a year to increase the wages of all 2.5 million Vietnamese garment workers from the average wage to a living wage. This is the equivalent of a third of the amount paid out to shareholders by the top five companies in the garment sector.The fortunes of the richest are often boosted by tax dodging – by rich individuals and by the corporations of which they are owners or shareholders. Using a global network of tax havens, as revealed in the Panama and Paradise Papers, the super-rich are hiding at least $7.6 trillion from the tax authorities. New analysis by economist Gabriel Zucman for this paper has shown that this means the top 1% is evading an estimated $200bn in tax. Developing countries are losing at least $170bn each year in foregone tax revenues from corporations and the super-rich. Even billionaires who have made their fortunes in competitive markets are often doing so by driving down the wages and conditions of workers, forcing countries into a suicidal race to the bottom on wages, labour rights and tax giveaways. At the same time the poorest children, and especially the poorest girls are condemned to die poor, as opportunities go to the children of richer families.

In order to make a profit, capitalists must exploit workers, in other words, pay them less than the value of the commodities that they produce. So, there will always be more total value on the market than what can be paid for (and consumed) by the domestic population. When markets become saturated, this causes what's called the crisis of overproduction. There's too much stuff, and the people will never—can never—be paid enough to buy it all.

The Negative Effects of Capitalism on Society

Beyond its economic effects, capitalism also has significant negative impacts on society. These effects include the erosion of social cohesion, the degradation of the environment, and the commodification of social goods.

Erosion of Social Cohesion:

One of the most significant negative effects of capitalism on society is the erosion of social cohesion. In a capitalist system, individuals are encouraged to pursue their own self-interest, often at the expense of others. This focus on individualism can weaken the bonds of community and social solidarity, as people become more focused on their own economic success than on the well-being of others. Economic inequality, which is a common feature of capitalist societies, can further erode social cohesion by creating divisions between different social classes. When wealth is concentrated in the hands of a small percentage of the population, it can lead to feelings of resentment and alienation among those who are excluded from economic opportunities. This division can result in social unrest, as marginalised groups demand greater access to resources and opportunities. Additionally, the commodification of social goods, such as education, healthcare, and housing, can weaken social cohesion by reducing access to these essential services. In a capitalist system, these goods are often treated as commodities to be bought and sold in the market, rather than as basic human rights. This commodification can lead to significant disparities in access to essential services, as those with greater wealth are able to afford better education, healthcare, and housing, while those with less wealth are left with inadequate options. These disparities can further divide society, as they create unequal opportunities for individuals to improve their economic and social standing.

Environmental Degradation:

Capitalism's focus on profit maximisation often leads to the degradation of the environment. In their pursuit of profits, businesses may engage in practices that harm the environment, such as deforestation, pollution, and over-extraction of natural resources. These practices are often driven by the desire to reduce costs and increase efficiency, without regard for the long-term environmental consequences. One of the key drivers of environmental degradation in capitalist economies is the externalisation of costs. In order to maximise profits, businesses may externalise the environmental costs of production, such as pollution or resource depletion, by shifting them onto society as a whole. For example, a factory may pollute a river in order to reduce the costs of waste disposal, without bearing the full cost of the environmental damage. This externalisation of costs allows businesses to increase their profits, but it also leads to significant environmental harm, as the true costs of production are not reflected in the price of goods and services. Another factor contributing to environmental degradation is the relentless pursuit of economic growth. In a capitalist system, businesses are incentivized to continuously expand their operations in order to increase profits. This drive for growth often leads to the over-extraction of natural resources, as businesses seek to increase production and reduce costs. This over-extraction can result in the depletion of natural resources, such as forests, fisheries, and fossil fuels, which are essential for the long-term sustainability of the environment. Furthermore, capitalism's focus on consumption as a driver of economic growth can lead to the overproduction of goods and services, which contributes to waste and pollution. In order to maximise profits, businesses may produce more goods than are necessary, leading to the disposal of excess products and the generation of waste. This overproduction not only harms the environment but also contributes to the depletion of natural resources and the degradation of ecosystems.

List of significant incidents of environmental degradation linked to capitalist practices. These examples demonstrate how the profit motive in capitalist systems has contributed to environmental damage --

1. Oil Spills

- Exxon Valdez Oil Spill (1989): In March 1989, the Exxon Valdez oil tanker struck a reef off the coast of Alaska, spilling over 11 million gallons of crude oil into Prince William Sound. This disaster resulted from cost-cutting measures and inadequate oversight by the corporation, severely affecting marine ecosystems.

- Deepwater Horizon Oil Spill (2010): In April 2010, BP's Deepwater Horizon oil rig exploded in the Gulf of Mexico, leading to the largest marine oil spill in history. BP's pursuit of cost-cutting in safety measures was partly blamed for the disaster, which released 4.9 million barrels of oil into the ocean.

2. Deforestation

- Amazon Rainforest Deforestation (Ongoing, 1960s–Present): Since the 1960s, large-scale deforestation has occurred in the Amazon rainforest, largely driven by agribusiness, cattle ranching, and logging companies seeking profits. These activities have led to loss of biodiversity and significant carbon emissions.

- Southeast Asia Palm Oil Plantations (1990s–Present): The expansion of palm oil plantations in Indonesia and Malaysia has resulted in widespread deforestation, loss of habitat for endangered species like orangutans, and increased carbon emissions. Corporate interests have prioritised profit over environmental conservation.

3. Air and Water Pollution

- Great Smog of London (1952): Although not directly a result of modern capitalism, the Great Smog of London was largely caused by industrial pollution, fueled by unchecked coal-burning industries prioritising profit over public health. This event led to thousands of deaths.

- Flint Water Crisis (2014): In 2014, cost-cutting measures in Flint, Michigan, led to the contamination of the city's water supply with lead, causing a public health crisis. The decision was partly motivated by economic concerns rather than safety, leading to significant long-term environmental and health damage.

4. Mining Disasters

- Cerro de Pasco Mining, Peru (Ongoing, 1900s–Present): The mining of silver, lead, and zinc by corporations in Cerro de Pasco has caused severe environmental degradation, including water contamination and soil pollution. The pursuit of profit by multinational mining companies has left the surrounding communities exposed to toxic heavy metals.
- Mountaintop Removal in Appalachia (1970s–Present): This coal mining technique involves removing entire mountaintops to access coal seams beneath. It has destroyed vast swaths of forest, altered ecosystems, and polluted waterways. The coal companies prioritise extraction efficiency and profit over environmental impact.

5. Industrial Waste and Chemical Pollution

- Love Canal, New York (1978): In the 1940s and 1950s, chemical companies, including Hooker Chemical, dumped toxic waste into the Love Canal site in Niagara Falls, New York. By the 1970s, this site caused severe health issues and environmental damage. Profit-driven neglect and lack of regulation led to this environmental catastrophe.
- Bhopal Disaster (1984): In December 1984, a Union Carbide chemical plant in Bhopal, India, leaked methyl isocyanate gas, killing thousands and causing long-term environmental contamination. Corporate negligence, partly due to cost-saving measures, was a significant factor in the disaster.

6. Climate Change

- Carbon Emissions from Fossil Fuels (Industrial Revolution–Present): Since the Industrial Revolution, fossil fuel industries have significantly contributed to greenhouse gas emissions, driving climate change. Oil, gas, and coal companies, driven by profit maximisation, have resisted regulations and efforts to reduce emissions.
- Clearance of Peatlands for Agriculture (1990s–Present): In Southeast Asia, vast peatlands have been cleared for palm oil and other agricultural activities. The draining and burning of these peatlands release massive amounts of carbon dioxide into the atmosphere, exacerbating climate change. This deforestation is driven by agribusiness seeking profit at the expense of the environment.

7. Waste and Overconsumption

- E-Waste Crisis (2000s–Present): The rise of consumer electronics, driven by capitalist consumerism, has resulted in millions of tons of electronic waste (e-waste) each year. Companies in the electronics industry often prioritise profits over sustainable practices, leading to environmental damage, particularly in developing countries where much of this waste is dumped.
- Plastic Pollution (1950s–Present): Since the 1950s, the production of plastic has grown exponentially, driven by industries focused on profit maximisation. Single-use plastics, particularly by companies in the packaging and food industries, have resulted in severe ocean pollution and damage to marine ecosystems.

8. Agricultural Practices

- Industrial Agriculture and Soil Degradation (1940s–Present): The rise of industrial agriculture in the mid-20th century, driven by corporations seeking to maximise yields and profits, has led to significant soil degradation, loss of biodiversity, and water pollution from chemical fertilisers and pesticides.
- Overfishing (1980s–Present): Commercial fishing industries have engaged in overfishing practices, severely depleting fish populations and damaging marine ecosystems. Profit-driven companies have prioritised short-term gains over long-term sustainability.

9. Logging and Timber Industry

- Siberian Forest Destruction (1990s–Present): The logging industry in Siberia, fueled by capitalist markets, has led to large-scale deforestation, threatening wildlife and contributing to climate change. This destruction is driven by timber companies seeking profit from global demand for wood and paper products.
- West African Forest Degradation (1990s–Present): Logging companies in West Africa have caused widespread deforestation, especially in countries like Liberia and Sierra Leone, driven by demand for timber. These companies often disregard the long-term environmental impact in favour of short-term financial gain.

10. Industrial Accidents

- Chernobyl Disaster (1986): While not directly a capitalist enterprise, the Chernobyl nuclear accident in the Soviet Union demonstrated the risks of prioritising industrial efficiency over safety. The environmental impact was catastrophic, causing long-lasting radioactive contamination. Some private firms involved in nuclear energy have also shown a similar pattern of cost-cutting at the expense of safety.

- Fukushima Daiichi Nuclear Disaster (2011): In March 2011, an earthquake and tsunami caused the failure of the Fukushima Daiichi Nuclear Power Plant in Japan, operated by TEPCO. While not entirely a result of capitalist practices, TEPCO faced criticism for inadequate safety measures driven by cost considerations, leading to environmental contamination.

11. Corporate Negligence in Environmental Regulation

- Volkswagen Emissions Scandal (2015): Volkswagen was found to have installed software in diesel vehicles to cheat emissions tests. The company prioritised profit over compliance with environmental regulations, leading to higher levels of pollutants being released into the atmosphere.
- DuPont's Teflon Pollution (1990s–2000s): DuPont knowingly contaminated waterways and soil with perfluorooctanoic acid (PFOA), a chemical used in the production of Teflon. The company prioritised profits over the environment and public health, resulting in widespread contamination and long-term health impacts.

Commodification of Social Goods:

In a capitalist system, goods and services are treated as commodities to be bought and sold in the market. While this commodification can lead to efficiency and innovation, it can also have negative effects on society, particularly when it comes to essential social goods, such as education, healthcare, and housing. When these essential services are treated as commodities, access to them is often determined by an individual's ability to pay, rather than by their need. This can lead to significant disparities in access to these services, as those with greater wealth are able to afford better education, healthcare, and housing, while those with less wealth are left with inadequate options. For example, in many capitalist economies, access to quality education is often determined by an individual's ability to pay for private schooling or to live in a wealthy neighbourhood with well-funded public schools. This can create significant disparities in educational outcomes, as children from lower-income families are often left with fewer opportunities to succeed academically. These disparities can have long-term consequences, as they limit social mobility and perpetuate economic inequality. Similarly, in capitalist healthcare systems, access to medical care is often determined by an individual's ability to pay for insurance or out-of-pocket expenses. This can result in significant disparities in health outcomes, as those with greater wealth are able to afford better healthcare, while those with less wealth may struggle to access the care they need. These disparities can have serious consequences for public health, as they contribute to the spread of preventable diseases and increase the overall burden on healthcare systems.The commodification of housing can also lead to significant social disparities, as access to affordable housing is often limited in capitalist economies. In many cities, rising property values and rental costs have made it increasingly difficult for lower-income individuals and families to find affordable housing. This has contributed to the rise of homelessness and housing insecurity, as well as to the displacement of communities due to gentrification.

Efforts to mitigate these negative effects have taken many forms, from government regulation and social welfare programs to the development of alternative economic systems, such as democratic socialism. (This book has a separate Chapter on Democratic Socialism) These efforts seek to address the inherent imbalances in capitalism and create a more equitable and sustainable economic system that prioritises human welfare and environmental sustainability over the relentless pursuit of profit. As the global economy continues to evolve, the challenges posed by capitalism will likely persist, requiring ongoing efforts to address its negative effects and to create a more just and sustainable economic system for future generations. The question remains whether capitalism can be reformed to address its shortcomings or whether a new economic system will emerge to take its place. Regardless of the outcome, it is clear that the negative effects of capitalism on the economy and society cannot be ignored and must be addressed in order to create a more equitable and sustainable future for all.

• • •

CHAPTER XI

Real Economic Growth Vs. Fake Economic Growth

In contemporary debates about economic systems and their impact on societal development, the distinction between real economic growth and fake economic growth is increasingly relevant. Real economic growth is often defined by its sustainability, inclusiveness, and focus on the well-being of the population as a whole. Fake economic growth, on the other hand, refers to short-term increases in economic output that are unsustainable, exploitative, and ultimately fail to improve the overall quality of life for the majority of people. My argues – that real economic development is never truly possible within a capitalist economy due to its structural incentives toward profit maximisation, inequality, and environmental degradation.

To begin with, we must clarify what constitutes real economic growth versus fake economic growth. Real economic growth is typically measured not just by increases in Gross Domestic Product (GDP), but by improvements in overall quality of life, including access to education, healthcare, housing, and other essential social services. It also involves sustainable practices that ensure future generations can enjoy the benefits of a robust economy without the depletion of natural resources or environmental degradation. In short, real economic growth contributes to the long-term well-being of the entire population, both economically and socially.

Fake economic growth, conversely, is often measured primarily by short-term increases in GDP or stock market performance without considering the negative externalities such as environmental harm, labour exploitation, or social inequality. This type of growth may appear impressive in economic reports but fails to translate into meaningful improvements in people's lives. In fact, it may worsen the living conditions of many by prioritising profits over social welfare and sustainability.

In capitalist economies, much of what is heralded as economic growth falls into the category of fake economic growth. It is growth that benefits a small segment of the population—namely, the owners of capital—while failing to uplift the majority. Furthermore, it often leads to environmental degradation, social inequality, and economic instability.

The definition I have given: —

Real Economic Growth

Real economic growth is characterised by improvements in quality of life and human well-being. It is not limited to increases in GDP or financial wealth but extends to social, environmental, and institutional aspects of a nation's development. Real growth requires investments in -

Education and Human Capital: Real economic growth necessitates robust investments in education, ensuring that all individuals have access to quality schooling, vocational training, and higher education. By improving the knowledge and skills of the population, economies can generate innovation, increase productivity, and ensure that individuals are equipped to contribute meaningfully to economic progress. Education also facilitates social mobility, helping individuals rise out of poverty and contribute to the overall development of society.

Healthcare and Well-being: A healthy population is essential for real economic growth. Investing in healthcare ensures that individuals can live longer, healthier lives, which in turn allows them to participate more fully in the economy. Access to healthcare also reduces the economic burden of preventable diseases and improves overall productivity. By ensuring that everyone, regardless of income level, has access to affordable healthcare, societies can create a foundation for sustainable development.

Infrastructure and Public Services: Real economic growth requires the development of infrastructure that supports economic activity, such as transportation systems, energy grids, and communication networks. These investments not only facilitate trade and commerce but also improve the quality of life for citizens by providing access to essential services like clean water, electricity, and internet connectivity.

Environmental Sustainability: Real economic growth must be sustainable over the long term, which means taking into account the impact of economic activity on the environment. This includes transitioning to renewable energy sources, reducing carbon emissions, conserving natural resources, and protecting ecosystems. Environmental sustainability ensures that future generations will have access to the resources they need to thrive, rather than depleting them for short-term economic gains.

Social Equity: Real economic growth requires an equitable distribution of wealth and resources. It should aim to reduce income inequality and provide opportunities for all individuals to participate in the economy. This includes ensuring fair wages, access to social services, and the protection of workers' rights. Societies that prioritise social equity are more stable and resilient, as they foster social cohesion and reduce the risk of unrest or conflict.

In summary, real economic growth is multidimensional, encompassing not just increases in economic output but also improvements in education, healthcare, infrastructure, environmental sustainability, and social equity. It focuses on the well-being of society as a whole and seeks to create a foundation for long-term, sustainable development.

Fake Economic Growth: The Illusion of Progress

Fake economic growth, by contrast, is often driven by short-term increases in economic output that do not translate into meaningful improvements in the quality of life for the majority of the population. This type of growth is typically measured by superficial indicators such as rising GDP, stock market performance, or real estate prices, but it fails to address the underlying social, environmental, and economic challenges that threaten long-term prosperity.

Speculative Bubbles: One of the most common manifestations of fake economic growth is the formation of speculative bubbles, where asset prices—whether in stocks, real estate, or commodities—are driven to unsustainable levels by excessive speculation. These bubbles create the illusion of economic growth as asset prices rise, but they are often disconnected from the underlying economic fundamentals. When these bubbles burst, they can lead to economic recessions, job losses, and widespread financial instability.

Short-Termism and Profit Maximization: In a capitalist economy, the focus on short-term profits often drives businesses and investors to prioritise immediate financial returns over long-term sustainability. This can result in practices such as cost-cutting measures that undermine the quality of goods and services, outsourcing jobs to low-wage countries, or engaging in environmentally destructive activities to reduce costs. While these practices may boost corporate profits in the short term, they often erode the foundations of real economic growth by reducing consumer trust, increasing inequality, and depleting natural resources.

Income Inequality and Concentration of Wealth: Fake economic growth often exacerbates income inequality by concentrating wealth in the hands of a small elite, while leaving the majority of the population behind. This type of growth is typically driven by financial speculation, corporate profits, and rising asset values, rather than by broad-based improvements in wages or living standards. As a result, the benefits of economic growth are not shared equitably, and the overall well-being of society is not improved.

Environmental Degradation: Fake economic growth frequently comes at the cost of environmental degradation. In pursuit of short-term profits, businesses may engage in practices such as deforestation, pollution, and resource extraction without considering the long-term environmental consequences. This type of growth may increase GDP in the short term, but it undermines the potential for sustainable development by depleting the natural resources and ecosystems that future generations will depend on.

Capitalism's Role in Fostering Fake Economic Growth

Capitalism, as an economic system, is structured in a way that often promotes fake economic growth. The primary drivers of this system—profit maximisation, competition, and capital accumulation—create incentives for businesses and investors to prioritise short-term financial gains over long-term sustainability and social welfare. Several aspects of capitalism contribute to the prevalence of fake economic growth:

Profit Motive and Short-Term Focus:

At the core of capitalism is the pursuit of profit. Businesses in a capitalist economy are driven by the need to maximise returns for their shareholders, often at the expense of broader social and environmental considerations. While profit generation is necessary for businesses to survive and thrive, the relentless focus on profit maximisation can lead to harmful outcomes for society as a whole.

One of the key ways in which capitalism undermines real economic growth is through its tendency to prioritise short-term financial gains over long-term sustainability. For example, many businesses engage in practices that boost their profits in the short term but have negative long-term consequences for the environment or for workers. This might include cutting corners on environmental regulations, paying workers low wages, or outsourcing production to countries with lax labour laws. While these practices can increase profits and contribute to economic growth in the short term, they often lead to greater social and environmental problems in the long run.

Additionally, the capitalist focus on profit maximisation encourages businesses to externalise costs. This means that businesses often shift the negative consequences of their activities—such as pollution, resource depletion, or health impacts—on society as a whole. By externalising these costs, businesses can increase their profits while avoiding the full responsibility for the harm they cause. This creates a situation where economic growth is measured in terms of increased production and profits, but the true costs of that growth are not accounted for.

For example, a company might cut down a forest to produce timber for construction, increasing its profits and contributing to GDP growth. However, the environmental costs of deforestation—such as loss of biodiversity, carbon emissions, and disruption of local ecosystems—are not reflected in the company's balance sheet. These costs are borne by society as a whole, leading to environmental degradation and reducing the potential for sustainable economic development in the future.

Speculation and Financialization:

In recent decades, financialization—the increasing dominance of financial markets, financial motives, financial institutions, and financial elites over the economy—has played a significant role in fostering fake economic growth. Financialization shifts the focus of the economy from producing goods and services to generating profits through financial transactions, often with little regard for the real economy.

One of the most prominent examples of financialization is the growth of the stock market. In capitalist economies, stock market performance is often used as a proxy for economic health. When stock prices rise, it is assumed that the economy is doing well, and when stock prices fall, it is assumed that the economy is in trouble. However, the stock market is not always reflective of the real economy. Stock prices can rise due to speculative investments, share buybacks, and other financial manoeuvres that have little to do with actual economic productivity.

For example, in the aftermath of the 2008 financial crisis, central banks around the world implemented policies such as quantitative easing (QE) and low-interest rates to stimulate economic growth. While these policies succeeded in boosting stock prices and creating wealth for investors, they did little to improve the real economy. Unemployment remained high, wages stagnated, and many people continued to struggle with debt and housing insecurity. In this sense, the growth of the stock market during this period was largely fake, as it did not translate into real improvements in people's lives.

Financialization also encourages short-term thinking among corporations. Instead of investing in long-term projects that could improve productivity and create jobs, corporations are incentivized to engage in financial manoeuvres such as share buybacks and mergers and acquisitions that boost their stock prices in the short term. This prioritisation of short-term financial gains over long-term investments in the real economy undermines real economic growth.

Furthermore, financialization has contributed to the growth of speculative bubbles in various asset markets, including real estate, commodities, and cryptocurrencies. These bubbles create the illusion of economic growth as asset prices rise, but they are unsustainable and often lead to economic crises when they burst. The collapse of these bubbles can result in significant losses for investors, job losses, and reduced economic output, further undermining real economic development.

Externalization of Costs:

One of the defining features of capitalism is the externalisation of costs, where businesses shift the negative consequences of their activities—such as pollution, resource depletion, or labour exploitation—onto society as a whole. By externalising these costs, businesses can increase their profits while avoiding the full responsibility for the harm they cause. This creates a situation where economic growth is measured in terms of increased production and profits, but the true costs of that growth are not accounted for, leading to environmental degradation, social inequality, and economic instability.

My friends, Capitalism's relentless pursuit of growth at any cost has led to profound environmental consequences, which further illustrate the distinction between real and fake economic growth.

In the capitalist model, natural resources are viewed primarily as inputs for production, with little regard for their long-term sustainability or the ecological systems they support.

• Climate Change and Capitalism

One of the most pressing environmental challenges of our time is climate change, a problem that is deeply intertwined with the capitalist mode of production. The burning of fossil fuels for energy, deforestation, industrial agriculture, and other activities that drive economic growth under capitalism are also the primary drivers of climate change. Despite overwhelming scientific consensus on the need to reduce greenhouse gas emissions to avoid catastrophic climate impacts, capitalist economies continue to prioritise short-term economic growth over the long-term health of the planet. The capitalist system's focus on profit maximisation makes it difficult to address climate change in a meaningful way. For example, fossil fuel companies have a financial incentive to continue extracting and selling oil, coal, and natural gas, even though these activities contribute to global warming. In many cases, these companies have lobbied against environmental regulations and funded misinformation campaigns to delay action on climate change, prioritising their profits over the future of the planet. The environmental costs of capitalism are often externalised, meaning that they are not borne by the companies that cause them, but by society as a whole. For example, the costs of climate change—such as increased natural disasters, rising sea levels, and declining agricultural productivity—are borne by communities around the world, particularly in developing countries that are least responsible for global emissions. These externalised costs are not reflected in GDP or corporate profits, creating the illusion of economic growth while the planet's ecological systems are degraded.

• Resource Depletion and Environmental Degradation

Beyond climate change, capitalism's growth model has led to the depletion of natural resources and the destruction of ecosystems. In many cases, capitalist economies prioritise the extraction of resources such as timber, minerals, and fossil fuels over the preservation of ecosystems and biodiversity. This extraction-based model of growth is inherently unsustainable, as it depletes the natural capital on which future economic development depends. For example, the over-extraction of fish stocks in the world's oceans has led to the collapse of fisheries, threatening the livelihoods of millions of people who depend on fishing for their food and income. Similarly, deforestation in the Amazon rainforest has destroyed vital ecosystems and contributed to the loss of biodiversity, with long-term consequences for the global climate and the well-being of indigenous communities. Despite these environmental costs, capitalist economies continue to pursue growth by extracting and exploiting natural resources. This creates the illusion of economic growth in the short term, as GDP rises and profits are generated, but it undermines the potential for long-term economic development by depleting the natural capital on which future generations depend.

An Example: The Exploitation of Natural Resources in Sub-Saharan Africa

Sub-Saharan Africa offers a compelling case study of how capitalist economies can create the illusion of economic growth through the exploitation of natural resources, while failing to deliver real, broad-based development. Many countries in the region are rich in natural resources such as oil, minerals, and timber, and their economies are heavily reliant on the extraction and export of these resources. However, despite periods of rapid GDP growth driven by resource extraction, many of these countries continue to experience high levels of poverty, inequality, and environmental degradation.

- Resource Extraction and Economic Growth

Countries such as Nigeria, Angola, and the Democratic Republic of Congo (DRC) have experienced periods of rapid economic growth driven by the extraction of oil, minerals, and other natural resources. For example, Nigeria is one of the largest oil producers in the world, and its oil industry has contributed significantly to GDP growth over the past several decades. Similarly, the DRC is rich in minerals such as cobalt, copper, and diamonds, which are in high demand on global markets. The extraction of these resources has driven periods of rapid economic growth, attracting foreign investment and generating significant revenue for governments and corporations. However, this growth has been highly uneven and has failed to translate into real economic development for the majority of people in these countries. Much of the wealth generated from resource extraction has been concentrated in the hands of a small elite, while the majority of the population remains impoverished. In many cases, the exploitation of natural resources has led to environmental degradation, displacement of communities, and violent conflict, further undermining the potential for real development.

- The Resource Curse

The phenomenon known as the "resource curse" explains why countries that are rich in natural resources often experience slower economic development and higher levels of poverty and inequality than resource-poor countries. The resource curse occurs when the extraction of natural resources becomes the dominant sector of the economy, crowding out other industries such as manufacturing and agriculture. In countries affected by the resource curse, governments and elites often prioritise short-term profits from resource extraction over long-term investments in education, infrastructure, and social welfare. This leads to a lack of economic diversification and makes countries highly vulnerable to fluctuations in global commodity prices. When resource prices fall, these economies often experience severe recessions, as they are overly reliant on a single sector. Moreover, resource-rich countries often suffer from weak institutions and governance, as the concentration of wealth in the hands of a small elite fosters corruption and undermines democratic accountability. In many cases, governments and corporations engage in rent-seeking behaviour, extracting as much wealth as possible from natural resources without investing in long-term development or the well-being of the population.

Inequality and Concentration of Wealth:

Capitalism's emphasis on competition and capital accumulation tends to concentrate wealth in the hands of a small elite, while leaving the majority of the population with stagnant wages and limited opportunities for upward mobility. This concentration of wealth exacerbates inequality and reduces the overall level of demand in the economy, as the wealthy are more likely to save and invest their money, rather than spend it on goods and services that drive real economic growth. (There will be a detailed discussion about this later)

Historical Evidence of Capitalism's Growth Illusions

- Post-World War II Economic Boom

The post-World War II period, particularly in the United States and Western Europe, is often referred to as the "Golden Age of Capitalism." This era saw high levels of economic growth, low unemployment rates, and rising living standards. However, much of this growth was based on unsustainable consumption patterns, industrial expansion, and government policies that favoured corporate profits over long-term societal well-being. The boom was largely fueled by consumer spending and government investments in infrastructure and defence, creating a robust economy in the short term. Yet, this growth relied heavily on the mass production and consumption of goods, which led to increased waste, environmental pollution, and resource depletion. The automobile industry, for instance, expanded rapidly, leading to urban sprawl, increased reliance on fossil fuels, and the destruction of natural habitats. Moreover, while living standards improved for many during this period, the benefits were unevenly distributed. Racial and gender inequalities persisted, and economic growth disproportionately favoured white men, while women and people of colour continued to face discrimination in employment, education, and housing. The economic prosperity of this era was also underpinned by exploitative labour practices in developing countries, where multinational corporations outsource production to take advantage of cheap labour and lax environmental regulations. Although the post-war economic boom appeared to bring prosperity, much of this growth was fake in the sense that it masked underlying social and environmental problems that would resurface in the following decades. The reliance on unsustainable consumption and production patterns eventually led to economic crises, environmental degradation, and the rise of neoliberal policies that further entrenched inequality.

- The Neoliberal Turn

The rise of neoliberalism in the late 20th century marked a significant shift in global economic policy. Neoliberalism, characterised by deregulation, privatisation, and the liberalisation of trade and capital flows, sought to reduce the role of the state in the economy and promote free-market principles. Proponents argued that these policies would lead to greater economic efficiency, innovation, and growth. However, in practice, neoliberalism has often exacerbated inequality, environmental degradation, and economic instability, contributing to fake economic growth. One of the key tenets of neoliberalism is the deregulation of financial markets. This has led to the growth of speculative bubbles, as seen in the 2008 global financial crisis. Deregulation allowed banks and financial institutions to engage in risky lending practices, creating the illusion of economic growth through the housing market and financial speculation. However, when the bubble burst, it revealed the fragility of this growth, leading to widespread economic devastation, job losses, and foreclosures. The crisis exposed how neoliberal policies prioritise short-term profits for financial elites over the long-term stability and well-being of the broader economy. Neoliberal policies have also led to the privatisation of public services, including education, healthcare, and infrastructure, further exacerbating inequality. Privatisation often results in reduced access to essential services for lower-income individuals, as private companies prioritise profit over the public good. This undermines real economic development, as access to quality education, healthcare, and infrastructure are essential for improving living standards and ensuring long-term economic growth. And also neoliberal trade policies have contributed to environmental degradation and the exploitation of labour in developing countries. The liberalisation of trade has encouraged multinational corporations to outsource production to countries with lower labour costs and weaker environmental regulations, leading to the exploitation of workers and the destruction of ecosystems. While this has resulted in economic growth for corporations and wealthy investors, it has often come at the expense of the well-being of workers and the environment in developing countries.

Neoliberalism and Inequality in Latin America: Latin America has been a key battleground for neoliberal economic policies, which have often resulted in widening inequality and social unrest. The region provides a stark example of how neoliberal capitalism can exacerbate inequality and undermine real economic development. In the 1980s and 1990s, many Latin American countries adopted neoliberal policies promoted by international financial institutions like the International Monetary Fund (IMF) and the World Bank. These policies included privatisation, deregulation, and trade liberalisation, which were intended to boost economic growth and attract foreign investment. While these policies did lead to periods of economic growth, they also resulted in significant inequality. Privatisation often led to the concentration of wealth and resources in the hands of a few, while the majority of the population saw little benefit. Deregulation allowed for the exploitation of workers and the environment, while trade liberalisation exposed domestic industries to competition from more developed economies, leading to job losses and declining wages. Countries like Argentina and Brazil experienced severe economic crises in the wake of neoliberal reforms, with soaring unemployment, rising poverty, and social unrest. These crises revealed the fragility of the neoliberal growth model, which prioritised the interests of multinational corporations and wealthy elites over the needs of the broader population. The case of Latin America demonstrates how neoliberal capitalism can lead to fake economic growth, where the benefits are concentrated among a small elite while the majority of the population is left behind. Inequality, social unrest, and economic instability are the inevitable outcomes of a system that prioritises short-term profits over long-term development.

The Need for a Shift Towards Real Economic Growth

To achieve real economic growth, societies must shift away from the profit-driven logic of capitalism and towards a more sustainable, equitable model of economic development. This requires:

1. Long-Term Investments in Human Capital: Real economic growth requires robust investments in education, healthcare, and social services that improve the well-being of the population as a whole. This includes ensuring that everyone has access to quality education, healthcare, and social safety nets, regardless of their income level.

2. Sustainable Development Practices: Real economic growth must be sustainable over the long term, which means taking into account the environmental impact of economic activity. This includes transitioning to renewable energy sources, reducing

carbon emissions, and protecting natural resources for future generations.

3. Equitable Distribution of Wealth: Real economic growth requires an equitable distribution of wealth and resources, ensuring that the benefits of economic progress are shared by all members of society. This can be achieved through progressive taxation, social welfare programs, and policies that promote fair wages and workers' rights.

4. Regulation of Financial Markets:To prevent the formation of speculative bubbles and promote real economic growth, governments must regulate financial markets and discourage short-term profit-seeking behaviour. This includes implementing policies that promote long-term investments in productive assets, rather than speculative investments in financial markets.

• • •

CHAPTER XII

Fake Economic Growth and Sad Reality

The consequences of fake economic growth are far-reaching and can undermine the long-term stability and prosperity of societies. While fake growth may boost economic output in the short term, it often leads to negative outcomes. A significant barrier to real economic development in a capitalist economy is the system's tendency to create speculative bubbles. These bubbles occur when asset prices are driven to unsustainable levels by excessive speculation, often fueled by cheap credit and loose monetary policy. While these bubbles can create the illusion of economic growth, they often result in significant economic instability when they inevitably burst. The global financial crisis of 2008 is a prime example of how speculative bubbles can lead to fake economic growth. In the years leading up to the crisis, housing prices in the United States were driven to unsustainable levels by speculative investments in mortgage-backed securities. This created a housing bubble that contributed to significant GDP growth and increased financial profits for banks and investors. However, when the bubble burst, it resulted in a severe economic downturn, with millions of people losing their homes, jobs, and savings. Another Example:The claim that India is the 5th largest economy in the world, while factually correct in terms of nominal GDP, does not accurately reflect the country's economic reality. The significant income inequality, poverty, unemployment, and inadequate health and education services indicate that the benefits of economic growth are not reaching the majority of the population. The presence of numerous Indian billionaires on the Forbes Richest People List further underscores the disparity between the wealthy and the poor. Speculative bubbles are a recurring feature of capitalist economies, as investors are often driven by the pursuit of short-term profits rather than long-term stability. These bubbles create the illusion of economic growth by inflating asset prices, but they do not contribute to real economic development. In fact, they often result in significant economic damage when they burst, leading to recessions, job losses, and reduced economic output.On the other side Real economic growth requires stable, sustainable investments in productive assets such as infrastructure, technology, and education, rather than speculative investments in financial markets. However, capitalism's focus on profit maximisation and short-term gains often encourages speculative behaviour, which undermines the potential for long-term economic development.

I will examine specific case studies that showcase the long-term negative repercussions of capitalist economies' pursuit of short-term profit maximisation and their inability to achieve genuine economic development. The distinction between genuine and fraudulent economic growth will be further illustrated through these case studies, which will also serve to bolster the argument that capitalism impedes genuine economic development.

- Case Study 1: The 2008 Global Financial Crisis —

The 2008 Global Financial Crisis (GFC) is one of the most significant examples of fake economic growth driven by speculative bubbles and financialization. Leading up to the crisis, the U.S. housing market experienced a massive boom fueled by the proliferation of subprime mortgages, securitization, and risky financial products like mortgage-backed securities (MBS) and collateralized debt obligations (CDOs). These financial instruments were designed to extract profit through complex financial engineering, with little regard for their long-term sustainability.

Pre-Crisis Growth and the Illusion of Stability —

In the years before the crisis, U.S. GDP was rising, unemployment was low, and corporate profits were surging. The housing market, in particular, appeared to be booming, as homeownership rates rose and housing prices reached unprecedented levels. This apparent prosperity was used to justify deregulation and the loosening of lending standards in the financial industry, with many arguing that the housing boom was a sign of healthy economic growth. However, the reality was that much of this growth was fake. The housing boom was built on a foundation of speculative investments and risky lending practices that were unsustainable in the long term. Subprime mortgages, which were given to borrowers with poor credit histories, were bundled into securities and sold to investors around the world. This created the illusion of stability and profitability, even as the underlying risks grew larger. Banks and financial institutions, driven by the pursuit of short-term profits, had little incentive to ensure that the loans they were making were sound. Instead, they focused on maximising their returns through the creation and sale of complex financial products. As housing prices continued to rise, investors and lenders were encouraged to take on even more risk, inflating the housing bubble further.

The Crisis Unfolds —

When housing prices inevitably began to fall in 2007, the entire system unravelled. Borrowers who had taken out subprime mortgages found themselves unable to make their mortgage payments, leading to a wave of foreclosures. The value of mortgage-backed securities plummeted, causing massive losses for banks, investors, and financial institutions. The interconnectedness of the global financial system meant that the crisis quickly spread beyond the housing market, leading to a global economic downturn. The GFC exposed the fragility of the economic growth that had been achieved in the years leading up to the crisis. It revealed that much of this growth had been built on speculative bubbles and financial manipulation, rather than real, productive investments in the economy. The fallout from the crisis was devastating, with millions of people losing their homes, jobs, and savings. In the U.S. alone, it is estimated that nearly 10 million families lost their homes to foreclosure. Governments around the world were forced to intervene to stabilise the financial system, using taxpayer money to bail out banks and financial institutions. The economic damage caused by the crisis was severe, with global GDP contracting by 2.1% in 2009, according to the World Bank. Unemployment rates skyrocketed, and millions of people were pushed into poverty. The crisis also had long-term consequences, contributing to rising inequality, political instability, and the erosion of trust in institutions.

Lessons Learned —

The 2008 Global Financial Crisis serves as a powerful example of how capitalist economies can generate fake economic growth through speculative bubbles and financial manipulation. While the economy appeared to be growing in the years before the crisis, much of this growth was illusory, built on a foundation of risky financial practices that ultimately collapsed. The crisis also highlights the social and economic costs of financialization, as the pursuit of short-term profits for financial elites came at the expense of long-term stability and the well-being of ordinary people.

- Case Study 2: The Irish Property Bubble —

Ireland's experience during the early 2000s is another example of how capitalism can foster fake economic growth through speculative bubbles. Ireland experienced rapid economic growth during this period, driven by a booming property market, deregulation of the banking sector, and foreign investment. This period, often referred to as the "Celtic Tiger" years, seemed to represent a model of successful capitalist development. However, the property boom proved to be unsustainable, and the subsequent crash had devastating effects on the Irish economy.

The Boom: Illusions of Prosperity —

In the late 1990s and early 2000s, Ireland's economy grew at an extraordinary rate, with GDP growth rates exceeding 10% in some years. This growth was largely driven by a construction boom, fueled by low interest rates, easy credit, and foreign investment. Housing prices skyrocketed, and construction accounted for a significant share of GDP. During this period, Ireland was hailed as an economic success story, with low unemployment, rising incomes, and an influx of foreign investment. The banking sector played a central role in financing the property boom, lending heavily to developers and homebuyers. Many banks took on excessive risk, believing that the property market would continue to grow indefinitely. The Irish government also contributed to the bubble by implementing tax incentives for property development and failing to regulate the banking sector effectively. As housing prices continued to rise, the construction sector became increasingly dominant, creating a sense of economic prosperity that masked the underlying risks.

The Crash: The Reality of Fake Growth —

By 2008, the Irish property market began to collapse, revealing the fragility of the country's economic growth. Housing prices plummeted, construction activity ground to a halt, and many developers and homeowners found themselves unable to repay their loans. The banking sector, which had heavily invested in the property market, was hit hard, with several major banks facing insolvency. The Irish government was forced to intervene, using taxpayer money to bail out the banks and prevent the collapse of the financial system. The cost of these bailouts was enormous, contributing to a sovereign debt crisis that required Ireland to seek financial assistance from the International Monetary Fund (IMF) and the European Union (EU). The economic impact of the property crash was severe, with Ireland experiencing a deep recession and rising unemployment. Many people lost their homes, and the country faced years of austerity measures to address the debt crisis. The construction boom that had driven much of the economic growth proved to be unsustainable, leading to a period of economic contraction and stagnation.

Lessons Learned —

The Irish property bubble is another example of how capitalism can generate fake economic growth through speculative bubbles. While the economy appeared to be growing rapidly during the Celtic Tiger years, much of this growth was based on unsustainable investments in the property market. When the bubble burst, it exposed the underlying weaknesses in the economy and led to a period of severe economic hardship. The case of Ireland also highlights the role of deregulation and government policy in fostering speculative bubbles, as well as the social costs of economic crises.

• • •

The Sad Reality ---

Widening Inequality: Another major barrier to real economic development in a capitalist economy is the system's inherent tendency to create and exacerbate economic inequality. Capitalism is based on the accumulation of capital, and those who control the most capital are able to accumulate even more wealth through investments, ownership of businesses, and other means. This creates a cycle where the rich get richer while the poor remain trapped in poverty. Economic inequality is not just a social issue; it also has significant economic consequences. When wealth is concentrated in the hands of a small elite, it reduces the overall level of demand in the economy. The wealthy are more likely to save and invest their money, rather than spending it on goods and services, which reduces consumption and limits economic growth. In contrast, lower-income individuals are more likely to spend their money on basic necessities, which can stimulate demand and drive economic growth. Moreover, economic inequality reduces social mobility and perpetuates cycles of poverty. In many capitalist societies, access to education, healthcare, and other essential services is determined by an individual's ability to pay. This creates a situation where those who are born into wealth are able to access better opportunities and improve their economic standing, while those who are born into poverty are left with limited options for upward mobility. This not only limits individual potential but also reduces the overall level of human capital in the economy, which is essential for long-term economic development. In addition, economic inequality can lead to social unrest and political instability. When large segments of the population are excluded from economic opportunities and see their living standards stagnate or decline, it can lead to frustration, resentment, and a loss of faith in the political and economic system. This can result in protests, strikes, and other forms of social unrest, which can disrupt economic activity and further undermine the potential for real economic development.

Undermining Human Development: Fake economic growth can impede human development and restrict the potential for long-term economic progress by prioritising short-term profits over investments in infrastructure, healthcare, and education. Societies that fail to invest in their human capital are less likely to generate the innovation, productivity, and social cohesion needed for sustainable economic growth. In a capitalist economy, essential social goods such as education, healthcare, and housing are often treated as commodities to be bought and sold in the market. This commodification of social goods creates significant disparities in access to these services, as those with greater wealth are able to afford better education, healthcare, and housing, while those with less wealth are left with inadequate options. The commodification of education, for example, can lead to significant disparities in educational outcomes. In many capitalist economies, access to quality education is determined by an individual's ability to pay for private schooling or to live in a wealthy neighbourhood with well-funded public schools. This creates a situation where children from lower-income families are left with fewer opportunities to succeed academically, which limits their potential for upward mobility and perpetuates cycles of poverty. Similarly, the commodification of healthcare can result in significant disparities in health outcomes. In capitalist healthcare systems, access to medical care is often determined by an individual's ability to pay for insurance or out-of-pocket expenses. This can result in lower-income individuals and families struggling to access the care they need, leading to poorer health outcomes and increased rates of preventable diseases. Housing is another essential social good that is often commodified in capitalist economies. Rising property values and rental costs have made it increasingly difficult for lower-income individuals and families to find affordable housing. This has contributed to the rise of homelessness and housing insecurity, as well as to the displacement of communities due to gentrification. In a system that prioritises profit over social welfare, the commodification of social goods creates significant disparities in access to essential services, which undermines the potential for real economic development. Real economic growth requires investments in public goods that improve the well-being of society as a whole, ensuring that everyone has access to the resources they need to thrive.

Labour exploitation: Around 56% of the global population lives on between $2 and $10 a day, including the majority of the world's workers and small-scale food producers. Women are heavily over-represented among the working poor. Recent estimates by the International Labour Organization (ILO) show that almost one in three workers in emerging and developing countries live in poverty. This includes two-thirds of workers in sub-Saharan Africa. Poverty wages in turn have knock-on impacts, with workers consistently working long hours of overtime just to earn enough to survive. While the value of what workers produce has grown dramatically, wages have not kept pace. The ILO has found that, in 91 of 133 rich and developing countries, wages have not kept pace with increased productivity and economic growth from 1995–2014. After the global financial crisis of 2008–09, growth in real wages at the global level recovered in 2010, but since 2012 they have decelerated, falling from 2.5% to 1.7% in 2015, the lowest level in four years. Common business models propose that companies focus on their self-identified specialisms and outsource all other activities. As a result, workers involved in the production process are easily considered non-critical, and thus a cost to be minimised, rather than an asset in which to invest. External contractors achieve their competitive advantage by lowering costs, and the most direct way to do so is by reducing wages. The most common way to reduce costs is by offshoring activities. When highly skilled labour is not needed, companies often look for the countries with the lowest costs,shifting production to wherever is cheapest. Governments around the world compete to provide the cheapest labour, in a suicidal race to the bottom. This results in the use of production workers who do not receive a fair share of the financial benefits enjoyed by the parent company, nor many of the rights observed in the country in which the company is headquartered. Such offshore workers' remuneration is commonly linked to the number of hours worked, decoupled from the performance of the companies that ultimately benefit from their labour. Job insecurity is the norm. In 2016, the International Trade Union Confederation (ITUC) stated that 50 of the world's largest companies, with a combined revenue of $3.4 trillion, maintained a 'hidden' work force of an estimated 116 million people in their supply chains –representing around 94% of the total workers employed. Their contracts are often outsourced across borders multiple times, and the workers are more likely to be on short-term contracts with minimal protections. They are likely to be women.Such global supply chains allow companies to take advantage of low paid workers but can also allow them to avoid government regulation for both labour conditions and taxation.

Perhaps the most shocking element of the global labour market today is the existence and the scale of modern slavery, including both forced labour and forced marriage. The ILO has estimated that 40 million people worldwide were enslaved in 2016 – 25 million of them in slave labour. According to its recent report, 'In many cases, the products they made and the services they provided ended up in seemingly legitimate commercial channels. Forced labourers produced some of the food we eat and the clothes we wear, and they have cleaned the buildings in which many of us live or work'. The ILO estimates that 71% of slaves today are women and girls and 4 million of those in slave labour are children.

Environmental Destruction: (There has been a lot of discussion on this topic before.) Fake economic growth often comes at the cost of environmental degradation, which can have long-term consequences for the health of ecosystems and the sustainability of economic development. Climate change, deforestation, and resource depletion are all consequences of a growth model that prioritises short-term profits over long-term sustainability.

In conclusion, real economic development is fundamentally incompatible with the capitalist economic system. Capitalism's focus on profit maximisation, inequality, environmental degradation, and speculative behaviour creates a situation where economic growth is often illusory and unsustainable. While capitalism may generate short-term increases in GDP and financial profits, it fails to deliver the broad-based, inclusive, and sustainable development that is necessary for the long-term well-being of society. To achieve real economic growth, we must explore alternative economic models that prioritise human well-being, sustainability, and social equity. Systems such as democratic socialism, mixed economies, or green economics may offer pathways to achieving real growth by balancing economic activity with the needs of society and the environment. These systems prioritise public goods, social welfare, and environmental stewardship, ensuring that economic development benefits everyone, rather than just a select few. Ultimately, real economic development requires a fundamental rethinking of the way we organise our economies and societies. It requires moving away from the profit-driven logic of capitalism and towards a more equitable and sustainable model of economic growth that prioritises the well-being of people and the planet.

• • •

CHAPTER XIII

Potential Alternative As a Path to Real Economic Growth

In contrast to capitalism's focus on profit maximisation and short-term gains, democratic socialism as The best potential alternative offers a model that prioritises human well-being, social equity, and environmental sustainability. Democratic socialism advocates for a mixed economy, where key industries and services are publicly owned or regulated, and the government plays an active role in ensuring that economic growth benefits all members of society.

Why democratic socialism is the best option ? To express the reason in one word - " Democratic socialism offers a vision of an economy that serves the needs of all people, rather than just the wealthy elite, and promotes long-term well-being over short-term profit."- Sajid Mollah

Why Democratic Socialism as a Pathway to Real Economic Development?

Democratic socialism emerges as the most compelling alternative to capitalism for achieving real economic development. Unlike capitalism, which prioritises profit maximisation for private individuals and corporations, democratic socialism emphasises the collective good, economic equality, and sustainability. The central premise of democratic socialism is that the economy should serve the needs of the entire population, not just a wealthy elite. In this section, I will explore how democratic socialism offers a framework for achieving real economic growth / Real Economic Development that benefits all members of society and fosters environmental stewardship.

Democratic Socialism and Economic Equality --

At the heart of democratic socialism is the belief that economic equality is essential for real economic development. In a capitalist economy, wealth and resources tend to accumulate at the top, leading to extreme inequality. This concentration of wealth undermines real economic growth by limiting access to education, healthcare, housing, and other essential services for large segments of the population. As a result, the potential of millions of people to contribute to the economy is stifled, creating a system in which only a select few benefit from economic growth. Democratic socialism seeks to address this inequality by ensuring that wealth and resources are distributed more equitably across society. This is achieved through progressive taxation, robust social safety nets, and public ownership of key industries and services. By redistributing wealth, democratic socialism creates a more inclusive economy in which all individuals have the opportunity to participate fully in economic life. This, in turn, leads to more sustainable and genuine economic growth, as more people are able to contribute their talents and skills to the economy. Countries that have adopted elements of democratic socialism, such as the Nordic nations of Denmark, Sweden, and Norway, provide compelling evidence of the benefits of this approach. These countries have some of the highest levels of economic equality in the world, thanks to their strong social welfare systems, progressive taxation, and commitment to public services such as healthcare and education. At the same time, they also have high levels of economic productivity, innovation, and overall well-being. By prioritising economic equality, these countries have been able to achieve real economic development that benefits all members of society.

Democratic Socialism and Public Ownership --

Another key feature of democratic socialism is the belief in public ownership of certain key industries and services. In a capitalist economy, essential services such as healthcare, education, and infrastructure are often privatised, leading to inequality in access and quality. Democratic socialism, on the other hand, advocates for public ownership of these services to ensure that they are available to all, regardless of income or social status. Public ownership allows for the prioritisation of long-term social and economic goals over short-term profits. For example, publicly owned utilities can focus on providing affordable and sustainable energy to all citizens, rather than maximising profits for shareholders. Publicly funded healthcare systems can prioritise the health and well-being of the population, rather than generating profits for private insurance companies. In this way, democratic socialism fosters real economic growth by ensuring that essential services are accessible to everyone and that economic resources are used to benefit the common good. Public ownership also promotes economic stability and resilience. In capitalist economies, privatised industries are often subject to market fluctuations, leading to instability and uncertainty for workers and consumers. Public ownership, by contrast, provides a stable foundation for the economy by ensuring that essential services remain accessible and affordable, even during economic downturns. This stability is essential for real economic growth, as it allows individuals and businesses to plan for the long term and invest in the future.

Democratic Socialism and Sustainability --

One of the most significant advantages of democratic socialism over capitalism is its potential to promote sustainable economic development. Capitalism's focus on profit maximisation often leads to the over-exploitation of natural resources and environmental degradation, as companies prioritise short-term profits over long-term ecological health. Democratic socialism, by contrast, places a greater emphasis on sustainability and environmental stewardship, recognizing that real economic growth must be compatible with the health of the planet. In a democratic socialist economy, environmental concerns are integrated into economic decision-making processes. This could involve government regulation of industries to ensure that they adhere to sustainable practices, public investment in renewable energy and green infrastructure, and policies that promote conservation and the responsible use of natural resources. By prioritising sustainability, democratic socialism seeks to create an economy that meets the needs of the present without compromising the ability of future generations to meet their own needs. Countries that have embraced elements of democratic socialism, such as Sweden and Denmark, are often leaders in environmental sustainability. These countries have implemented policies that promote renewable energy, reduce carbon emissions, and protect natural ecosystems, while also maintaining strong economies and high standards of living. This demonstrates that it is possible to achieve real economic growth while also protecting the environment—a goal that is often elusive in capitalist economies.

The Role of the State in Democratic Socialism --

In a democratic socialist system, the state plays a central role in guiding the economy and ensuring that it serves the public good. This is in stark contrast to capitalism, where the state's role is often limited to protecting private property and enforcing market rules. Under democratic socialism, the state takes on a more active role in managing the economy to promote equality, sustainability, and long-term economic stability. One of the key functions of the state in a democratic socialist economy is to regulate industries to ensure that they operate in the best interests of society. This could involve setting labour standards, ensuring fair wages, protecting the environment, and preventing monopolies. By regulating industries, the state can ensure that economic growth is inclusive and sustainable, rather than driven solely by the pursuit of profit. In addition to regulation, the state also plays a key role in providing public goods and services. In a democratic socialist system, the state is responsible for ensuring that all citizens have access to education, healthcare, housing, and other essential services. This not only promotes economic equality but also fosters long-term economic growth by ensuring that all individuals have the resources they need to contribute to the economy. Furthermore, the state can play a critical role in promoting innovation and economic development through public investment. In a capitalist economy, investment decisions are often driven by the pursuit of short-term profits, which can stifle innovation and long-term development. In a democratic socialist system, the state can invest in areas such as education, research and development, and infrastructure, which are essential for real economic growth. By taking a long-term view of economic development, the state can ensure that resources are allocated in a way that promotes innovation and productivity, rather than just short-term profits.

Participatory Economics and Worker Control --

Democratic socialism also offers a vision of an economy in which workers have greater control over their workplaces and economic decisions. In contrast to capitalism, where decision-making is often concentrated in the hands of corporate executives and shareholders, democratic socialism promotes the idea of participatory economics, in which workers and communities have a say in how the economy is run. This can take the form of worker cooperatives, where workers collectively own and manage their businesses. In a cooperative, decisions about production, wages, and working conditions are made democratically, with each worker having an equal say. This not only promotes economic equality but also fosters a sense of ownership and responsibility among workers, leading to more sustainable and productive enterprises. Participatory economics can also extend to the broader economy, with democratic decision-making processes used to determine how resources are allocated and how economic priorities are set. This could involve the use of participatory budgeting, where citizens have a direct say in how public funds are spent, or the establishment of economic planning councils, where representatives from different sectors of society come together to develop long-term economic strategies. By giving workers and communities a greater voice in economic decision-making, democratic socialism promotes real economic growth that is more inclusive and responsive to the needs of the population. This stands in stark contrast to capitalism, where economic decisions are often made by a small elite with little regard for the well-being of workers or the broader society.

• • •

Critics of democratic socialism often argue that it stifles innovation, reduces individual incentives, and leads to inefficiency. However, these criticisms are often based on a misunderstanding of how democratic socialism works in practice. (Details are given in chapter number twenty)

So we understand why democratic socialism is the best option. To express the reason in one word - " Democratic socialism offers a vision of an economy that serves the needs of all people, rather than just the wealthy elite, and promotes long-term well-being over short-term profit." All criticisms of democratic socialism are logically refuted in chapter 20. In this chapter I have analysed democratic socialism in more detail. By reading this chapter we can absorb almost all of democratic socialism.

• • •

CHAPTER XIV

The Illusion of India as the 5th Largest Economy

India's ascension to the position of the 5th largest economy in the world is often celebrated as a symbol of its economic prowess and growth. However, critics argue that this ranking, based on nominal GDP, is superficial and masks deeper, more troubling issues within the country. One of the most significant of these issues is the stark income inequality and wealth concentration. This discussion will delve into why India's status as the 5th largest economy holds little real value for the majority of its citizens, highlighting the pervasive inequality that plagues the nation. We will also explore how the presence of numerous Indian billionaires on the Forbes Richest People List underscores this inequality.

Income Inequality in India

Despite its impressive GDP figures, India's wealth distribution is highly unequal. The economic growth has not been inclusive, and a large portion of the population remains marginalised.

Oxfam Report on Wealth Distribution -

According to Oxfam's reports, the richest 1% of Indians own more than 40% of the country's wealth. Meanwhile, the bottom 50% of the population holds less than 5% of the total wealth. This extreme concentration of wealth means that economic benefits are not being shared equitably among all citizens, but are instead accruing to a small elite.

Thomas Piketty and Lucas Chancel's Study -

In their comprehensive study, economists Thomas Piketty and Lucas Chancel highlight that the top 10% of India's population captures a disproportionate share of the national income. This exacerbates social and economic disparities, making it difficult for the majority to benefit from the country's economic growth.

1. Economic Disparities: The study shows that the income growth of the top 10% far outpaces that of the bottom 90%, leading to widening economic disparities.

2. Social Inequity: This economic divide also translates into social inequity, where access to quality education, healthcare, and opportunities is largely determined by one's economic standing.

The Forbes Richest People List: A Sign of Inequality

The presence of many Indian billionaires on the Forbes Richest People List is often touted as a sign of India's economic success. However, this concentration of wealth among a few individuals is a clear indicator of the deep-rooted inequality in the country.

1. Mukesh Ambani: As of the latest reports, Mukesh Ambani, chairman of Reliance Industries, is consistently ranked among the top 10 richest people in the world. While Ambani's wealth grows, many Indians struggle with basic necessities.

2. Gautam Adani: Gautam Adani, chairman of the Adani Group, has seen his wealth increase exponentially in recent years. His rise in wealth, amidst claims of crony capitalism, further highlights the disparity between the rich and the poor.

3. Other Billionaires: India is home to dozens of billionaires, whose combined wealth is astronomical compared to the per capita income of the average Indian. This disparity is not only unjust but also indicative of systemic issues within the country's economic structure.

The Real Value of GDP Rankings

While nominal GDP is a common measure of economic size, it does not capture the full picture of economic health and well-being. Several reasons highlight why India's status as the 5th largest economy holds little real value:

Lack of Inclusive Growth -

Economic growth should ideally lead to improved living standards for all citizens. However, in India, growth has been skewed in favour of the wealthy. The lack of inclusive growth means that a significant portion of the population remains marginalised despite the overall economic progress.

1. Marginalised Populations: Large segments of the population, including rural communities and urban poor, do not benefit equally from economic growth.

2. Quality of Life: Improvements in GDP have not necessarily translated into better quality of life for the average Indian. Issues such as inadequate housing, poor healthcare, and lack of clean water persist for many.

Persistent Poverty -

Despite being the 5th largest economy, India has one of the highest numbers of people living in poverty.

1. World Bank Data: According to the World Bank, over 20% of Indians live on less than $1.90 a day. This indicates that economic growth has not significantly reduced poverty levels.

2. Living Conditions: Many Indians continue to live in substandard conditions, with limited access to basic services and amenities.

Unemployment and Underemployment -

High unemployment and underemployment rates further diminish the significance of GDP rankings.

1. Centre for Monitoring Indian Economy (CMIE): The CMIE reports an unemployment rate of around 7-8% in recent years. Youth unemployment is particularly high, indicating a mismatch between education and job market requirements.

2. Underemployment: Many employed individuals are underemployed, working in low-paying or insecure jobs that do not utilise their skills or provide financial stability.

Health and Education: The Neglected Sectors

Economic growth has not significantly improved health and education outcomes in India, which are critical for long-term sustainable development.

Healthcare -

1. World Health Organization (WHO) Data: India spends only about 1.28% of its GDP on healthcare, significantly lower than the global average. This underfunding results in inadequate healthcare infrastructure and services.

2. Access to Healthcare: Many Indians, particularly in rural areas, lack access to basic healthcare services, leading to poor health outcomes and financial distress due to out-of-pocket healthcare expenses.

Education -

1. Annual Status of Education Report (ASER): The report reveals that learning outcomes in rural areas are alarmingly low, with many students unable to read basic texts or perform simple arithmetic.

2. UNESCO Report: According to UNESCO, India has the highest number of out-of-school children in the world, indicating issues with access to and quality of education.

Environmental Concerns

India's rapid economic growth has also led to severe environmental degradation.

Air Pollution -

1. WHO Data: Several Indian cities are listed among the most polluted globally, with air pollution causing significant health and economic costs.

2. Health Impact: Air pollution contributes to respiratory illnesses, reduced productivity, and increased healthcare costs.

Water Crisis -

1. NITI Aayog Report: India is facing a severe water crisis, with many parts of the country experiencing acute water shortages. This affects agriculture, industry, and daily living conditions.

2. Sustainability: The water crisis poses a significant threat to sustainable development and economic stability.

Structural Issues

Critics point to various structural issues that need to be addressed for sustainable growth.

Infrastructure Deficits -

1. Global Competitiveness Report: According to the World Economic Forum's report, poor infrastructure is a significant bottleneck for economic growth in India.

2. Transportation and Utilities: Issues with transportation, electricity, and other utilities hamper economic activities and reduce overall productivity.

Bureaucratic Inefficiencies -

1. Ease of Doing Business: Although India has improved in the World Bank's Ease of Doing Business rankings, bureaucratic red tape and corruption continue to pose challenges for businesses and investors.

2. Regulatory Framework: The complex and often inconsistent regulatory framework can deter foreign investment and hinder domestic business growth.

Perspectives from Economists

Amartya Sen -

Nobel Laureate Amartya Sen emphasises that GDP growth is not a comprehensive measure of economic progress. He argues that true development should focus on improving human capabilities and quality of life, which includes addressing inequality, health, and education.

Jean Drèze -

Development economist Jean Drèze highlights that India's economic policies have largely favoured the rich, leading to increased inequality. He stresses the need for social policies that ensure equitable distribution of resources and opportunities.

Abhijit Banerjee -

Nobel Laureate Abhijit Banerjee points out that India's economic policies often fail to address the needs of the poor. He advocates for better-targeted welfare programs and increased public spending on health and education to reduce inequality.

- The narrative of India as the 5th largest economy must be re-evaluated in the context of income inequality. True economic progress is not just about high GDP figures but also about ensuring that the benefits of growth are shared equitably among all citizens. Addressing income inequality is essential for achieving sustainable and inclusive development that truly reflects the nation's economic potential.

While India's economic achievements are commendable, they lose their value when juxtaposed with the harsh realities of poverty and inequality. The challenge lies in transforming economic growth into economic justice, where every individual has the opportunity to thrive. Only then can India's status as the 5th largest economy be a true indicator of its progress and development.

References -

1. Oxfam Inequality Report
2. Thomas Piketty and Lucas Chancel's Study on Income Inequality
3. World Bank Data on Poverty
4. National Sample Survey Office (NSSO) Reports

5. Centre for Monitoring Indian Economy (CMIE) Unemployment Data

6. Economic Survey of India

7. World Health Organization (WHO) Healthcare Data

8. Lancet Study on Healthcare Expenditure

9. Annual Status of Education Report (ASER)

10. UNESCO Report on Out-of-School Children

11. World Health Organization (WHO) Data on Air Pollution

12. NITI Aayog Report on Water Crisis

13. World Economic Forum's Global Competitiveness Report

14. Amartya Sen's Research on Development Economics

15. Jean Drèze's Publications on Social Policy

16. Abhijit Banerjee's Work on Poverty Alleviation

CHAPTER XV

The Worst Curse of Mankind

Unemployment, corruption, and economic inequality are often regarded as some of the most harmful man-made conditions afflicting societies globally. These three phenomena act as a collective curse on both social and economic systems, exacerbating social instability, stunting economic growth, and deepening inequality. Each one represents a failure of societal structures to deliver prosperity and well-being to all individuals. This essay will argue, through an examination of the economic, social, and political ramifications of these issues, that they are indeed the worst curses of mankind.

1. Unemployment: The Destruction of Human Potential

Unemployment is a destructive force both economically and socially. It is not just a matter of lost wages for individuals, but a systemic problem that erodes the economic potential of entire societies. The absence of work is not merely an individual burden but one that compounds across the economy. Economically, unemployment represents a colossal waste of human capital. Every unemployed individual is a potential worker who could be contributing to the production of goods and services. When these individuals are sidelined, the economy operates below its potential, leading to lower GDP and stagnating growth. Moreover, high unemployment often leads to a vicious cycle: without jobs, people have less disposable income, leading to lower consumer spending, which in turn reduces demand for goods and services, causing businesses to shrink further and lay off more workers. This cycle of low demand and low employment leads to long-term economic stagnation, sometimes described as a "negative multiplier effect."

Socially, unemployment is linked to increased levels of stress, mental illness, and social disintegration. The inability to find work robs individuals of their sense of purpose, dignity, and social standing, often leading to depression, substance abuse, and family breakdowns. High unemployment rates can also lead to increased crime, as people without jobs turn to illicit means to survive. This social breakdown further weakens the fabric of society, creating a breeding ground for unrest and instability. Historically, countries suffering from prolonged unemployment often experience severe political repercussions. The rise of extremism, populism, and even authoritarianism can be traced back to periods of mass unemployment, where large sections of the population feel disenfranchised and disillusioned with the political and economic system. The Great Depression of the 1930s, which led to widespread unemployment, is often cited as a contributing factor to the rise of fascism in Europe.

2. Corruption: The Cancer of Governance and Social Trust

Corruption is another man-made curse that inflicts significant harm on both social and economic systems. It erodes trust in institutions, undermines economic efficiency, and exacerbates inequality. Corruption occurs when individuals in positions of power use their authority for personal gain, at the expense of the public good. Economically, corruption distorts markets and undermines the efficiency of resource allocation. In corrupt systems, contracts, licences, and government contracts are often awarded based on personal relationships, bribes, or favouritism rather than merit or need. This leads to suboptimal use of resources, as projects are awarded to less qualified individuals or companies that may not be capable of delivering high-quality results. Corruption also deters investment, both domestic and foreign, as businesses are reluctant to invest in markets where they must pay bribes or navigate opaque regulatory systems. In addition, corruption creates barriers to entrepreneurship and innovation. Small businesses and startups often cannot afford to pay bribes or navigate corrupt systems, leading to a concentration of economic power in the hands of a few well-connected elites. This stifles competition and innovation, further entrenching inequality and limiting economic growth. Socially, corruption undermines the legitimacy of institutions and erodes public trust. When people believe that their leaders and public officials are corrupt, they lose faith in the system and become less likely to engage in civic life, vote, or participate in public affairs. This creates a vicious cycle where corruption breeds apathy, which in turn allows corruption to flourish unchecked. In extreme cases, corruption can lead to state failure, as public institutions become so compromised that they are unable to function effectively. The collapse of Somalia in the 1990s and the ongoing struggles in countries like Venezuela are stark reminders of the devastating consequences of unchecked corruption. Furthermore, corruption exacerbates inequality, as it allows the wealthy and powerful to manipulate the system in their favour, while the poor and marginalised are left with limited access to justice, services, and opportunities. Corrupt officials often syphon off public funds that are meant for essential services like education, healthcare, and infrastructure, depriving the most vulnerable members of society of the resources they need to improve their lives.

3. *Economic Inequality: The Root of Social Unrest and Economic Stagnation*

Economic inequality, perhaps the most visible and pervasive of the three curses, is deeply interwoven with both unemployment and corruption. It refers to the unequal distribution of wealth, income, and opportunity within a society. While some degree of inequality is natural in any economic system, extreme inequality poses significant dangers to both social cohesion and economic growth. Economically, inequality can lead to slower growth and economic instability. When wealth is concentrated in the hands of a small elite, overall demand in the economy is reduced, as the wealthy tend to save more and consume less as a proportion of their income. In contrast, middle- and lower-income individuals spend a larger proportion of their income on goods and services, stimulating demand and driving economic growth. When inequality is high, this demand is suppressed, leading to lower economic growth and higher levels of unemployment. Inequality also undermines productivity, as it limits access to education, healthcare, and other essential services for large segments of the population. When people are unable to access the resources they need to develop their skills and talents, the economy as a whole suffers. This is particularly evident in developing countries, where extreme inequality often prevents children from attending school or receiving adequate healthcare, perpetuating cycles of poverty and limiting the potential for economic development. Socially, extreme inequality leads to increased levels of social unrest, crime, and political instability. When people perceive that the system is rigged against them and that they have little chance of improving their circumstances, they become disillusioned and angry. This can lead to protests, strikes, and even violence, as people demand a fairer distribution of wealth and opportunities. The Arab Spring, which began in 2010, was driven in part by widespread economic inequality and frustration with corrupt and autocratic regimes that had failed to provide economic opportunities for their populations. Political instability, in turn, can have devastating economic consequences. Investors are less likely to invest in countries with high levels of inequality and social unrest, leading to reduced investment and slower economic growth. In extreme cases, inequality can lead to the breakdown of social and political order, as seen in countries like South Africa during apartheid or more recently in Venezuela, where extreme inequality and corruption have contributed to a severe economic and political crisis.

4. Combined Impact: The Vicious Cycle of Decline

These three man-made phenomena— unemployment, corruption, and economic inequality— do not exist in isolation. Rather, they are deeply interconnected and often reinforce one another. High levels of unemployment can exacerbate inequality, as people without jobs have limited access to opportunities for upward mobility. Similarly, corruption often deepens inequality by allowing the wealthy and powerful to manipulate the system in their favour, while the poor and marginalised are left with limited access to resources and opportunities. At the same time, economic inequality can lead to higher levels of corruption, as those with wealth and power use their resources to influence public officials and secure favourable treatment. Inequality also contributes to higher levels of unemployment, as the concentration of wealth in the hands of a few reduces overall demand in the economy, leading to lower levels of job creation. Together, these three phenomena create a vicious cycle that traps societies in a state of economic stagnation, social unrest, and political instability. They represent a fundamental failure of the social contract, as they prevent large segments of the population from participating fully in economic and social life.

As such, Unemployment, corruption, and economic inequality can be seen as the worst curses of mankind—man-made conditions that perpetuate suffering, undermine prosperity, and threaten the very foundations of society. They are not just economic issues but profound social problems that destroy human potential, erode trust in institutions, and foster environments of exploitation and injustice. Their combined impact creates a cycle of hardship that is difficult to break, perpetuating poverty, inequality, and instability across generations. These afflictions are the product of flawed human systems and governance, and their eradication is essential for achieving a just, equitable, and prosperous society.

The Need for Systemic Change -

To break free from this cycle, we must address the root causes of these issues and work toward creating systems that prioritise human well-being, social equity, and sustainable development over short-term profits and power. Policies that promote job creation, reduce inequality, and combat corruption are essential for creating more just and prosperous societies. This includes investments in education, healthcare, and infrastructure, as well as measures to ensure that wealth and power are distributed more equitably. It also requires strengthening institutions and governance systems to reduce corruption and ensure that public officials are held accountable for their actions.

Ultimately, unemployment, corruption, and economic inequality are not inevitable. They are the result of specific policy choices and societal structures that can be changed. By addressing these issues, we can create a world where economic and social systems work for everyone, rather than just a select few. This requires a collective effort to rethink the way we organise our economies and societies, and to prioritise the well-being of all individuals over the narrow interests of a small elite. In doing so, we can lift the curse of unemployment, corruption, and inequality, and create a world that is more just, equitable, and prosperous for all.

• • •

CHAPTER XVI

The Links between Corruption, Inequality, and Unemployment

Unemployment, corruption, and inequality interact to build a complex network influencing social and economic reality all around. Although these components are sometimes taken separately, their interdependence usually aggravates structural problems and drives a difficultly breakable cycle. Development of policies and sustainable development depend on an awareness of the causal links among several elements. Considering the multidimensional nature of this link, this study will look at the interactions among unemployment, corruption, and inequality. Investigating the theoretical frameworks, empirical data, and real-world case studies from many sites will help me to understand the degree of this interconnection. Before investigating the link among unemployment, corruption, and inequality, definitions of these terms must be clear:

1. Unemployment: This refers to the situation where individuals who are willing and able to work cannot find employment. Unemployment can be cyclical (caused by economic downturns), structural (due to mismatches between skills and job requirements), or frictional (temporary, as workers move between jobs).
2. Corruption: Corruption is the abuse of entrusted power for private gain. It includes activities such as bribery, embezzlement, and nepotism. Corruption distorts governance, public trust, and economic performance.
3. Inequality: Inequality refers to the unequal distribution of wealth, income, or access to opportunities within a society. It can be economic, social, or political in nature and often leads to

disparities in living standards.

These three phenomena, while distinct, are interconnected through various mechanisms that contribute to socio-economic imbalances.

The Nexus Between Unemployment and Inequality -

Unemployment and inequality are deeply linked, with one often exacerbating the other. High levels of unemployment tend to increase inequality, as individuals without jobs lose income, social security, and opportunities for upward mobility. The effects of unemployment are more profound for marginalised groups, such as women, ethnic minorities, and people with lower levels of education, which widens the inequality gap.

- Cyclical and Structural Unemployment: During periods of economic recession, cyclical unemployment spikes as businesses downsize or close due to reduced demand. This disproportionately affects low-skilled workers, who are often the first to lose their jobs. Structural unemployment, on the other hand, results from technological changes or shifts in the economy that render certain jobs obsolete. These structural changes often leave behind workers who do not have the skills needed for emerging industries, further deepening economic inequality.
- Youth Unemployment and Long-Term Inequality: High levels of youth unemployment create long-lasting impacts on income distribution. Individuals who are unable to secure employment at the beginning of their careers often struggle with lower lifetime earnings, poor health outcomes, and diminished social mobility. The result is a generational perpetuation of inequality, with each cycle of unemployment worsening the socio-economic divide.

Corruption's Role in Unemployment and Inequality -

Corruption exacerbates both unemployment and inequality by preventing access to services, diverting resources from productive investments, and undermining the rule of law. In countries where corruption is widespread, public funds that could have been allocated to job creation programs, education, or healthcare are diverted for personal gain, thereby perpetuating poverty and inequality. Corruption distorts the allocation of resources, making it difficult for the government to implement policies that can reduce unemployment. For example, in many developing countries, government contracts for infrastructure projects are often awarded based on bribes rather than merit. This misallocation results in poorly executed projects, wasted resources, and missed opportunities for job creation. Furthermore, corruption in education systems restricts access to quality education for disadvantaged groups, limiting their chances of securing employment and exacerbating income inequality. In many cases, political corruption leads to rent-seeking behaviour, where the elites use their positions to extract wealth from the economy without contributing to productivity. This form of corruption undermines the ability of institutions to function effectively, leading to inefficiencies in labour markets and reduced job opportunities. Rent-seeking also widens income disparities, as the benefits of corruption are concentrated among a small, wealthy elite, while the broader population suffers from underdevelopment and limited economic opportunities.

The Vicious Cycle: How Unemployment Fuels Corruption and Inequality

The relationship between unemployment, corruption, and inequality can be viewed as a self-perpetuating cycle, where each factor intensifies the others. When unemployment rises, especially for extended periods, it creates conditions that are ripe for corruption to thrive. The lack of economic opportunities pushes individuals into desperation, where some may turn to corrupt practices to secure income, be it through bribery, fraud, or involvement in the informal and illicit economy. As more people engage in corruption, the system becomes more dysfunctional, with resources and opportunities being funnelled towards those who have the means to pay bribes or who have connections to power. This distorted distribution of resources exacerbates inequality, leaving the most vulnerable further marginalised. The psychological and social consequences of unemployment deepen the cycle. Long-term unemployment erodes trust in institutions as individuals lose faith in the government's ability to create jobs or ensure fair access to opportunities. Disillusionment with the system pushes people to circumvent formal channels in favour of informal networks, which are often plagued by corruption. For instance, individuals might bribe officials to secure public sector jobs or pay to avoid bureaucratic delays. This culture of corruption creates barriers for those who lack the financial means to participate in corrupt activities, which locks them out of the labour market and other essential services. As corruption entrenches itself in the system, those with connections or wealth enjoy greater access to education, healthcare, and jobs, while the majority remain excluded, thereby increasing economic inequality. In societies where corruption is widespread, unemployment also drives a shift towards the informal economy, which typically lacks the regulatory oversight of the formal sector. The informal economy often thrives on under-the-table deals, evasion of taxes, and disregard for labour laws, all of which feed into a broader cycle of corruption. Workers in the informal sector are especially vulnerable to exploitation, receiving lower wages, minimal protections, and no access to benefits like health care or pensions. This creates a stark division between those in the formal economy, who are more secure, and those in the informal economy, who are more prone to poverty and exploitation. As inequality between these two groups widens, so does the gap in access to political influence and social mobility. Those entrenched in poverty and unemployment remain politically marginalised, while the wealthier elite—who benefit from corruption—consolidate their power, further deepening economic inequality. Moreover, high unemployment creates fertile ground for political corruption, as politicians and officials may exploit the desperation of the jobless to maintain power. In some cases, political leaders may promise jobs in exchange for votes, further entrenching clientelism and rent-seeking behaviour. This type of political corruption undermines democracy and accountability, as those in power prioritise their own interests over effective governance. When political leaders use unemployment as a tool for maintaining control, it becomes even harder for governments to implement policies that could reduce joblessness and improve economic equality. This political manipulation worsens the cycle, as unemployment persists and inequality grows, while corruption continues to undermine the functioning of institutions. Finally, unemployment can also fuel social unrest and conflict, which in turn exacerbates corruption and inequality. In areas where joblessness is rampant, frustrations may boil over into protests, riots, or even rebellion. Political instability often creates an environment in which corruption flourishes, as law enforcement and the judiciary become weakened or compromised. In these contexts, elites may use the unrest to justify authoritarian measures or to reinforce systems of patronage that protect their interests. This only deepens inequality as political and economic power becomes more concentrated in the hands of a few, while the majority of the population struggles with unemployment and poverty. The cycle becomes increasingly difficult to break, as corruption and inequality reinforce each other, fueled by the desperation created by widespread unemployment.

In my conclusion, the vicious cycle that links unemployment, corruption, and inequality is present at various societal levels, ranging from individual behaviours to institutional practices. Unemployment fosters an environment that is conducive to corruption, as both individuals and governments endeavour to circumvent the formal systems that have failed them. This corruption, in turn, exacerbates economic inequality by allocating resources to those who are already in positions of authority, thereby further marginalising the unemployed and impoverished. Not only does the persistence of this cycle erode social cohesion and political stability, but it also makes it increasingly challenging for societies to implement the types of reforms that could alleviate unemployment, reduce corruption, and promote greater economic equality.. The links between these three phenomena will continue to perpetuate systemic injustice and limit opportunities for millions around the world unless concerted efforts are made to break the cycle.

Empirical Evidence: Regional and Global Perspectives -

Depending on their political and economic structures, various regions of the world exhibit varying degrees of unemployment, corruption, and inequality. In spite of this, certain global patterns appear, showing the causal connections between these three phenomena:

- Latin America: In many Latin American countries, corruption is deeply entrenched in both public and private sectors, contributing to high levels of unemployment and inequality. For example, Brazil's Operation Car Wash scandal revealed massive corruption in state-run companies, which drained public resources and limited the government's ability to invest in job-creating programs. Meanwhile, the region struggles with high levels of inequality, as wealth remains concentrated among a small elite.

- Sub-Saharan Africa: Countries in Sub-Saharan Africa are plagued by both high unemployment rates and systemic corruption. The misappropriation of public funds in countries like Nigeria and Zimbabwe has hindered economic growth and job creation. Corruption in these countries also exacerbates inequality, as the benefits of economic growth are captured by corrupt elites, while the majority of the population remains impoverished.

- South Asia: In South Asia, particularly India, corruption and inequality are closely linked. The persistence of corruption in the bureaucracy and the unequal distribution of economic opportunities have limited the ability of the government to address unemployment effectively. For example, corruption in the allocation of public goods and services has reinforced social inequalities, particularly along caste and religious lines.

- Eastern Europe and Central Asia: In post-Soviet states, the transition to market economies has been accompanied by high levels of corruption and inequality. In countries like Ukraine and Russia, oligarchic structures have emerged, where powerful business elites exert significant control over political and economic systems. This concentration of power has led to widespread inequality, while high unemployment rates persist due to the inefficiencies created by corrupt governance.

Policy Responses and Interventions - Addressing the causal links between unemployment, corruption, and inequality requires a multi-faceted approach. Policymakers must focus on creating an environment that promotes transparency, accountability, and equal access to opportunities. Several interventions have proven effective in breaking the cycle:

1. Strengthening Institutions: Building strong institutions that promote transparency and accountability is essential for combating corruption and reducing inequality. Anti-corruption bodies should be independent and well-resourced, with the power to investigate and prosecute corrupt practices.
2. Social Safety Nets and Employment Programs: Governments must invest in social safety nets that provide support to unemployed individuals and vulnerable populations. Public works programs and job training initiatives can help reduce unemployment and mitigate the impacts of inequality.
3. Educational Reforms: Improving access to quality education is critical for addressing both unemployment and inequality. Governments must focus on reforming education systems to ensure that all citizens, regardless of their socio-economic background, have the skills needed to participate in the labour market.

4. Inclusive Economic Policies: Economic policies that promote inclusive growth, such as progressive taxation and investment in public infrastructure, can help reduce inequality while creating jobs. These policies should target marginalised groups and regions that have been left behind by economic development.

5. Global Cooperation: Corruption and inequality are not just national issues; they are global challenges that require international cooperation. Efforts to combat tax evasion, money laundering, and illicit financial flows can help ensure that resources are used for the public good rather than being syphoned off by corrupt elites.

● ● ●

CHAPTER XVII

Impact of Economic Inequality on Unemployment

Economic inequality—particularly in terms of income and wealth distribution—plays a significant role in shaping employment outcomes. Inequality not only determines access to opportunities but also has profound macroeconomic implications, influencing everything from aggregate demand to labour market dynamics. The relationship between inequality and unemployment is complex and multifaceted, with income and wealth inequality contributing to higher unemployment rates and exacerbating economic instability. In this analysis, I will explore how income and wealth inequality contribute to unemployment, and how the unequal distribution of wealth affects consumption patterns and aggregate demand, ultimately impacting job creation and economic growth.

1. Income and Wealth Inequality and Unemployment

Income inequality refers to the uneven distribution of income across a population, while wealth inequality refers to the uneven distribution of assets and financial resources. Both forms of inequality have direct and indirect effects on unemployment. The concentration of income and wealth in the hands of a few creates imbalances in the economy, where the majority of people lack sufficient purchasing power, leading to decreased demand for goods and services. This reduction in demand, in turn, negatively impacts job creation and employment levels. Income inequality often manifests in low wages for a large segment of the population, particularly for low- and middle-income workers. When wages are stagnant or insufficient to meet basic needs, it diminishes the purchasing power of workers. As a result, consumer spending declines, which directly affects businesses that rely on a steady flow of demand to maintain operations and expand. When demand for goods and services declines, businesses may be forced to cut costs by laying off workers or reducing their hours, which further exacerbates unemployment. Additionally, income inequality creates a labour market where certain groups of people—often those from disadvantaged backgrounds—are more vulnerable to unemployment. Low-income workers are often the first to be laid off during economic downturns, as businesses seek to cut labour costs. Moreover, low wages make it difficult for workers to invest in education, training, or other forms of skill development that could help them secure better-paying, more stable jobs. This creates a cycle where low-income individuals remain trapped in low-wage, insecure employment, contributing to higher overall unemployment rates. Wealth inequality also plays a significant role in shaping unemployment dynamics. When wealth is concentrated in the hands of a small elite, the majority of people are left with limited financial resources. This limits their ability to invest in education, start businesses, or take entrepreneurial risks that could create jobs and stimulate economic growth. The concentration of wealth in the hands of a few also reduces the overall level of economic dynamism, as wealth is often hoarded or invested in speculative financial markets rather than being used to create jobs or drive productive economic activity. Furthermore, wealth inequality contributes to economic instability, which can increase unemployment. When wealth is concentrated in speculative investments, such as real estate or stock markets, it can lead to asset bubbles that eventually burst, resulting in economic recessions and widespread job losses. The global financial crisis of 2008 is a prime example of how wealth inequality and speculative behaviour can lead to economic instability and high unemployment rates.

2. Unequal Distribution of Wealth and Its Effects on Consumption Patterns

The unequal distribution of wealth has profound implications for consumption patterns and aggregate demand, both of which are critical drivers of employment and economic growth. When wealth is concentrated in the hands of a few, it skews consumption patterns and reduces overall demand for goods and services, leading to slower economic growth and higher unemployment rates. One of the key ways in which wealth inequality affects consumption patterns is through the concept of the marginal propensity to consume (MPC). The MPC refers to the proportion of additional income that a person spends on consumption, as opposed to saving. Lower-income individuals tend to have a higher MPC, meaning that they are more likely to spend any additional income they receive on goods and services. In contrast, wealthier individuals tend to have a lower MPC, meaning that they are more likely to save or invest additional income rather than spending it on consumption. When wealth is concentrated in the hands of a small elite, it reduces overall consumption in the economy. Since wealthier individuals spend a smaller proportion of their income on goods and services, their wealth does not contribute as much to aggregate demand as the income of lower- and middle-income individuals. This creates a situation where the economy operates below its full potential, as there is insufficient demand to support higher levels of production and employment. Moreover, because consumption is a key driver of economic growth, reduced consumption due to wealth inequality can lead to slower economic growth and higher unemployment rates. Businesses that rely on consumer spending may struggle to generate enough revenue to maintain operations and expand, leading to layoffs and reduced hiring. In contrast, if wealth were more evenly distributed, lower- and middle-income individuals would have more purchasing power, which would boost demand for goods and services and drive job creation. Wealthy individuals often allocate a significant portion of their resources to investments rather than consumption. While investment can be beneficial for the economy, much of the investment made by the wealthy is directed toward speculative financial markets or luxury assets, such as real estate, rather than toward productive economic activities that generate jobs. This type of investment behaviour contributes to asset bubbles and economic instability without creating sustainable employment opportunities. For example, in many countries, wealthy individuals invest heavily in real estate, driving up property prices and contributing to housing bubbles. While this may increase the value of their assets, it does little to create jobs or stimulate economic growth. In fact, rising property prices can reduce the purchasing power of lower- and middle-income individuals, as they are forced to spend a larger proportion of their income on housing, leaving them with less money to spend on other goods and services. This, in turn, reduces aggregate demand and contributes to higher unemployment rates.

3. *The Effects of Wealth Inequality on Aggregate Demand*

Aggregate demand, the total demand for goods and services in an economy, is a key determinant of economic growth and employment levels. When aggregate demand is strong, businesses are more likely to expand production and hire more workers, leading to lower unemployment rates. Conversely, when aggregate demand is weak, businesses may cut back on production and reduce their workforce, leading to higher unemployment rates. Wealth inequality undermines aggregate demand by concentrating wealth in the hands of individuals who are less likely to spend it on goods and services. As mentioned earlier, wealthier individuals have a lower marginal propensity to consume, meaning that they spend a smaller proportion of their income on consumption compared to lower-income individuals. This creates a situation where aggregate demand is suppressed, as there is insufficient spending in the economy to support robust economic growth and job creation. The relationship between aggregate demand and employment is well-established in macroeconomic theory. When aggregate demand is strong, businesses are more likely to increase production in order to meet the higher demand for goods and services. This often requires businesses to hire more workers, leading to lower unemployment rates. Conversely, when aggregate demand is weak, businesses may reduce production, lay off workers, or delay hiring, leading to higher unemployment rates. Wealth inequality weakens aggregate demand by reducing the purchasing power of lower- and middle-income individuals, who are more likely to spend their income on goods and services. This creates a situation where there is insufficient demand for businesses to justify expanding production or hiring more workers, leading to higher unemployment rates. In contrast, a more equitable distribution of wealth would increase the purchasing power of a larger segment of the population, boosting aggregate demand and driving job creation. Wealth inequality can create a vicious cycle of weak aggregate demand and high unemployment. When wealth is concentrated in the hands of a small elite, it reduces the purchasing power of the majority of the population, leading to weaker aggregate demand. This, in turn, leads to higher unemployment rates, as businesses cut back on production and reduce their workforce in response to the lower demand for goods and services. High unemployment further weakens aggregate demand, as unemployed individuals have less income to spend on goods and services. This creates a feedback loop where weak aggregate demand leads to higher unemployment, which in turn leads to even weaker aggregate demand. This vicious cycle can be difficult to break, as it requires significant policy interventions to redistribute wealth and stimulate demand.

4. Inequality and Labor Market Segmentation

Another way in which inequality contributes to unemployment is through labour market segmentation. Inequality creates divisions within the labour market, where certain groups of workers—often those from disadvantaged backgrounds—are excluded from stable, well-paying jobs and are instead relegated to precarious, low-wage employment. This segmentation of the labour market contributes to higher unemployment rates among disadvantaged groups, as they are more likely to be laid off during economic downturns and less likely to have access to opportunities for upward mobility. Labour market segmentation is often driven by discrimination based on race, gender, and socioeconomic status. In many capitalist economies, marginalised groups—such as racial and ethnic minorities, women, and individuals from low-income backgrounds—are disproportionately affected by unemployment due to systemic discrimination in hiring practices, wages, and working conditions. For example, studies have shown that racial and ethnic minorities are more likely to experience higher unemployment rates compared to their white counterparts, even when controlling for education and experience. This is partly due to discriminatory hiring practices, as well as the concentration of minority workers in low-wage industries that are more vulnerable to economic downturns. Similarly, women are often concentrated in lower-paying, part-time, or precarious jobs, which increases their vulnerability to unemployment during periods of economic instability.

Reducing unemployment and advancing economic equality depend on confronting labour market discrimination. This calls for policies aimed at equal access to education, training, and employment opportunities for underprivileged groups as well as actions to counteract hiring practices and pay discrimination. Improving employment results depends on education and training; but, inequality creates obstacles to access to these chances. Higher unemployment rates among underprivileged groups can be a result of people from low-income backgrounds often having great difficulties acquiring the education and skills required to land well-paying employment. As it limits access to quality education, vocational training, and other kinds of human capital development, wealth disparity aggravates these obstacles. In a more fair society, training and education would be available to every person regardless of their social level. Through ensuring that every worker possesses the skills and credentials required to enter the labour market, this would help lower unemployment. Furthermore, funding training and education will increase output and economic growth, so generating more employment possibilities and lowering unemployment.

In conclusion, income and wealth inequality have profound and far-reaching effects on unemployment and economic instability. The concentration of wealth and income in the hands of a small elite undermines aggregate demand, weakens consumption patterns, and creates labour market divisions that contribute to higher unemployment rates. Inequality also exacerbates the vicious cycle of weak aggregate demand and unemployment, creating a self-perpetuating system that is difficult to break without significant policy interventions. To address the negative impact of inequality on unemployment, policymakers must focus on redistributing wealth and income, promoting equal access to education and training, and combating labour market discrimination. By creating a more equitable economy, we can boost aggregate demand, drive job creation, and promote sustainable, inclusive economic growth that benefits all members of society, rather than just a privileged few.

● ● ●

CHAPTER XVIII

The Harmful Nexus of Dictatorial Power and Capitalist Interests

An economic situation that is profoundly detrimental to the general society of a country can be established by a dictatorial government and a small number of capitalists who are acting in collusion. This scenario frequently leads to widespread corruption, increased economic inequality, and heightened unemployment, as a small elite possesses the power to manipulate economic and political systems to their advantage. The subsequent comprehensive analysis logically investigates the mechanism by which this occurs, with the assistance of pertinent data and historical precedents. The political power of a dictatorial government is inherently centralised in the hands of a single individual or a small ruling elite. This lack of accountability enables policies that disproportionately benefit those in power and their economic allies—capitalists who have a vested interest in supporting the status quo. These capitalists frequently consist of large corporations, oligarchs, or industrialists who wield substantial influence over economic policies through cronyism, favouritism, or outright bribery.

The Nexus of Corruption

In a dictatorial regime, the lack of political pluralism and accountability creates an environment where corruption can flourish. Dictatorships often lack independent institutions to oversee and check the actions of the ruling elite. When combined with capitalism, where large amounts of wealth can be accumulated by a few, this lack of oversight can result in widespread corruption. For example, in many authoritarian regimes, officials may exploit their positions for personal gain, embezzling state funds or accepting bribes from businesses. Capitalists, in turn, may engage in corrupt practices to secure favourable regulations, contracts, or monopolies, further perpetuating a cycle of corruption. In Russia, where Vladimir Putin's administration has been described as authoritarian, oligarchs with close ties to the government have accumulated immense wealth, often through corrupt means. This has led to policies that benefit these oligarchs, perpetuating economic inequality and undermining democratic processes. (Supporting Document: Analysis from 'Freedom House' and 'The Carnegie Moscow Center' offers insights into how authoritarianism and capitalism interact to create economic disparities and corruption in Russia.)

Capitalists may influence or outright control regulatory agencies, ensuring that laws and regulations are written in ways that protect their interests. In this scenario, government agencies that are supposed to regulate industries instead serve as tools for industry leaders to entrench their dominance. For example, environmental regulations might be weakened, or labour laws might be ignored to maximise corporate profits. Dictators and their regimes may demand kickbacks from businesses in exchange for government contracts or the ability to operate without interference. This breeds a culture of patronage where only those businesses that are loyal to the regime are allowed to succeed. Dictatorial governments may grant monopolies to their capitalist allies, stifling competition and innovation. This leads to higher prices for consumers and fewer job opportunities as smaller businesses are pushed out of the market.

Supporting Evidence: Transparency International's Corruption Perceptions Index consistently shows that countries with dictatorial governments rank among the most corrupt nations. For instance, countries such as Venezuela, North Korea, and Zimbabwe, where dictatorships and close relationships with certain business elites persist, regularly score at the bottom of the index. Venezuela under Hugo Chávez and Nicolás Maduro, corruption has been a major issue, with significant impact on the economy and society. Studies by the World Bank have shown that corruption, especially when institutionalised in governments with authoritarian regimes, leads to the misallocation of resources, inefficiencies in public services, and reduced foreign investment—all of which harm long-term economic growth.

Economic Inequality: The Result of Power Concentration and Capitalist Exploitation

Under a dictatorial regime, the ruling elite often have substantial control over economic resources and decisions. When combined with capitalism, where wealth accumulation is a central feature, this can exacerbate economic inequality. The concentration of wealth in the hands of a few individuals or families leads to significant disparities in income and access to resources. For example, in countries like Egypt under Hosni Mubarak, economic reforms favouring privatisation and liberalisation were implemented in a way that disproportionately benefited a small group of elites and foreign investors. This led to significant wealth disparities and left the majority of the population with limited economic opportunities.

Dictatorial governments often implement policies that redistribute wealth upward, rather than downward. This can include tax cuts for the wealthy, privatisation of public assets that benefit only a small elite, and the removal of social safety nets that protect the lower and middle classes. Dictatorial regimes are notorious for suppressing labour unions and workers' rights, often to the benefit of capitalist elites. This allows businesses to keep wages low, maximise profits, and avoid investments in worker safety or benefits. In countries like Egypt under Mubarak and in modern-day Belarus, labour unions have been severely restricted, leaving workers with little bargaining power and perpetuating poverty. Workers may have limited ability to organise or advocate for better wages and working conditions. This suppression can prevent fair wage distribution and contribute to widening income inequality. For instance, in countries like Saudi Arabia, where the government exerts significant control and labour rights are restricted, the wealth generated by capitalist enterprises is often concentrated among the elite, with little benefit trickling down to the general workforce. Dictators often facilitate speculative bubbles in industries like real estate or finance, which disproportionately benefit the wealthy. Meanwhile, the general populace struggles with rising living costs without corresponding wage increases.

Historical Evidence -

- Chile under Pinochet : The neoliberal reforms implemented by Pinochet's dictatorship in Chile in the 1970s are a prime example of how economic inequality can be exacerbated under dictatorial rule. While some sectors of the economy, particularly finance and large corporations, benefited greatly from deregulation and privatisation, poverty rates soared, and inequality widened dramatically.
- Brazil under the Military Dictatorship (1964-1985) : The military dictatorship in Brazil created an economy that concentrated wealth among a small group of industrialists and landowners, while poverty and inequality deepened for the rest of society. Economic policies focused on growth through industry and infrastructure development without addressing the needs of the working class, resulting in long-term inequality.

Unemployment: A Consequence of Economic Mismanagement and Structural Inefficiency

Unemployment often rises under dictatorial regimes because of economic mismanagement, corruption, and a lack of competitive markets. When a small elite controls the economy, innovation is stifled, productivity declines, and job creation is minimised. Additionally, government spending is frequently redirected towards maintaining the regime's power rather than investing in sectors that could create jobs. Dictatorial governments often rely on a few key industries, particularly those controlled by their capitalist allies, rather than promoting diversification. This can lead to job shortages in sectors not favoured by the government. For example, in oil-dependent dictatorships like Saudi Arabia, employment opportunities outside the energy sector remain limited, contributing to high unemployment rates among youth and women. For instance, in many authoritarian regimes with significant oil wealth, such as Libya, the economy can become overly reliant on a single commodity. When global oil prices fall, these economies suffer from high unemployment and economic instability due to their lack of diversification. As capital and resources are concentrated in the hands of a few, opportunities for entrepreneurship diminish. Smaller businesses find it harder to compete with large monopolistic firms that receive government support. This stifles job creation and innovation, perpetuating unemployment. When resources are allocated based on personal relationships rather than economic need or potential, inefficiency prevails. Projects that could generate employment may be overlooked in favour of those that provide short-term gains to the elite.

Supporting Evidence -

- Zimbabwe under Robert Mugabe : Mugabe's dictatorial regime led to massive unemployment in Zimbabwe due to corruption, economic mismanagement, and the prioritisation of loyalty over competence in public and private sectors. By 2008, unemployment rates in Zimbabwe exceeded 90%, a direct result of the regime's destructive economic policies.
- North Korea : Unemployment and underemployment in North Korea are rampant due to the regime's centralised control of the economy and its prioritisation of military spending over economic development. The country's rigid and corrupt economic system has created massive inefficiencies, resulting in chronic job shortages.

(Supporting Document: The 'OECD Economic Surveys' often highlight how inefficient resource allocation and corruption in authoritarian regimes can lead to higher unemployment and economic stagnation. The 'IMF's World Economic Outlook' often discusses the impact of lack of economic diversification and the resulting high unemployment in economies controlled by authoritarian regimes.- Reports from 'Human Rights Watch' and Reports from 'The Economist' and 'BBC News')

The social impact of unemployment, corruption, and economic inequality is profound. When a small elite controls the majority of resources and wealth, while the rest of society struggles, social tensions inevitably rise. Public dissatisfaction often leads to unrest, protests, and in some cases, revolutions. When individuals feel that they cannot achieve economic success or stability due to systemic corruption and inequality, they become alienated from society. This alienation can lead to crime, radicalization, and social fragmentation. And as inequality grows, so too does the potential for political instability. Dictatorial regimes may face increasing resistance from the populace, leading to crackdowns on civil liberties, protests, and even violent repression. Historical examples include the Arab Spring, where widespread corruption, unemployment, and inequality fueled mass uprisings across the Middle East and North Africa.

In summary, the economic and social environment is significantly harmed by the collaboration between capitalist elites and dictatorial governments. Corruption is the result of the concentration of power, as those in power manipulate laws and institutions for personal gain. This corruption, in turn, exacerbates economic inequality by syphoning wealth and resources from the majority of the population to benefit a small elite. As a consequence of economic inefficiencies and the suppression of competition, unemployment increases. This situation is a curse on society that has been imposed by humans, resulting in widespread poverty, social unrest, and political instability. The combination of dictatorial rule and capitalist exploitation is profoundly detrimental to the general welfare of a country, as evidenced by historical examples and the analysis of the underlying economic mechanisms.

• • •

CHAPTER XIX

A Few Capitalists with the BJP Government's Support

The development of monopolies is not a new phenomenon in capitalism; it has historical roots dating back to the industrial revolution. During the late 19th and early 20th centuries, countries like the United States and the United Kingdom saw the rise of massive corporations such as Standard Oil, U.S. Steel, and Carnegie Steel. These companies leveraged technological advancements, economies of scale, and aggressive business tactics to dominate entire sectors. Similarly, India experienced the rise of monopolistic entities during the colonial era, where the British East India Company exemplified a state-sanctioned monopoly that controlled trade, resources, and the economic fate of the country.

Post-independence India initially adopted a mixed economy with a focus on state-led development and industrialization. However, over time, particularly after the liberalisation reforms of 1991, the economy began transitioning toward a more market-oriented system. These reforms opened up the Indian economy to globalisation, foreign investment, and privatisation, laying the groundwork for the rise of capitalist monopolies in key sectors. In modern India, the rise of business oligarchs—wealthy and influential capitalists who dominate entire industries—has become a defining feature of the economy. These figures have built vast business empires, often spanning multiple sectors such as telecommunications, infrastructure, retail, and energy. Some of the most prominent examples include Mukesh Ambani of Reliance Industries and Gautam Adani of the Adani Group.

- Mukesh Ambani (Reliance Industries): Mukesh Ambani has built Reliance into one of the largest and most powerful conglomerates in India, with a presence in sectors as diverse as telecommunications (Jio), petrochemicals, retail, and digital services. Ambani's wealth and influence have allowed him to shape market dynamics, often outcompeting smaller players through sheer financial clout and economies of scale. For example, Jio's aggressive pricing strategy in the telecommunications market drove several competitors, including smaller companies, out of business, solidifying Reliance's near-monopolistic hold over the industry.

- Gautam Adani (Adani Group): Gautam Adani's rise to power is similarly remarkable. The Adani Group controls a wide range of industries, including ports, airports, power generation, and coal mining. Adani's close ties to the political establishment, particularly the BJP government, have drawn attention to the role of political patronage in facilitating the growth of monopolistic enterprises. Adani's rapid expansion in sectors like infrastructure and energy has positioned his group as a dominant force in the Indian economy.

These oligarchs have not only amassed personal wealth but have also accumulated significant political influence. Their businesses benefit from government policies that favour large corporations, creating a feedback loop where economic and political power reinforce each other.

In capitalist economies, monopolisation usually happens in a predictable way: big companies use a variety of tactics to get rid of or beat out smaller competitors, which makes the market more concentrated and lowers the level of competition. These are some of the strategies:

- Large corporations can afford to engage in predatory pricing, where they temporarily lower prices to a level that smaller competitors cannot match. This forces smaller businesses out of the market, allowing the larger corporation to dominate once competitors have been eliminated. This was evident in the telecommunications sector when Jio, owned by Reliance Industries, offered highly discounted data and voice services. Competitors like Vodafone and Idea struggled to keep up with such low prices, leading to mergers and exits, further consolidating Reliance's market share.

- Another strategy used by monopolistic firms is vertical integration, where companies control not only the production of goods but also the distribution and supply chains. This reduces dependency on external suppliers and gives firms greater control over the entire value chain. Reliance Industries, for example, has pursued vertical integration by owning both upstream and downstream businesses in sectors like petrochemicals, refining, and retail, giving it a competitive edge over firms that rely on external partners.

- One of the most common routes to monopoly is through mergers and acquisitions. By absorbing competitors, a company can rapidly increase its market share and reduce competition. The recent merger between Vodafone and Idea in the Indian telecom sector is an example of how consolidation is used to survive in a highly competitive market dominated by giants like Reliance Jio. In other sectors, such as aviation, banking, and pharmaceuticals, mergers and acquisitions are a common means by which large firms consolidate their power.

- Large corporations often engage in lobbying and influence-peddling to shape regulations in their favour. Regulatory capture occurs when government agencies or officials tasked with regulating an industry become sympathetic to, or even controlled by, the very industries they are supposed to regulate. In India, there have been numerous allegations that certain regulatory frameworks have been tailored to benefit large corporations. For example, changes to environmental regulations, land acquisition laws, and labour laws have sometimes been seen as favouring big businesses like those owned by Ambani and Adani, giving them an edge over smaller competitors who lack the resources to navigate these changes.

Specific Sectors Dominated by Monopolies in India

Several sectors in India have witnessed the rise of monopolistic or oligopolistic control, with a few large players dictating the market. Let's take a closer look at some of these sectors:

1. Telecommunications: The telecom sector is one of the most visible examples of monopolisation in India. Reliance Jio's entry into the market with heavily discounted data and voice services led to a massive shake-up. Smaller players were either forced out or absorbed by larger companies. The result is a market dominated by a few large firms, with Reliance Jio holding a significant share. This monopolistic control has raised concerns about consumer choice, fair pricing, and innovation in the sector.

2. Energy and Power: The energy sector, particularly coal mining and power generation, is increasingly dominated by the Adani Group. Adani's involvement in coal mining, power plants, and renewable energy projects has made it a dominant player in the energy market. The group's ability to secure favourable contracts and government support has allowed it to expand rapidly, often at the expense of smaller, less politically connected firms. The privatisation of coal mines and the push for renewable energy have further strengthened Adani's hold over this critical sector.

3. Retail and E-Commerce: Reliance Retail and JioMart, backed by the deep pockets of Reliance Industries, have expanded rapidly across India's retail sector. The company's foray into e-commerce, competing with global giants like Amazon and Walmart-owned Flipkart, has raised concerns about the impact on small retailers and local kirana shops. As Reliance integrates its telecommunications, digital services, and retail arms, it is positioning itself as a dominant force in both online and offline retail. This consolidation threatens to undermine the livelihoods of small business owners who are unable to compete with the

pricing power and technological infrastructure of Reliance.

4. Infrastructure and Ports: The Adani Group's dominance in the infrastructure sector, particularly ports and airports, is another example of monopolistic tendencies in the Indian economy. Adani Ports and Special Economic Zone (APSEZ) is India's largest commercial ports operator, and the group has secured control over several key airports through government privatisation initiatives. This consolidation of infrastructure under a single corporate entity raises concerns about competition, pricing, and access to essential services.

It is common for politicians to favour certain businesses and people, which has led to the growth of monopolies in India. Big businesses that are politically connected to the government can use those ties to get better policies, contracts, and changes to the rules. This mutually beneficial relationship between big business and political power makes it possible for a small group of capitalists to gradually take over the economy. People have said that Narendra Modi's BJP government favours some business groups with its policies and public projects. People are worried about crony capitalism because the government has close ties with powerful businessmen like Mukesh Ambani and Gautam Adani. Some people say that government actions, like giving out contracts for infrastructure or loosening rules on some industries, have helped these capitalists too much, letting them grow their businesses while limiting competition. This isn't just regulatory support; it also includes getting land, resources, and contracts from the government. One example is that the Adani Group has been given contracts to build airports and power plants, often in ways that critics say favour the conglomerate over other bidders. In the same way, Reliance Jio's quick rise to the top of the telecom industry was helped by good spectrum auction rules and regulatory decisions.

The rise of monopolies has huge effects on society and the economy as a whole. Some capitalists are getting stronger, which makes the economy less fair, hurts small businesses, and limits consumer choice. Big companies take over the market, which hurts competition. In a free market economy, competition is what drives new ideas, efficiency, and fair prices. On top of that, monopolies have big effects on society and politics. When a small group of people have a lot of economic power, that power often translates into political power. This lets the capitalists change laws and rules in ways that strengthen their control. This hurts democratic government and makes it so that economic and political elites look out for each other's best interests, even if it means hurting the public good. Monopolies can make economic inequality worse and also damage the environment and cause social problems. Because they want to make as much money as possible, big businesses may put short-term gains ahead of long-term sustainability. This can lead to unfair actions like taking too many natural resources, polluting the environment, and forcing communities to move. In industries like mining and energy, for example, when companies like Adani control all the resources, it destroys the environment and forces people to move.

India's rise of capitalist monopolies, made easier by a political climate that encourages them, shows how capitalism tends to concentrate power and wealth in the hands of a few. Oligarchs of today are people like Mukesh Ambani and Gautam Adani who have a lot of power in the economy and politics. These businessmen have taken over important parts of the Indian economy through tactics like predatory pricing, vertical integration, and mergers. There are many effects on society from this monopolisation, including changes in economic equality, consumer choice, competition, and the environment. India's economy will continue to be shaped by a small group of powerful individuals without strong regulatory frameworks and political accountability. This will often be bad for smaller businesses and regular people. Going forward, it will be hard to find a balance between promoting economic growth and making sure that it is fair, includes everyone, and lasts.

Government Policies Favouring Capitalists

Government policies play a central role in shaping the economic landscape and determining the distribution of wealth and resources. Under the BJP government, several policies have been implemented that disproportionately benefit large capitalists and corporations, often at the expense of smaller businesses and the broader population. These policies have contributed to the creation of monopolies and oligopolies, consolidating economic power in the hands of a few.

A. Deregulation and Privatisation

1. Deregulation: Reducing Government Oversight

Deregulation refers to the reduction or elimination of government regulations in various sectors of the economy. The BJP government has pursued an agenda of deregulation across several industries, including banking, energy, telecommunications, and agriculture. While deregulation is often promoted as a way to stimulate growth, encourage competition, and increase efficiency, in practice, it can disproportionately benefit large corporations that have the resources to dominate newly deregulated markets.

- Banking Sector Deregulation: In the banking sector, deregulation has led to increased privatisation of public sector banks and the relaxation of lending norms. Large corporate entities benefit from easier access to credit, while small businesses often face difficulties in securing loans. This preferential access to finance enables large corporations to expand their operations, acquire smaller competitors, and further consolidate their market position.

- Agricultural Deregulation (Farm Laws): The introduction of the three controversial farm laws in 2020 is another example of deregulation favouring big capital. The laws were intended to liberalise agricultural markets by removing restrictions on the sale, pricing, and storage of farm produce. However, these reforms were widely criticised for favouring large agribusinesses and corporate entities, allowing them to exert greater control over the agricultural supply chain. This deregulation would have undermined the bargaining power of small farmers, potentially forcing them into unfavourable contracts with large corporations. Massive protests by farmers eventually led to the repeal of these laws.

- Energy Sector Deregulation: In the energy sector, deregulation has led to the privatisation of coal mining and the expansion of private participation in the renewable energy market. The Adani Group, for example, has benefited significantly from deregulation in coal mining, becoming one of the largest players in the sector. Similarly, deregulation in the renewable energy sector has allowed large corporations to dominate the market, reducing opportunities for smaller players.

2. Privatisation: Selling Off Public Assets

Privatisation involves transferring ownership of state-owned enterprises and assets to private companies. The BJP government has accelerated the privatisation of public sector enterprises (PSEs) across various sectors, including aviation, railways, defence, and energy. The justification for privatisation is often framed in terms of improving efficiency and reducing the fiscal burden on the government. However, privatisation frequently results in the concentration of economic power in the hands of a few large corporations, leading to monopolistic practices.

- Aviation Industry Privatisation: The privatisation of Air India, India's national carrier, serves as a key example. After years of financial struggles, the government sold the airline to the Tata Group in 2021. While the sale was hailed as a successful privatisation effort, it raised concerns about the growing concentration of power in the aviation sector, where a few large players now dominate the market. This consolidation reduces competition and can lead to higher prices for consumers.

- Railways Privatization: The Indian Railways, one of the largest employers in the world, has also been the subject of privatisation efforts. The BJP government has introduced private trains and allowed private companies to bid for rail routes. While this move is presented as a way to modernise the railways and improve services, it raises concerns about the potential monopolisation of profitable routes by a few large corporations, such as the Adani and Tata Groups, reducing the government's ability to control pricing and accessibility.

- Defence and Energy Sector Privatization: The defence and energy sectors have also seen significant privatisation. The entry of private companies into defence production, for example, has allowed major conglomerates like Reliance and Adani to secure lucrative contracts for manufacturing military equipment. Similarly, privatisation in the energy sector has enabled companies like the Adani Group to dominate the coal and renewable energy markets. This concentration of power reduces competition and places critical infrastructure in the hands of a few large players, which may not prioritise national interests or public welfare.

B. Tax Policies and Incentives

1. Corporate Tax Cuts

One of the most significant policy changes benefiting capitalists under the BJP government has been the reduction of corporate tax rates. In 2019, the government announced a sharp reduction in corporate tax rates from 30% to 22% for existing companies, and to 15% for new manufacturing firms. This was one of the largest tax cuts in India's history, and it was intended to boost investment, stimulate economic growth, and create jobs.

Who Benefits from Corporate Tax Cuts?

While corporate tax cuts can stimulate investment, they disproportionately benefit large corporations that already have substantial profits. Large conglomerates like Reliance Industries, Adani Group, and Tata Group have been able to significantly reduce their tax liabilities, freeing up capital for expansion and further consolidation. Meanwhile, smaller businesses, which often struggle with tight profit margins, do not benefit as much from these cuts, as they are less able to reinvest the saved capital.

- The reduction in corporate tax rates has also had a significant impact on government revenue. The government has been forced to reduce spending on public services such as healthcare, education, and social welfare programs, which disproportionately affects lower-income groups. This creates a situation where the benefits of tax cuts accrue primarily to the wealthy, while the burden of reduced public spending falls on the poor and middle class.

2. Special Economic Zones (SEZs) and Other Incentives

Special Economic Zones (SEZs) are designated areas where businesses enjoy tax breaks, relaxed regulations, and other incentives to encourage investment and export-oriented growth. The BJP government has expanded SEZs as a key policy tool for attracting foreign investment and promoting industrial development. However, the benefits of SEZs tend to flow disproportionately to large corporations that have the resources to invest in these zones.

- SEZs and Corporate Monopolies: Companies such as Reliance Industries and the Adani Group have taken advantage of SEZs to establish large industrial complexes and export-oriented businesses. The tax breaks and regulatory relaxations provided in SEZs reduce the cost of doing business for these large corporations, allowing them to dominate their respective sectors. This creates an uneven playing field for smaller businesses that cannot afford to set up operations in SEZs or take advantage of the same incentives.

- Displacement and Land Acquisition: The creation of SEZs often involves the acquisition of large tracts of land, which can lead to the displacement of local communities, particularly farmers and indigenous populations. Large corporations frequently benefit from government support in acquiring land at low prices, while the displaced populations receive inadequate compensation. This creates social unrest and exacerbates economic inequality, as the benefits of SEZs accrue primarily to wealthy capitalists while the costs are borne by marginalised communities.

C. Infrastructure Development and Public Contracts

1. Favouritism in Awarding Contracts

Infrastructure development is a key priority for the BJP government, which has launched ambitious projects such as the Bharatmala project (a highway development initiative) and the Sagarmala project (a port development initiative). These projects require significant investment and the participation of private companies through public-private partnerships (PPPs). However, the awarding of contracts for these projects has often been criticised for favouring a few large corporations, particularly those with close ties to the government. The Adani Group, for example, has been awarded numerous contracts for the development and operation of ports, airports, and power plants. Similarly, Reliance Industries has secured contracts for telecommunications infrastructure and digitization projects. This favouritism in awarding contracts allows these large conglomerates to further entrench their dominance in key sectors of the economy, reducing competition and limiting opportunities for smaller players. The lack of transparency in the awarding of public contracts has raised concerns about crony capitalism, where business interests are closely aligned with political power. Allegations of favouritism and corruption in the bidding process undermine public trust in the government and create an environment where a few powerful capitalists are able to secure lucrative contracts at the expense of fair competition.

2. The Impact on Small and Medium Enterprises (SMEs)

Large infrastructure projects and public contracts tend to favour companies with significant financial resources and technical expertise, which often leaves SMEs at a disadvantage. SMEs, which are the backbone of the Indian economy in terms of employment and contribution to GDP, often struggle to compete with large corporations for government contracts. This marginalisation of SMEs reduces economic diversity and limits opportunities for entrepreneurship and innovation. As large corporations continue to secure the lion's share of infrastructure contracts, smaller businesses are often crowded out of the market. This consolidation of economic power not only stifles competition but also limits the ability of SMEs to contribute to economic growth and job creation. The concentration of wealth and resources in the hands of a few large players exacerbates income inequality and reduces economic mobility for smaller businesses and entrepreneurs.

The BJP government's policies of deregulation, privatisation, tax incentives, and infrastructure development have played a significant role in consolidating economic power in the hands of a few large capitalists. While these policies are Often justified in terms of promoting economic growth and attracting investment, they have disproportionately benefited large corporations and wealthy individuals, leading to increased market concentration and reduced competition. The result is a growing monopoly of economic power by a few key players, such as the Adani Group and Reliance Industries, who have leveraged their political connections and access to government contracts to expand their dominance across multiple sectors. This concentration of power not only undermines the principles of free competition but also exacerbates income inequality, marginalises small businesses, and erodes democratic accountability.

The Illusion of Economic Growth --

- Economic growth is often measured by metrics such as GDP, which can present an overly simplistic view of economic progress. High GDP growth rates can be achieved through various means, including increased production and investment by large corporations. However, these figures may not reflect the distribution of benefits across the population or the long-term sustainability of growth. In India, the BJP government has highlighted GDP growth as a key achievement, promoting it as evidence of economic success. However, this growth is frequently accompanied by rising income inequality and the concentration of economic power among a few capitalists. The benefits of growth are not equally distributed, and many segments of the population may not experience improved living standards.

- The dominance of large corporations can have adverse effects on small and medium enterprises (SMEs). As monopolistic practices become more prevalent, SMEs often struggle to compete with the resources and market power of large firms. This can lead to the closure of smaller businesses and a reduction in economic diversity. Additionally, the focus on large-scale projects and investments can marginalise SMEs, which may not have the capacity to participate in or benefit from government initiatives. This concentration of economic power can stifle innovation and limit opportunities for smaller businesses to thrive.

Socioeconomic Consequences --

- The concentration of wealth among a few capitalists, coupled with supportive government policies, contributes to increased income inequality. Large corporations and wealthy individuals often accumulate significant wealth, while lower-income groups may experience stagnating wages and limited economic mobility. This widening gap between rich and poor can lead to social tensions and reduced social cohesion.
- The pursuit of profit and the expansion of large conglomerates can have negative environmental and social consequences. For instance, aggressive business practices such as resource extraction and industrial pollution can lead to environmental degradation. Additionally, the displacement of local communities and exploitation of labour are often associated with the operations of large corporations.
- The close relationship between large capitalists and the government can undermine democratic institutions and processes. When economic power is concentrated in the hands of a few, it can lead to the undue influence of wealthy individuals and corporations on political decisions. This can result in policies that favour business interests over public welfare and diminish democratic accountability.

The challenges associated with capitalism and its propensity to establish monopolistic conditions are exemplified by the consolidation of economic power among a small number of capitalists, with the backing of the BJP government. Although the government may emphasise economic growth metrics, the reality of this growth frequently entails the concentration of wealth and power, environmental degradation, and increased inequality.

It is imperative to fortify regulatory frameworks that foster competition and prevent monopolistic practices in order to resolve the issues that result from the concentration of economic power. The implementation of effective antitrust laws and regulatory oversight can contribute to the reduction of the dominance of large corporations and the establishment of a level playing field. Inclusive growth that benefits all segments of society should be the primary objective of economic policies. The following are included: addressing income inequality, investing in education and healthcare, and supporting SMEs. A more equitable distribution of economic benefits can be achieved through public investment in social infrastructure. It is imperative that economic policies are in the public interest, and transparency and accountability in both government and business practices are essential for this sake. The adverse consequences of concentrated economic power can be alleviated through measures such as transparency in government contracts, public oversight of corporate practices, and anti-corruption initiatives.

• • •

CHAPTER XX

Democratic Socialism: A Detailed Analysis

Democratic socialism is a political and economic philosophy that seeks to combine the ideals of socialism with the principles of democracy. The goal of democratic socialism is to create an economy and society that is more equitable, fair, and just, where wealth and power are distributed more equally among all citizens rather than concentrated in the hands of a few. Unlike authoritarian forms of socialism that rely on centralised control and state dominance, democratic socialism emphasises the importance of democratic institutions, individual rights, and the rule of law, while advocating for greater public ownership and control of key economic resources. At its core, democratic socialism seeks to address the inherent inequalities of capitalism by ensuring that economic decisions are made in a way that serves the broader public interest rather than the profit motives of private capital.

Democratic socialism is defined as having a socialist economy in which the means of production are socially and collectively owned or controlled alongside a democratic political system of government. Democratic socialists reject most self-described socialist states, which followed Marxism–Leninism. Democratic socialism is also sometimes used as a synonym for social democracy, although many say this is misleading because democratic socialism advocates social ownership of the means of production, whereas social democracy does not . In simple terms, Democratic Socialism as an ideology is an extension of the liberal propagation of democracy altered to suit the needs of all the countries of the world . The ideology believes that democracy and socialism are one and indivisible, there cannot be a true democracy without a true socialism, and there cannot be a true socialism without a true democracy . The two come together in equality, social justice, fair share for all and an irreversible shift in the balance of wealth and power to workers and their families.

The Democratic Socialists of America (DSA), defines democratic socialism as a decentralised socially-owned economy and rejecting both authoritarian socialism and social democracy, stating: "Capitalism is a system designed by the owning class to exploit the rest of us for their own profit. We must replace it with democratic socialism, a system where ordinary people have a real voice in our workplaces, neighbourhoods, and society. We believe there are many avenues that feed into [democratic socialism]. Our vision pushes further than historic social democracy and leaves behind authoritarian visions of socialism in the dustbin of history."

Tony Benn, a prominent left-wing Labour Party politician, described democratic socialism as socialism that is "open, libertarian, pluralistic, humane and democratic; nothing whatever in common with the harsh, centralised, dictatorial and mechanistic images which are purposely presented by our opponents and a tiny group of people who control the mass media in Britain."

Democratic socialism can be characterised as follows:

- Much property held by the public through a democratically elected government, including most major industries, utilities, and transportation systems
- A limit on the accumulation of private property
- Governmental regulation of the economy
- Extensive publicly financed assistance and pension programs
- Social costs and the provision of services added to purely financial considerations as the measure of efficiency

Publicly held property is limited to productive property and significant infrastructure; it does not extend to personal property, homes, and small businesses. And in practice in many democratic socialist countries, it has not extended to many large corporations.

The key principles of democratic socialism revolve around democracy, social ownership, and economic planning. First and foremost, democratic socialism prioritises the extension of democratic principles to the economic sphere. This means that workers and communities should have a direct say in economic decision-making, whether through cooperatives, worker councils, or government oversight. It also means that political power must be distributed in a way that ensures that all citizens, regardless of their wealth or social status, have an equal voice in shaping the laws and policies that affect their lives. Social ownership is another fundamental principle, which holds that key industries and services should be owned or controlled collectively rather than privately. This does not necessarily mean that the entire economy should be nationalised; rather, democratic socialists advocate for public control of sectors that are considered essential to the well-being of society, such as energy, healthcare, and education. Finally, democratic socialism emphasises the need for economic planning and regulation to ensure that the economy functions in a way that meets the needs of all citizens. This includes measures to prevent monopolies, reduce inequality, and promote sustainable development.

Comparison with Other Forms of Socialism

To better understand the uniqueness of democratic socialism, it is useful to compare it with other forms of socialism, such as Marxist-Leninist socialism, social democracy, and libertarian socialism. Marxist-Leninist socialism, also known as state socialism, is characterised by the centralization of political and economic power in the hands of the state. In this model, the state owns and controls all means of production, and economic planning is carried out by a central authority. This form of socialism is often associated with one-party rule and the suppression of political opposition. While Marxist-Leninist regimes have achieved some successes in terms of economic development and social welfare, they have also been criticised for their authoritarianism, lack of political freedoms, and inefficiencies in economic planning. In contrast, democratic socialism rejects the concentration of power in a single party or leader and instead advocates for a pluralistic and participatory democracy where citizens have a direct role in shaping both the political and economic systems.

Social democracy, while closely related to democratic socialism, differs in its approach to the economy. Social democracy advocates for a mixed economy where the private sector coexists with a strong welfare state and significant government intervention to address market failures and reduce inequality. Social democrats do not seek to abolish capitalism but rather to reform it through progressive taxation, social welfare programs, and regulation. While social democracy has been successful in many countries, particularly in Europe, democratic socialists argue that it does not go far enough in addressing the root causes of inequality and exploitation within the capitalist system. Democratic socialism, by contrast, seeks a more fundamental transformation of the economy through the extension of public ownership and democratic control over key sectors.

Libertarian socialism, also known as anarcho-socialism, is another form of socialism that advocates for a stateless society where workers directly control the means of production through decentralised, self-managed cooperatives and communes. Unlike democratic socialism, which accepts the need for a democratic state to regulate and plan the economy, libertarian socialism is sceptical of any form of centralised authority and seeks to abolish the state altogether. While both democratic and libertarian socialists share a commitment to worker self-management and social equality, they differ in their views on the role of the state and the means by which socialism should be achieved.

Views on the compatibility of democracy and socialism

One of the foremost scholars who have argued that socialism and democracy are compatible is the Austrian-born American economist Joseph Schumpeter, who was hostile to socialism. In his book Capitalism, Socialism and Democracy (1942), Schumpeter emphasised that "political democracy was thoroughly compatible with socialism in its fullest sense". However, it has been noted that he did not believe that democracy was a sound political system and advocated republican values.

In a 1963 All India Congress Committee address, Indian Prime Minister Jawaharlal Nehru stated: "Political democracy has no meaning if it does not embrace economic democracy. And economic democracy is nothing but socialism."

Political historian Theodore Draper wrote: "I know of no political group which has resisted totalitarianism in all its guises more steadfastly than democratic socialists."

Historian and economist Robert Heilbroner argued that "[t]here is, of course, no conflict between such a socialism and freedom as we have described it; indeed, this conception of socialism is the very epitome of these freedoms", referring to open association of individuals in political and social life; the democratisation and humanization of work; and the cultivation of personal talents and creativity.

Bayard Rustin, a long-time member of the Socialist Party of America and National Chairman of the Social Democrats, USA, wrote: "For me, socialism has meaning only if it is democratic. Of the many claimants to socialism only one has a valid title—that of socialism which views democracy as valuable per se, which stands for democracy unequivocally, and which continually modifies socialist ideas and programs in the light of democratic experience. This is the socialism of the labour, social-democratic, and socialist parties of Western Europe."

Economic anthropologist Jason Hickel and his colleague Dylan Sullivan argue that in order to transcend the problems associated with the persistent underdevelopment in the contemporary "imperialist world economy", where "continued capital accumulation may create pressures for cheapening labour" which "works against the goals of human development," and also the top-down authoritarian socialism as experienced in the Soviet Union and Maoist China, which they argue is "at odds with the socialist goals of workers' self-management and democratic control over production," it will be necessary to adopt a "socialist strategy in the twenty-first century that is radically democratic, extending democracy to production itself."

Marxist theorist and revolutionary Leon Trotsky wrote that: "Socialism needs democracy like the human body needs oxygen". In particular, he believed that central planners in the Soviet Union, regardless of their intellectual capacity, operated without the input and participation of the millions of people who participate in the economy and so they would be unable to respond to local conditions quickly enough to effectively coordinate all economic activity.

The term "democratic socialism" is sometimes used synonymously with "socialism"; the adjective "democratic" is often added to distinguish it from the Marxist – Leninist brand of socialism, which is widely viewed as being "non – democratic" in practice.

Busky, Donald F. (July 20, 2000). Democratic Socialism: A Global Survey. Praeger. pp. 7–8. ISBN 978-0275968861. "Democratic socialism is the wing of the socialist movement that combines a belief in a socially owned economy with that of political democracy. Sometimes simply called socialism, more often than not, the adjective democratic is added by democratic socialists to attempt to distinguish themselves from Communists who also call themselves socialists. All but communists, or more accurately, Marxist-Lenininsts, believe that modern-day communism is highly undemocratic and totalitarian in practice, and democratic socialists wish to emphasise by their name that they disagree strongly with the Marxist-Leninist brand of socialism."

Democratic socialism represents a political and economic philosophy that combines the principles of democracy with the goals of socialism. It seeks to create an egalitarian society where wealth and resources are distributed more equitably while maintaining democratic governance and individual freedoms. This philosophy contrasts sharply with more authoritarian forms of socialism, such as Marxism-Leninism, and aims to integrate social ownership with democratic management of enterprises and institutions. In this comprehensive analysis, we will address and refute common criticisms and misconceptions of democratic socialism, emphasising its potential to promote equality, social cohesion, and human flourishing.

Common Misconceptions about Democratic Socialism

- Misconception 1: Equating Democratic Socialism with Totalitarianism

One of the most pervasive misconceptions is the belief that democratic socialism inevitably leads to totalitarianism. Critics often cite historical examples like the Soviet Union or Maoist China, where socialist principles were enforced through authoritarian means. However, democratic socialism is fundamentally different, advocating for socialism through democratic means, ensuring political freedoms, and safeguarding human rights. The Scandinavian countries, particularly Sweden and Norway, are prime examples of democratic socialism in action, where strong social safety nets coexist with robust democratic institutions.

- Misconception 2: Confusing Democratic Socialism with Marxism-Leninism

Another common misconception is the conflation of democratic socialism with Marxism-Leninism. While both advocate for socialism, their methods and end goals differ significantly. Marxism-Leninism seeks to establish a classless society through revolutionary means, often resulting in a one-party state. In contrast, democratic socialism emphasises gradual reforms within a democratic framework, striving to balance social ownership with individual liberties. Democratic socialism aims to achieve social equity without compromising democratic governance.

- Misconception 3: Misunderstanding Economic Policies

Critics often misunderstand the economic policies of democratic socialism, assuming it entails complete state control over the economy. However, democratic socialism advocates for a mixed economy, where both private enterprise and social ownership coexist. Key industries and services, such as healthcare, education, and utilities, are often socialised to ensure universal access, while other sectors remain in private hands to foster innovation and competition. This hybrid approach aims to combine the efficiency of the market with the equity of social ownership.

My Response to Common Criticisms

Criticism 1: Inefficiency -
Critics argue that democratic socialism leads to economic inefficiency, claiming that state-run enterprises lack the incentives for productivity and innovation inherent in private businesses. They assert that without the profit motive, public services become bloated and inefficient, leading to higher costs and lower quality.

My Counter Argument -
While there are instances of inefficiency in any economic system, the claim that democratic socialism inherently leads to inefficiency is unfounded. Many democratic socialist countries have demonstrated high levels of efficiency and productivity, particularly in public services. For example, the healthcare systems in countries like Sweden and Denmark are often more efficient than those in the United States, delivering higher quality care at a lower cost per capita.

Examples of Efficiency in Democratic Socialist Policies -
In healthcare, countries with democratic socialist policies often achieve better health outcomes with lower expenditures. The

National Health Service (NHS) in the United Kingdom, though facing challenges, provides comprehensive care to all citizens and is considered one of the most efficient healthcare systems globally. Additionally, public transportation systems in cities like Copenhagen and Helsinki are models of efficiency, offering reliable and affordable services that reduce traffic congestion and environmental impact.

Criticism 2: Lack of Innovation -

Another criticism is that democratic socialism stifles innovation by removing the profit motive that drives entrepreneurial activity. Critics argue that without the incentives of market competition, there is little impetus for businesses and individuals to innovate, leading to technological stagnation and economic decline.

My Counter Argument -

Contrary to this criticism, democratic socialist policies can foster innovation by providing a stable and supportive environment for research and development. By ensuring that basic needs such as healthcare, education, and housing are met, individuals are free to pursue innovative endeavours without the pressure of immediate financial survival. Furthermore, public investment in research and development can drive significant technological advancements, as seen in the Scandinavian countries.

Examples of Innovation under Democratic Socialist Policies -

Finland, with its strong social safety net, consistently ranks high in innovation indices. The Finnish education system, heavily supported by public funds, produces some of the world's best-educated individuals, who contribute to high levels of innovation and economic productivity. Similarly, Sweden's investment in green technologies and renewable energy has positioned it as a global leader in environmental innovation.

Criticism 3: Loss of Individual Freedom -

A common criticism is that democratic socialism leads to a loss of individual freedom, as increased government intervention and regulation encroach on personal liberties. Critics argue that a larger role for the state in economic and social affairs limits individual autonomy and choice.

My Counter Argument -

Democratic socialism aims to enhance, not diminish, individual freedom by ensuring that all citizens have the means to live fulfilling and autonomous lives. Economic security and access to essential services such as healthcare and education are fundamental to true freedom. Without these, individuals are often constrained by economic pressures and inequality, limiting their real choices and opportunities.

Examples of Preserved and Enhanced Freedoms in Democratic Socialist States -

In democratic socialist countries, citizens often enjoy high levels of political and personal freedom. The Scandinavian countries, for example, have robust democratic institutions and strong protections for civil liberties. Moreover, the social safety nets in these countries provide individuals with the freedom to pursue education, career changes, and entrepreneurial ventures without the crippling fear of financial ruin.

Economic Policy of Democratic Socialism

The economic policies of democratic socialism are grounded in the belief that the economy should serve the needs of the people rather than the interests of capital. This requires a fundamental restructuring of the economy to prioritise social welfare, equality, and sustainability over profit maximisation. Democratic socialists advocate for a range of economic policies, including progressive taxation, regulation of markets, wealth redistribution, and public ownership of key industries.

Progressive taxation is a central element of democratic socialist economic policy. Under a progressive tax system, those with higher incomes and greater wealth are taxed at higher rates, which helps to reduce inequality and generate revenue for social programs. Democratic socialists argue that a progressive tax system is essential for ensuring that the wealthy pay their fair share and that the burden of funding public services does not fall disproportionately on low- and middle-income individuals. In addition to income taxes, democratic socialists often support taxes on wealth, such as inheritance taxes and capital gains taxes, as a means of addressing the concentration of wealth in the hands of a small elite.

Regulation of markets is another key component of democratic socialist economic policy. Democratic socialists believe that markets should be regulated to prevent monopolies, protect workers' rights, and ensure that businesses operate in a way that is socially and environmentally responsible. This includes regulations on labour practices, such as minimum wage laws, worker safety standards, and protections against discrimination and exploitation. It also includes environmental regulations aimed at reducing pollution, conserving natural resources, and promoting sustainable development. Democratic socialists argue that without proper regulation, markets are prone to exploitation, inequality, and environmental degradation.

Wealth redistribution is a core principle of democratic socialism, and this is achieved through both taxation and social welfare programs. Democratic socialists advocate for a robust welfare state that provides universal access to healthcare, education, housing, and other essential services. They argue that access to these services should be considered a basic human right, rather than something that is contingent on one's ability to pay. In addition to providing social services, democratic socialists support policies that promote income redistribution, such as universal basic income, guaranteed minimum wages, and progressive labour laws that empower workers and reduce income inequality.

Public ownership of key industries is another pillar of democratic socialist economic policy. Democratic socialists argue that certain industries—such as healthcare, education, energy, and transportation—are too important to be left to the whims of the market and should be publicly owned and democratically controlled. Public ownership can take different forms, from full nationalisation of industries to cooperative ownership models where workers and consumers have a direct say in the management of businesses. The goal of public ownership is to ensure that these essential services are provided in a way that meets the needs of the public, rather than being driven by the profit motives of private corporations.

Benefits of Democratic Socialism

Democratic socialist policies are intended to foster economic stability and social welfare by addressing the underlying causes of inequality and guaranteeing that the economy is in the public interest. Democratic socialist policies attempt to establish a more equitable and just society in which all individuals have access to the resources necessary for their success by emphasising social ownership, wealth redistribution, and market regulation. The regulation of markets and the provision of social services are two of the primary methods by which democratic socialist policies foster economic stability. Democratic socialist policies mitigate the risks of economic crises and guarantee that all individuals have access to the resources necessary for survival and prosperity by ensuring that markets are appropriately regulated and that essential services are publicly provided. For instance, universal healthcare alleviates the financial burden on families and individuals and prevents medical bankruptcies, which can have catastrophic consequences for both the personal and broader economy. In the same way, the availability of free or low-cost education guarantees that all individuals have the chance to acquire the necessary skills and knowledge to engage in the economy, thereby reducing unemployment and enhancing productivity. Social welfare is also promoted by democratic socialist policies, which reduce inequality and establish a safety net for the most vulnerable. Social welfare programs guarantee that all individuals have access to fundamental necessities, including healthcare, education, housing, and food, while progressive taxation and wealth redistribution contribute to the reduction of the wealth disparity between the wealthy and the impoverished. Democratic socialist policies establish a more stable and cohesive society in which all individuals have the chance to succeed by reducing inequality and addressing the fundamental needs of all citizens.

Numerous countries have implemented democratic socialist policies to varying degrees, and these case studies provide valuable insights into the potential outcomes of such policies. One of the most well-known examples of democratic socialism in practice is the Nordic model, which has been implemented in countries such as Sweden, Denmark, Norway, and Finland. These countries have achieved high levels of social welfare, low levels of inequality, and strong economic performance through a combination of progressive taxation, public ownership, and social welfare programs. For example, Sweden has a robust welfare state that provides universal access to healthcare, education, and social services, while also maintaining a competitive market economy. The success of the Nordic model demonstrates that it is possible to achieve both economic prosperity and social welfare through democratic socialist policies.

I will now examine the experiences of countries such as Sweden, Denmark, Norway, and Venezuela, as well as the effects of their adoption of democratic socialist policies on their economies and societies. ------

Sweden is often cited as a successful example of democratic socialism. The country has implemented a combination of progressive taxation, wealth redistribution, and public ownership of key industries to create a more equitable and just society. Sweden's social welfare programs, including universal healthcare, education, and social security, are funded by high levels of taxation, particularly on the wealthy. The country also has a strong tradition of labour rights and worker participation in decision-making, with many businesses being owned and controlled by workers. As a result, Sweden has one of the highest standards of living in the world, with low levels of poverty and inequality, and a highly educated and healthy workforce. Sweden's democratic socialist policies have helped to create a stable and prosperous economy, with low levels of unemployment and a high degree of social cohesion.

Denmark is another country that has successfully implemented democratic socialist policies. Like Sweden, Denmark has a strong social welfare system, funded by high levels of taxation on the wealthy. The country also has a high degree of public ownership of key industries, such as healthcare, education, and transportation, which ensures that these essential services are accessible to all citizens. Denmark's democratic socialist policies have helped to create a stable and prosperous economy, with low levels of poverty and inequality, and a high degree of social welfare. Moreover, Denmark's commitment to environmental sustainability and worker participation in decision-making has made it a global leader in green technology and innovation.

Norway is another example of a country that has successfully implemented democratic socialist policies. Norway's economy is heavily reliant on public ownership of key industries, particularly in the oil and gas sector. The country's wealth from oil and gas is managed by the government, which has created a sovereign wealth fund to ensure that the benefits of this wealth are shared broadly across society. Norway's democratic socialist policies have helped to create a high standard of living, with low levels of poverty and inequality, and a strong social welfare system. The country also has a high degree of worker participation in decision-making, with many businesses being owned and controlled by workers.

Another example of democratic socialism in practice can be found in the policies of the United Kingdom under the Labour government of the mid-20th century. Following World War II, the Labour government implemented a range of democratic socialist policies, including the nationalisation of key industries such as coal, steel, and railways, as well as the creation of the National Health

Service (NHS), which provides free healthcare to all citizens. These policies helped to reduce inequality and promote social welfare, while also contributing to the post-war economic boom in the UK. However, the limitations of the UK's experience with democratic socialism also highlight some of the challenges of implementing such policies, particularly in the face of political opposition and changing economic conditions.

In an overview, democratic socialism provides a vision for a society that is more equitable and just, in which economic decisions are made democratically and wealth is distributed more equitably. Democratic socialism aims to establish a system that prioritises economic stability, social welfare, and individual freedoms by integrating socialist economic principles with democratic political values. Although democratic socialist policies have been implemented in a variety of countries and contexts, the ultimate objective remains consistent: to establish a society in which all individuals have the chance to prosper, irrespective of their economic or social status.

● ● ●

CHAPTER XXI

Religious Support for Democratic Socialism

When you look at how political and religious views affect each other, you can see that the main ideas of many of the world's religions are very similar to the ideas behind democratic socialism. Even though each religion has its own rules and customs, most of them agree on some basic ideas, like fairness in the economy, helping those who are less fortunate, and promoting social justice. These are the same ideas that are at the heart of democratic socialism.

This chapter tries to show how democratic socialism is deeply linked to the teachings of Islam, Christianity, Judaism, Buddhism, and Hinduism. All of these religions want everyone to be happy and healthy, for everyone to have equal access to wealth and power, and for everyone to put the needs of others ahead of their own selfish desires. There is a common goal of a fair society that is similar to democratic socialism. This goal can be seen in the Christian call to "love thy neighbour," the Islamic focus on charity and zakat, the Jewish goal of "repairing the world," and the Buddhist and Hindu principles of compassion and dharma.

In what comes next, I'll talk more about the teachings of each of these religions and look at how they support democratic socialism. By understanding these similarities, we can better understand why democratic socialism is so popular around the world as a way to make the world more fair and kind, in line with the moral teachings of the world's major religions.

Support for democratic socialist ideas in Christianity ----

Theological and moral teachings in Christianity, especially those that stress social justice, compassion, and the well-being of the community, strongly support democratic socialist ideas. Throughout history, different Christian groups and leaders have used their faith's teachings to push for economic systems that put people's well-being, fair sharing of resources, and human dignity first. These ideas are very similar to democratic socialism.

Jesus Christ taught that we should care for the poor, the outcast, and the abused. These teachings are at the heart of Christianity. In the Gospels, Jesus speaks out for compassion and social justice many times. For example, in the Parable of the Good Samaritan and the Beatitudes, Jesus blesses the poor, the humble, and those who hunger for righteousness. For Christians, these teachings give them a moral reason to support democratic socialist ideas, which try to fix systemic inequality and make sure everyone has access to basic needs and opportunities.

In the Acts of the Apostles, we learn that the early Christian community lived together in a way that is similar to democratic socialism. From Acts 4:32–35, we learn that early Christians "shared everything they had" and gave things "to anyone who had need." This model of shared ownership and distribution shows how deeply Christians care about fairness in the economy and people's well-being, which are values that are similar to the goals of democratic socialism.

Catholic social teaching has long pushed for economic and social justice, drawing on the church's history of defending each person's worth and the greater good. Popes' encyclicals, like Rerum Novarum (1891) by Pope Leo XIII and Laudato Si (2015) by Pope Francis, stress the need for fair wages, workers' rights, and the right way to use resources. These papers criticise the bad things about unchecked capitalism and call for a more fair economic system that looks out for everyone's well-being. This is very similar to democratic socialist ideas.

In particular, Pope Francis has spoken out against economic inequality and environmental damage, which are issues that are very important to democratic socialism. He has spoken out against the "idolatry of money" and the way the poor are taken advantage of many times, calling for systemic changes that would protect the environment and promote social justice. In his encyclical Laudato Si, he talks about how environmental and social problems are linked and calls for economic and social policies that work together to help everyone.

There has also been a lot of support for democratic socialist ideas from Protestant groups. In the late 1800s and early 1900s, the Social Gospel movement arose. Its goal was to use Christian ethics to solve social problems like poverty, inequality, and forced labour. Leaders such as Walter Rauschenbusch and Washington Gladden said that Christians should take an active role in social reform by fighting for things like worker rights, public health measures, and social welfare programs.

Martin Luther King Jr., a famous Protestant leader, was a person who lived out both Christian faith and democratic socialism. King thought that economic justice was an important part of the civil rights movement and pushed for policies that would fight poverty and inequality. In his idea of the "Beloved Community," King stressed the importance of a democratic socialist economic system that makes sure everyone has an equal share of resources and opportunities.

Support for democratic socialist ideas among Christians isn't just found in the past or in theology; it's still having an effect on politics and social movements today. A lot of Christian groups and leaders support progressive policies that are similar to democratic socialism. These policies include fair labour practices, affordable housing, and health care for everyone. In the US, for example, the Religious Left fights for social and economic justice by using Christian teachings to push for systemic changes that reduce inequality and make life better for everyone.

The Christian community around the world has also shown support for democratic socialist movements around the world. In Latin America, for example, Christian liberation theology uses both Christian teachings and Marxist ideas to fight for the rights of the poor and oppressed. People like Oscar Romero and Gustavo Gutiérrez have done a lot to promote economic and social justice, stressing that faith requires active participation in the fight for a fair society.

Finally, Christianity supports democratic socialist ideas because it teaches about fairness, kindness, and looking out for the community's well-being. The early Christians lived together as a community, and this is still done today through papal encyclicals and social movements. Christian principles are very similar to democratic socialism's goals of economic equality and social welfare. Through examples from the past and the present, it is clear that Christianity provides a strong moral and ethical basis for policies that aim to make society more fair and just, ultimately making the world a more compassionate and just place.

Support for democratic socialist ideas in Islam ----

You can understand why Islam supports democratic socialist ideas by looking at its basic teachings on fairness in society, the economy, and how everyone should be treated morally. At its core, Islam stresses the importance of caring for others and sharing resources fairly. These are ideas that are very similar to democratic socialism. The Islamic economic system, which is based on the Quran and the Hadith, supports fair distribution of wealth, social welfare, and economic justice. This is very similar to the ideas behind democratic socialism.

Zakat, which means "charitable giving," is one of the most important parts of Islam. It shows that Muslims care about fairness in the economy and responsibility to society. Muslims are required by Zakat to give some of their wealth to people who need it. This makes sure that wealth flows around the community and reduces economic inequality. This idea is similar to the goal of democratic socialism, which is to redistribute wealth to make things more fair in the economy. Sadaqah, which means "voluntary charity," also encourages Muslims to give more than they are required to, which helps build a culture of kindness and support for those who are less fortunate.

Islamic teachings also stress how important it is to protect human dignity and do what is right (adl). It is clear in the Quran that economic exploitation and monopolistic practices are wrong. Instead, it supports fair trade and protecting workers' rights. Islam is in line with democratic socialist ideas because the Prophet Muhammad stressed doing business in an honest way and treating workers fairly. In this situation, Islamic leaders and scholars have often called for policies that guarantee fair wages, safe jobs, and good working conditions. These are all important parts of democratic socialism.

As a Muslim, you should provide social services and welfare because you believe in social justice. In Islam, welfare (taqwa) is more than just giving money to people in need. It's the government's job to meet the basic needs of its citizens, like housing, education, and medical care. Historical examples of Islamic government, like the welfare state in the early Caliphate period, show how Islamic principles have been used to make societies fair and just. These examples show that Islamic government can work with democratic socialist ideas, in which the government is very important for making sure everyone is safe and the economy is fair.

In the past, many important Muslim leaders and scholars have supported ideas that are similar to democratic socialism. For instance, the philosopher and poet Muhammad Iqbal imagined an Islamic government that combines spiritual and temporal aspects and fights for fairness in society and the economy. In the same way, modern Islamic movements like those that were influenced by Sayyid Qutb and Ali Shariati have stressed the need for social and economic changes to fix the problems that capitalism and colonialism caused.

In today's politics, Islamic groups and leaders still back policies that are in line with democratic socialist ideas. In Turkey, for example, the Justice and Development Party (AKP) has put in place economic policies and social welfare programs that are meant to lower poverty and raise living standards. In the same way, the Islamic Republic of Iran has set up social welfare systems and subsidies to help its people. This shows that it is committed to social justice based on Islamic principles.

The Muslim community around the world has also shown support for democratic socialist movements that fight for social and economic justice. Often, countries with a majority of Muslims have backed international efforts to fight poverty, support fair trade, and make sure everyone has equal access to resources. This global view makes it clear that Islamic principles can be used to solve any social or economic problem in the modern world.

As a conclusion, Islam supports democratic socialist ideas because it teaches about fairness in society, the economy, and community duty. The faith's focus on zakat, doing business in an honest way, and social welfare is very similar to democratic socialism's goals. It gives policies that try to make society fair and just a moral and ethical base. Through examples from the past and the present, it is clear that Islamic principles can support and improve democratic socialist projects, making the world more fair and caring.

Support for democratic socialist ideas in Judaism ----

There are many religious and moral traditions in Judaism that support democratic socialist ideas. These traditions stress social justice, community responsibility, and fair distribution of resources. Throughout Jewish history and practice, these ideas have been ingrained deeply. This is why Jews support democratic socialism, an economic system that puts people's rights, social welfare, and fairness first.

Jewish beliefs are based on the idea of tzedakah, which is sometimes translated as "charity" but is really more like "justice" or "righteousness." Giving to the poor and looking out for the community's well-being is a basic mitzvah (commandment) that all Jews must follow. This idea is very similar to the democratic socialist idea of redistribution of wealth to reduce economic inequality and help people who need it. The Talmud and other works by rabbis give detailed instructions on how to do tzedakah. They stress that it is not just a nice thing to do, but a moral and religious duty.

Tikkun olam, which means "repairing the world," is another important Jewish idea that fits well with democratic socialism. As a sign of commitment to social justice and the betterment of society, tikkun olam tells Jews to work for a more fair and just world. Jews have been involved in social justice movements and backed policies that support economic fairness, workers' rights, and social welfare because of this principle. These are all important ideas in democratic socialism.

There are many commandments in the Torah that stress how important it is to protect the weak and do right by the economy. Some of the rules for the Sabbatical year (Shmita) and the Jubilee year (Yovel) say that debts must be forgiven, slaves must be freed, and land must be returned to its original owners. These laws show a strong desire to make sure that everyone has access to economic opportunities and that wealth and power don't get too concentrated in the hands of a few. The democratic socialist goal is to stop economic monopolies and make sure that resources are shared fairly. These steps are in line with that goal.

Fair labour practices and workers' rights are also very important in Jewish teachings. The Torah says that workers should be paid on time and not be taken advantage of. These ideas are explained in more detail in the Talmud, which also calls for safe working conditions and fair treatment of workers. The democratic socialist view that workers' rights should be protected and fair wages and working conditions should be guaranteed is in line with these teachings.

Leaders and thinkers among the Jews have always understood these principles in ways that support democratic socialist ideas. In the late 1800s and early 1900s, for example, Jewish moral teachings had a big impact on the Jewish labour movement in both the US and Europe. A lot of the Jewish immigrants who worked in the clothing industry were very important in setting up labour unions and fighting for workers' rights, fair wages, and social welfare programs. To fight for economic and social changes, this movement used Jewish ideas of fairness and duty to the community.

A lot of well-known Jews have also talked about a social justice vision that is similar to democratic socialism. Rabbi Abraham Joshua Heschel, a famous Jewish theologian and civil rights activist, stressed how important it is to fix social and economic problems. His work in the civil rights movement and in writings about social justice show how much he cared about making a society that respected everyone's rights and dignity. Heschel's writings show that Jewish teachings and democratic socialist ideas can work together.

Many Jewish groups and leaders still support policies that are similar to democratic socialism in the modern world. A lot of different groups, like the Jewish Labour Committee and Jews for Racial and Economic Justice, use Jewish moral teachings to fight for issues like economic inequality, workers' rights, and social justice. These groups stress that Jews want to make the world a fair and just place to live, which is very similar to democratic socialist goals.

In Judaism, the idea of communal responsibility includes the whole world, showing a dedication to social justice around the world. Jewish teachings say that strangers should be treated fairly and weak people should be protected. These ideas are similar to the democratic socialist focus on human rights and global equality. This global view is shown by the fact that Jews support international efforts to fight poverty, support fair trade, and deal with climate change.

In the end, Judaism supports democratic socialist ideas because it teaches about fairness in society, community duty, and fair economic conditions. The Jewish teachings of tzedakah and tikkun olam, as well as the role that Jewish leaders and groups have played in social justice movements throughout history and today, are very similar to the goals of democratic socialism. These shared values give strong moral and ethical support to policies that aim to make society more fair and just, making the world a better place for everyone.

Support for democratic socialist ideas in Buddhism and Hinduism----

Buddhism, Hinduism, and other eastern religions teach about compassion, social justice, and the well-being of the community. These teachings are similar to democratic socialism. Both religions stress moral behaviour, caring for others, and fair sharing of resources. These ideas strongly align with the democratic socialist goal of making society fair and just.

Siddhartha Gautama, also known as the Buddha, started Buddhism more than 2,500 years ago. Its main goals are to end suffering (dukkha) and to develop compassion (karuna) and loving-kindness (metta) towards all living things. The Eightfold Path, which includes right livelihood and right action, is at the heart of Buddhist ethics. It tells people how to live in a way that doesn't hurt others and helps society as a whole. This moral framework backs up democratic socialist ideas by pushing for an economic system that puts people's well-being and dignity ahead of making money.

The idea of interdependence (pratitya-samutpada), which says that all living things are connected, is a key part of Buddhism that fits well with democratic socialism. This understanding makes people feel responsible for their community and motivates them to act in ways that help everyone, not just themselves. The focus of democratic socialism on community welfare and fair distribution of resources is strongly supported by Buddhist teachings in this situation.

Also, the Buddhist principle of dana (generosity) stresses how important it is to help those in need by sharing your money and other resources. As a Buddhist, Dana is seen as one of the highest virtues and is shown by doing good things for other people. This principle is very similar to the goal of democratic socialism, which is to redistribute wealth to fix economic inequality and make sure that everyone can get food, shelter, and medical care.

Buddhist societies from the past show how these ideas were put into practice. For example, Ashoka, the Indian emperor in the 3rd century BCE, became a Buddhist and made rules that were in line with Buddhist teachings about right and wrong. Ashoka's orders pushed for programs to help people, the building of hospitals and schools, and the care for animals and the environment. People often point to his rule as an early example of government based on democratic socialist ideas.

In the modern world, Buddhist leaders and groups still fight for fair economic and social conditions. People like the Dalai Lama have spoken out against the bad things about capitalism and pushed for economic systems that put people's health and the health of the environment first. The Dalai Lama has called for a "spiritual revolution" that meets both material and spiritual needs. This is in line with the democratic socialist view of addressing the well-being of society as a whole.

Hinduism is one of the world's oldest religions, and some of its ideas are similar to democratic socialism. In Hindu teachings, dharma (duty or righteousness) and doing what you're supposed to do for society are emphasised. The idea of dharma includes moral behaviour, social justice, and protecting the weak, which is in line with democratic socialist goals of making society fair and just.

The Hindu principle of seva, or selfless service, stresses how important it is to help others and make the community a better place. Seva is an important part of spiritual practice, and people often show it by doing good things for other people. This idea fits well with democratic socialism's focus on policies and programs that help people and work for the common good.

The idea of artha (material prosperity) and the moral pursuit of wealth are also influenced by Hindu teachings on economic justice. According to Hinduism, people should be good with their money and share resources fairly so that everyone can live a good life. Mahabharata is an epic book in Hinduism. It has many parts that talk about how to treat workers fairly, how to share wealth fairly, and how to protect the poor and vulnerable. The goals of democratic socialism, which are economic equality and social justice, are similar to these teachings.

People often get the wrong idea that the Varna system is a strict caste system. Originally, it was meant to make sure that everyone did their fair share of work based on their skills and responsibilities. Even though the system has changed over time, its basic idea of doing what you need to do for the good of society is similar to the democratic socialist idea of working for the common good.

In modern times, Hindu groups and leaders have pushed for changes in society and the economy that are in line with these moral teachings. Mahatma Gandhi, who was a major figure in India's fight for independence, used Hindu ideas to promote fairness in the economy, social justice, and peace between communities. Gandhi's ideas about ahimsa (nonviolent resistance) and Sarvodaya (welfare for all) are similar to democratic socialist ideas about how society should be. His focus on self-sufficient communities, fair distribution of resources, and social justice has continued to fuel movements for changes in the economy and society.

Modern Hindu groups, like the Swadhyaya movement and the Self-Employed Women's Association (SEWA), work to improve the lives of people and give them more economic power, especially those who are less fortunate. The moral teachings of Hinduism are used by these groups to push for democratic socialist goals like fair wages, equal access to education and health care, and the protection of workers' rights.

Finally, Eastern religions like Buddhism and Hinduism teach about compassion, social justice, and the well-being of the community, which are ideas that are similar to democratic socialism. Ethical behaviour, social responsibility, and fair sharing of resources are important parts of both religions. This gives strong moral and ethical support to policies that aim to make society fair and just. Buddhist and Hindu leaders and movements from the past and present show how these ideas can be put into practice. This shows that Eastern religious teachings have always been relevant in supporting democratic socialist ideas and making the world a better place for everyone.

• • •

CHAPTER XXII

The Fabian Socialism

In the previous section, I talked about the idea of democratic socialism. This is an ideology that wants to achieve socialism through democratic means, making sure that the people, not a small elite, run the political and economic systems. We looked at how democratic socialism stresses a slow change from capitalism to socialism by changing taxes, redistributing wealth, giving more power to the government, and increasing welfare. Democratic socialism avoids the authoritarian tendencies of other socialist ideas by pushing for change within the framework of existing democratic institutions. Instead, it focusses on improving individual freedoms and civil liberties while working for social justice and economic equality.

Democratic socialism is not a single ideology, though. It has used a lot of different strategies to reach its goals, some of which have been more extreme than others. Fabian socialism, a school of thought that started in Britain in the late 1800s, is one of the most important and influential ideas in this larger tradition. Like democratic socialism, Fabian socialism stresses the need for slow, democratic changes instead of big, revolutionary changes. On the other hand, it is different in that it focusses on changing laws and policies as the main way to reach socialism.

We will learn more about Fabian socialism in this chapter. We will look at its history, the important thinkers who contributed to it, and its unique way of working towards a socialist society. We will also look at how Fabian socialism is different from other types of socialism, especially Marxism, and how it has affected the socialist movement in Britain and around the world. We will learn more about the different types of socialist ideas and the different plans that have been put forward to make society more fair and just this way.

Fabian socialism takes its name from the Roman general Quintus Fabius Maximus, who was known for his strategy of delay and gradualism in his battles against the Carthaginian general Hannibal. Rather than engage in direct, decisive confrontation, Fabius adopted a strategy of wearing down his opponent through a series of smaller, incremental actions. The founders of the Fabian Society saw this approach as a model for their own strategy of achieving socialism—one that would be marked by patience, gradualism, and reform rather than revolution.

The Fabian Society was founded in London in 1884 by a group of intellectuals, including Sidney Webb, Beatrice Webb, George Bernard Shaw, and Graham Wallas. Unlike many other socialist groups of the time, which were influenced by Marxist ideas of class struggle and revolution, the Fabians rejected the notion that socialism could only be achieved through a violent overthrow of the capitalist system. Instead, they believed that socialism could be brought about through a series of gradual reforms, implemented by the state through democratic means. The Fabians saw the existing political system as a vehicle for change, rather than an obstacle to be overthrown, and they sought to work within the system to promote policies that would lead to greater social and economic equality.

The Fabians were deeply influenced by the political and economic conditions of late 19th-century Britain, a time when the industrial revolution had brought about profound changes in society. While industrialization had created enormous wealth for some, it had also led to widespread poverty, poor working conditions, and stark social inequalities. The Fabians saw these problems as the result of an unchecked capitalist system, and they believed that the state had a responsibility to intervene in the economy to correct these injustices. At the same time, they were also wary of the more radical, revolutionary forms of socialism that were gaining popularity in Europe, particularly in the wake of the 1848 revolutions and the rise of Marxist thought.

The Fabian Society quickly became a significant force within British politics, particularly within the growing labour movement. Unlike many other socialist groups, which remained on the fringes of political life, the Fabians sought to influence mainstream politics by forming alliances with the Labour Party and advocating for social reforms that could be implemented through the existing parliamentary system. Their influence was particularly strong in the early 20th century, when the Labour Party began to emerge as a significant political force in Britain. The Fabians provided much of the intellectual and policy framework for the Labour Party's early platforms, particularly in the areas of welfare reform, education, and public ownership of key industries.

Fabian socialism is unique among socialist ideologies in its commitment to gradual, reformist change through democratic means. The Fabians believed that socialism could be achieved without the need for violent revolution or the overthrow of the existing political system. Instead, they argued that the state could be used as a tool for social and economic reform, gradually transforming capitalism into socialism through a series of incremental policy changes.

Political Theory

At the core of the Fabian Society's view of state and society was a deep belief in the possibility of social progress through constitutional means which Barnard described as *"resolute constitutionalism". Because of this belief, Fabian leaders and other socialists of that time had a difference of opinion. The Fabian leaders never accepted the political theory of Marxism. They did not see the state as a tool for one social class to dominate another class or classes. In Fabian theory the state is a class-neutral institution. According to them, the state is a weapon especially necessary for the management of society.

Fabian socialism also differs from other forms of socialism, such as anarchism and syndicalism, in its emphasis on the importance of the state and centralised governance. While anarchists and syndicalists advocate for the abolition of the state and the establishment of decentralised, worker-controlled systems of governance, the Fabians believe that the state has an essential role to play in managing the economy and implementing social policies. They argue that modern industrial society is too complex to be managed by decentralised, local institutions, and that a strong, centralised state is necessary to ensure that the benefits of socialism are distributed fairly and efficiently.

Fabian socialists never recognized the class character of state authority and the need to analyze and discuss the class character of the state. They believed that by effecting the necessary state-administrative reforms, it would be easily possible to gradually introduce a socialist socio-economic and state system by influencing the state machinery. To achieve this objective, as their most preferred political strategy, they first try to promote socialism to the educated people of the society and present the ideal of socialism as an acceptable state ideology. Because, they believed that gradually the ideas and beliefs of the people at the top of the society will come down to the people at the bottom of the society. In this way the 'ideology of socialism' will become acceptable to the common people. They called this technique the "percolation" process. The Fabian theorists never condoned the usurpation of state power by any force. Thus, it appears that there is no room for revolutionizing Marxian ideas in Fabian political theory.

The Fabian leaders accepted the path of parliamentary democracy and the principle of gradualism or 'gradualism' as the most acceptable method for establishing socialism. Fabian leaders rejected the two methods of utopianism on the one hand and attempts to establish socialism in a destructive way (catastrophism) and adopted the method of gradualism as their alternative. The Fabian leadership was deeply opposed to any massive effort by the working class to bring about a social revolution by violent means. They considered the development of local governance, trade unions and cooperative societies as the spontaneous development of society. That is why they emphasized on establishing socialism gradually through marginal reforms. They accept 'gradualism' and promote its historical "incvitability". And there is complete unanimity among the top leaders of the Fabian group that industrial production should be headed by the requisite trained bureaucrats and technicians.

The Fabian leaders aimed to bring educated, middle-class people from various professions to socialism in order to establish their own ideals of socialism. That is why they adopted the propaganda methods of publishing booklets, writing articles, giving speeches, taking part in various propaganda activities, and organizing discussion and debate meetings. Through this method, they hoped to propagate the weaknesses of capitalism and the superiority of socialism to the educated, middle and upper middle class people of the society. The Fabian leaders believed that it was possible to change people's political opinions if they were properly persuaded. The strategy of the members of the Fabian Society was to infiltrate an organization, collect information, use logic and, if necessary, serve the information in favor of socialism in an organizational diplomatic manner, and gradually build public opinion in favor of socialism, avoiding direct conflict within the organization.

As 'political ideal', the Fabian Society adopted the ideals of liberal democracy promoted by British political philosophers John Locke, Jeremy Bettham and John Stuart Mill. They insisted on establishing socialism through parliamentary democracy based on universal suffrage. Eliminating the evils of capitalism through laws made in parliament in a democratic manner and properly administering the laws made to protect the common people from capitalist deprivation is the essence of Fabian's political speech.

The Fabian leaders were completely opposed to the laissez-faire ideals of capitalism. But they did not accept the Marxist arguments and arguments against capitalism. The Fabian leaders were largely influenced by the writings of British 'utopian socialists' such as William Morris and Robert Owen to arrive at the conclusion that capitalism did not and could not bring about the overall welfare of society. On the other hand, the anti-capitalist and anti-state philosophies of anarchist socialists like Klopotkin' or Bakunin were considered unrealistic by the Fabian leaders and therefore did not accept them.

Thus it appears that the Fabian socialists opposed three ideologies simultaneously in terms of political philosophy: laissez-faire political philosophy of liberalism, Marxism, and anarchism. These three types of state ideologies did not seem acceptable to the Fabian socialists. The Fabian leaders felt the need to free the common people from the exploitation and deprivation of capitalism in society, the entire society Fabian theorists wanted to convince through their argument that capitalism is exclusionary and socialism is inclusive. And if the faults of capitalism can be shown to the educated people of the society by making them intelligent and acceptable, then the social system can be changed and taken towards socialism. The social system can be changed and led to socialism only if the faults of Jibad can be pointed out. The Fabian socialists did not want to admit any special or individual role of the working class in the establishment of socialism and in the administration of the socialist state system. And it was a good and just decision. In Fabian political theory the state is a neutral institution. Fabian socialism stands on the foundation of liberal pluralistic social philosophy. The leaders of the Fabian Society never saw the state as an instrument of class interest. They believed that the welfare of the people could be achieved through a liberal-democratic state administration. That is why they wanted to establish democratic socialism for the benefit of all sections of the society by putting an end to capitalist deprivation by the people employed in the state administration.

Fabian Socialism and Marxism

No clear theory of history can be found in the writings of the Fabian leaders. Their thinking was developed under the influence of some famous philosophies of history of the 19th century, and that is why it was difficult for Fabian theorists to develop a theory of history of their own. The thought leaders of the Fabian Society were all informed by the philosophy of history of Comte, Spencer, Hegel and Marx. The evolutionist perspective can be seen in the essays in Fabian Essays in Socialism (1889), the only authoritative text on Fabian discourse. The authors of the essay all indicated that they believed in the multiple causation in history explanation.

While admitting that the eventual establishment of socialism was inevitable in history, they pointed out several psychological reasons for this inevitability, such as:

(1) The zeitgeist or spirit of the time in Western Europe.

(2) the uninterrupted propagation of revolution-related ideas since the French Revolution (1789);

(3) intellectual disillusionment with 'laissez faire ideology', and

(4) Creating a strong conviction among people about the failure of individualism-individualism in building a healthy, non-exploitative society, etc.

Among the political reasons, they pointed out several other issues, such as:

(1) Unstoppable progress of democratic ideology and governance,

(2) competition between political parties for popular support, and (3) the growing awareness of the public about the need to put into practice the ideals of collectivist social life more than ever before, etc.

Economic factors include -

(1) Expansion of the commercial system of production with the end of feudalism,

(2) Industrial Revolution,

(3) emergence of a landless working class and unemployment due to industrial revolution,

(4) Birth of Monotheism,

(5) Concentration of economic power in the hands of fewer and fewer people in society, etc.

From the above factors of social development, it can be seen that the theory of history of Fabian socialists was basically eclectic. Although Marx's-Engels' historical thought influenced some of the early Fabian theorists, they came to different conclusions when taking up political activities.

On behalf of the Fabian Society as an eternal worshiper of democratic socialism, the following essay from his book Fabian Essays in Socialism edited by Bernard Shaw is quoted here so that my reading friends may understand their ideology correctly -

Historic

By Sidney Webb

LL.B., Barrister At Law, Lecturer On Political Economy At The City Of London College.

The Development Of The Democratic Ideal.

IN discussing the historic groundwork of Socialism, it is worth remembering that no special claim is made for Socialism in the assertion that it possesses a basis in history. Just as every human being has an ancestry, unknown to him though it may be; so every idea, every incident, every movement has in the past its own long chain of causes, without which it could not have been. Formerly we were glad to let the dead bury their dead: nowadays we turn lovingly to the records, whether of persons or things; and we busy ourselves willingly among origins, even without conscious utilitarian end. We are no longer proud of having ancestors, since every one has them; but we are more than ever interested in our ancestors, now that we find in them the fragments which compose our very selves. The historic ancestry of the English social organization during the present century stands witness to the irresistible momentum of the ideas which Socialism denotes. The record of the century in English social history begins with the trial and hopeless failure of an almost complete industrial individualism, in which, however, unrestrained private ownership of land and capital was accompanied by subjection to a political oligarchy. So little element of permanence was there in this individualistic order that, with the progress of political emancipation, private ownership of the means of production has been, in one direction or another, successively regulated, limited and superseded, until it may now fairly be claimed that the Socialist philosophy of to-day is but the conscious and explicit assertion of principles of social organization which have been already in great part unconsciously adopted. The economic history of the century is an almost continuous record of the progress of Socialism. Socialism too, has in the record of its internal development a history of its own. Down to the present generation, the aspirant after social regeneration naturally vindicated the practicability of his ideas by offering an elaborate plan with specifications of a new social order from which all contemporary evils were eliminated. Just as Plato had his Republic and Sir Thomas More his Utopia, so Babœuf had his Charter of Equality, Cabet his Icaria, St. Simon his Industrial System, and Fourier his ideal Phalanstery. Robert Owen spent a fortune in pressing upon an unbelieving generation his New Moral World; and even Auguste Comte, superior as he was to many of the weaknesses of his time, must needs add a detailed Polity to his Philosophy of Positivism. The leading feature of all these proposals was what may be called their statical character. The ideal society was represented as in perfectly balanced equilibrium, without need or possibility of future organic alteration. Since their day we have learned that social reconstruction must not be gone at in this fashion. Owing mainly to the efforts of Comte, Darwin, and Herbert Spencer, we can no longer think of the ideal society as an unchanging State. The social ideal from being static has become dynamic. The necessity of the constant growth and development of the social organism has become axiomatic. No philosopher now looks for anything but the gradual evolution of the new order from the old, without breach of continuity or abrupt change of the entire social tissue at any point during the process. The new becomes itself old, often before it is consciously recognized as new; and history shows us no example of the sudden substitutions of Utopian and revolutionary romance. Though Socialists have learned this lesson4 better than most of their opponents, the common criticism of Socialism has not yet noted the change, and still deals mainly with the obsolete Utopias of the pre-evolutionary age. Parodies of the domestic details of an imaginary Phalanstery, and homilies on the failure of Brook Farm or Icaria, may be passed over as belated and irrelevant now that Socialists are only advocating the conscious adoption of a principle of social organization which the world has already found to be the inevitable outcome of Democracy and the Industrial Revolution. For Socialism is by this time a wave surging throughout all Europe; and for want of a grasp of the series of apparently unconnected events by which and with which it has been for two generations rapidly coming upon us—for want, in short, of knowledge of its intellectual history, we in England to-day see our political leaders in a general attitude of astonishment at the changing face of current politics; both great parties drifting vaguely before a nameless undercurrent which they fail utterly to recognize or understand. With some dim impression that Socialism is one of the Utopian dreams they remember to have heard comfortably disposed of in their academic youth as the impossible ideal of Humanity-intoxicated Frenchmen, they go their ways through the nineteenth century as a countryman blunders through Cheapside. One or two are history fanciers, learned in curious details of the past: the present eludes these no less than the others. They are so near to the individual events that they are blind to the onward sweep of the column. They cannot see the forest for the trees. History not only gives the clew to the significance of contemporary events; it also enables us to understand those who have not yet found that clue. We learn to class men and ideas in a kind of geological order in time. The Comte de Paris gives us excellent proofs that in absolute monarchy lies the only safety of social order. He is a survival: the type flourished in the sixteenth century; and the splendid fossils of that age can be studied in any historic museum. Lord Bramwell will give cogent reasons for the belief that absolute freedom of contract, subject to the trifling exception of a drastic criminal law, will insure a perfect State. His lordship is a survival from a nearer epoch: about 1840 this was as far as social science had got; and there are still persons who have learned nothing of later date. When I see the Hipparion at South Kensington I do not take his unfamiliar points to be those of a horse of a superior kind: I know that he is an obsolete and superseded pattern, from which the horse has developed. Historic fossils are more dangerous; for they are left at large, and are not even excluded from Downing Street or Westminster. But against the stream of tendencies they are ultimately powerless. Though they sometimes appear victorious, each successive struggle takes place further down the current which they believe themselves to be resisting. The main stream which has borne European society toward Socialism during the past 100 years is the irresistible progress of Democracy. De Tocqueville drove and hammered this truth into the reluctant ears of the Old World two generations ago; and we have all pretended to carry it about as part of our mental furniture ever since. But like most epigrammatic commonplaces, it is not generally realized; and De Tocqueville's book has, in due course, become a classic which every one quotes and nobody reads. The progress of Democracy is, in fact, often imagined, as by Sir Henry Maine, to be merely the substitution of one kind of political machinery for another; and there are many political Democrats to-day who cannot understand why social or economic matters should be mixed up with politics at all. It was not for this that they broke the power of the aristocracy: they were touched not so much with love of the many as with hatred of the few; and, as has been acutely said—though usually by foolish persons—they are Radicals merely because they are not themselves lords. But it will not long be possible for any man to persist in believing that the political organization of society can be completely altered without corresponding changes in economic and social relations. De Tocqueville expressly pointed out that the progress of Democracy meant nothing less than a complete dissolution of the nexus by which society was held together under the old régime. This dissolution is followed by a period of anarchic spiritual isolation of the individual from his fellows, and to that extent by a general denial of the very idea of society. But man is a social animal; and after more or less interval there necessarily comes into existence a new nexus, differing so entirely from the old-fashioned organization that the historic fossil goes about denying that it is a nexus at all, or that any new nexus is possible or desirable. To him, mostly through lack of economics, the progress of Democracy is nothing more than the destruction of old political privileges; and, naturally enough, few can see any beauty in mere dissolution and destruction. Those few are the purely political Radicals abhorred of Comte and Carlyle: they are in social matters the empiricist survivals from a prescientific age. The mere Utopians, on the other hand, who wove the baseless fabric of their visions of reconstructed society on their own private looms, equally failed, as a rule, to comprehend the problem of the age. They were, in imagination, resuscitated Joseph the Seconds, benevolent despots who would have poured the old world, had it only been fluid, into their new molds. Against their crude plans the Statesman, the Radical, and the Political Economist were united; for they took no account of the blind social forces which they could not control, and which went on inexorably working out social salvation in ways unsuspected by the Utopian. In the present Socialist movement these two streams are united: advocates of social reconstruction have learned the lesson of Democracy, and know that it is through the slow and gradual turning of the popular mind to new principles that social reorganization bit by bit comes.

All students of society who are abreast of their time, Socialists as well as Individualists, realize that important organic changes can only be --

(1) democratic, and thus acceptable to a majority of the people, and prepared for in the minds of all;

(2) gradual, and thus causing no dislocation, however rapid may be the rate of progress;

(3) not regarded as immoral by the mass of the people, and thus not subjectively demoralizing to them; and

(4) in this country at any rate, constitutional and peaceful.

Socialists may, therefore, be quite at one with Radicals in their political methods. Radicals, on the other hand, are perforce realizing that mere political leveling is insufficient to save a State from anarchy and despair. Both sections have been driven to recognize that the root of the difficulty is economic; and there is every day a wider consensus that the inevitable outcome of Democracy is the control by the people themselves, not only of their own political organization, but, through that, also of the main instruments of wealth production; the gradual substitution of organized coöperation for the anarchy of the competitive struggle; and the consequent recovery, in the only possible way, of what John Stuart Mill calls "the enormous share which the possessors of the instruments of industry are able to take from the produce." The economic side of the democratic idea is, in fact, Socialism itself.

Anyway guys,

They did not accept the materialist interpretation of history because they felt that Marx ultimately gave only one explanation of social development and did not consider other factors. So in this case there is no need for theory of history. However, Fabian theorists believed that the emergence of socialism was inevitable in the course of social development. This is all they admit. Fabian leaders also strongly objected to Marx's class conflict. The Fabian leaders believed that there was no need for class conflict in a democratic state system. Conflicts of interest in society can easily be resolved through bureaucratic means. However, Fabian theorists, like Marxists, defined social class based on the ownership of the means of production, but they believed that class divisions and conflicts could be mitigated or even eliminated through parliamentary democracy. So they were optimistic about social development through peaceful means and did not entertain any fear of counter-revolution in Britain. Fabian socialists argued that universal suffrage would enable workers and socialists to exercise state power. So according to them it is the duty of socialists to explain this possibility to the public.

The Fabian leaders did not deny the conflict between various economic interest groups in the society. But they did not accept the Marxist idea that socialism should be established only through class struggle in the struggle against worship. According to Sidney Webb, by the end of the 19th century most people in Britain were willingly or unwillingly inclined to accept socialism, and no party had strong objections to the expansion of the state.

Where the Fabian socialists agreed with the Marxists was that the interests of the working class could be protected by establishing socialism and that the building of new socialist social relations would require awakening the "class consciousness" of the working class. But the difference between them was that Fabian socialists felt no need for violent revolution to awaken the class consciousness of the workers. They emphasized on educating the working class, promoting socialism through speeches etc. and influencing people's minds in favor of socialism through arguments. They never supported workers' strikes, employers' lock-outs or unemployed riots.

The Fabian socialists took the administrative difficulties in the way of establishing socialism very seriously and hoped to gradually bring the anti-socialists to the side of socialism without class struggle. The Fabian Socialists strongly believed that since the workers were the majority in Britain, by gaining a majority in Parliament with their support, it would be possible to gradually erode the privileges of the capitalist class through legislation and create favorable conditions for socialism. In this case, the biggest disagreement between Marxism and Fabian socialism can be seen. Because Marxist politics is the politics of blood sport. They want to take away the common sense of justice and injustice from the common people. Their politics is not to educate the stupid; Driving stupidity into the darkness of more stupidity. To put an end to people's good thoughts.

The Marxian doctrine of the class character of the state in the process of social development is outright rejected in Fabian polity. In the Fabian doctrine, the state was not seen as an instrument for the dominant class of society to dominate other classes. The state is seen as an institution whose two main parts are parliament and bureaucracy. This is the essence of Fabian Socialism, which will gradually destroy capitalism through these two state units and establish socialism subject to the consent of the largest part of the people.

In order to establish socialism, it is clearly stated in Marxism that it is absolutely necessary to establish social ownership of the means of production. But the Fabian doctrine strongly rejects this statement of Marx. Fabian socialist thought recognizes the recognition of private enterprise and ownership in the production system. If necessary, they have said that some industries in the production system should be brought under the control of social ownership through nationalization. Their point is that the goal of socialism is to bring and maintain equality of income in the society and if this goal is achieved fairly without destroying private enterprise, then the socialist state will not only tolerate private ownership, but the above will come forward to help him. .

Fabian Socialism and Revolution

The Fabian socialists wanted to establish socialism as a system of government in Britain and therefore emphasized the need to elect a greater number of socialist supporters to Parliament. He needs some kind of violent revolution to change the state or establish socialism. Never admitted. Socialism can only be established by gradually reducing the power of the worshipers in society by establishing the rule of law enacted by Parliament. This was the conviction of the Fabian leaders. They believed that the establishment of socialism by any other means was neither safe nor possible. This statement about social change is what Sidney Webb describes as the "inevitability of gradualness".

Political change brought about by the voluntary consent of the people is much more permanent and strong than the change brought about by coercion. If all the resources that are created in the capitalist economic system, such as industries, factories, etc. are destroyed, the socialism itself will be damaged, at least the possibility of establishing socialism will be disrupted. Bernard Shaw's eloquent view on this matter is noteworthy: Returning a majority of Socialists to Parliament will not by itself reconstruct the whole economic system of the country in such a way as to produce equality of income. Still less will burning and destroying buildings or killing several of the opponents of Socialism, and getting several Socialists killed in doing so. You cannot wave a wand over the country and say "Let there be Socialism": at least nothing will happen if you do. Therefore, the Fabian socialist wants to advance only on the path of parliamentary struggle for the purpose of establishing socialism to get rid of the exploitation and deprivation of capitalism; He did not intend to establish socialism by violent means following Marxist or anarchist doctrines.

Fabian socialists admit that many laws and regulations will be necessary to establish socialism in the parliamentary democratic way. Many expressed the fear that the abundance and excess of state laws and regulations could endanger the freedom of the individual, such was the idea of the supporters of liberalism in British society. In response to this, the Fabian theorists say: It is absolutely wrong to think that the absence of laws or restrictions means the development of individual freedom. Fabian socialists clearly argued that social customs and capitalist deprivations controlled people far more than the laws of the state controlled them. In fact, socialism seeks to satisfy individual needs by removing obstacles to human development, to secure the freedom of the socially conscious individual, and hence to establish socio-economic equality in society. In a socialist socio-economic system, all individuals must earn a living, as no one is allowed to live on unearned income. This compulsory labor cannot be called tyranny to establish a beautiful society without deprivation. There is no place for fools or idle vagabonds in a socialist social system.

For the Fabian Society, history was comparable to a flowing river. Just as a river inevitably flows towards its goal, the Fabian socialists felt that society would inevitably move slowly towards socialism and that it was their duty to guide the course of society through legislation and administration by applying reason and removing all obstacles to its evolution. .

The revolution to seize state power is bound to be violent and this kind of revolution will shake the institutions and structures of the society in a big way. Even if worship ends, the course of the society will be blocked and the kind of equality that will be established will cause deep disappointment in the minds of many people in the society. It is only through legislation in parliaments administered by socialists elected on the basis of universal suffrage that inequality and deprivation can be permanently put an end to society, because only that type of equality has the moral support of the largest section of the people.

Morality and collectivism – The Fabian perspective

The basic moral claim of the socialist is that every human being should have equal responsibilities in the society and that is why all should earn their living through mental or manual labor and should not share the produce of others without doing any labor based only on property ownership. This is the moral statement of socialism. The 'ideal' principle of socialism is that no individual should own the means of production and should not be entitled to any "unearned income" such as rent or interest arising from such ownership.

What the Fabian socialists wanted was that there should be no stratification in society based on the ownership of land and/ or capital, but that there should be social differentiation based on the services that individuals contribute to social production. The moral support of Fabian socialism was for the unhindered fullest development of the individual. According to the Fabian socialists, "socialist morality" means "only the expression of the eternal passion of life seeking its satisfaction through the striving of each individual for the freest and fullest activity."

Fabian socialists never wanted society to be divided into classes. They said about establishing equality among different classes in the society. If socialism is established, each person will build mutual sanya and brotherhood among themselves as fellow human beings and colleagues in social life. Christianity and its ethics have no deep conflict with the ethics of socialism or collectivism. Jesus Christ told the rich to share wealth with the poor, and the Lord Jesus never wanted the poor to take away the wealth of the rich by violent means. The Fabian Ethos merely attempted to state that a Christian could maintain his religious beliefs and morals while accepting the ideology of socialism they proposed.

In the Fabian doctrine, the goal of liberty is leisure. 'Leisure' refers to a period of time which a person can use as he pleases or wishes in the midst of his daily activities. Therefore, the socialist state and social system should be built in such a way that people's leisure time increases and the opportunity to enjoy leisure can be enjoyed equally by everyone in the society. Sidney and Beatrice Webb gave another explanation of equality in the Fabian doctrine. Their statement criticizing guild socialism: "Equity demands that every healthy adult without exception should put into the common stock of commodities and services at least the equivalent of what he consumes, in order that the world may not be the poorer for his presence." It was undoubtedly a very high concept in terms of moral standards.

Another proof of the Fabian Society's high opinion of moral standards can be found in the following essay. From the book Fabian Essays in Socialism edited by Bernard Shaw on behalf of the Fabian Society, this is presented to my reading friends –

"Illth."

It is sometimes said that during this grotesquely hideous march of civilization from bad to worse, wealth is increasing side by side with misery. Such a thing is eternally impossible: wealth is steadily decreasing with the spread of poverty. But riches are increasing, which is quite another thing. The total of the exchange values produced in the country annually is mounting perhaps by leaps and bounds. But the accumulation of riches, and consequently of an excessive purchasing power, in the hands of a class, soon satiates that class with socially useful wealth, and sets them offering a price for luxuries. The moment a price is to be had for a luxury, it acquires exchange value, and labor is employed to produce it. A New York lady, for instance, having a nature of exquisite sensibility, orders an elegant rosewood and silver coffin, upholstered in pink satin, for her dead dog. It is made; and meanwhile a live child is prowling barefooted and hunger-stunted in the frozen gutter outside. The exchange-value of the coffin is counted as part of the national wealth; but a nation which cannot afford food and clothing for its children cannot be allowed to pass as wealthy because it has provided a pretty coffin for a dead dog. Exchange value itself, in fact, has become bedeviled like everything else, and represents, no longer utility, but the cravings of lust, folly, vanity, gluttony, and madness, technically described by genteel economists as "effective demand." Luxuries are not social wealth: the machinery for producing them is not social wealth: labor skilled only to manufacture them is not socially useful labor: the men, women, and children who make a living by producing them are no more self-supporting than the idle rich for whose amusement they are kept at work. It is the habit of counting as wealth the exchange values involved in these transactions that makes us fancy that the poor are starving in the midst of plenty. They are starving in the midst of plenty of jewels, velvets, laces, equipages, and racehorses; but not in the midst of plenty of food. In the things that are wanted for the welfare of the people we are abjectly poor; and England's social policy to-day may be likened to the domestic policy of those adventuresses who leave their children half-clothed and half-fed in order to keep a carriage and deal with a fashionable dressmaker. But it is quite true that while wealth and welfare are decreasing, productive power is increasing; and nothing but the perversion of this power to the production of socially useless commodities prevents the apparent wealth from becoming real. The purchasing power that commands luxuries in the hands of the rich, would command true wealth in the hands of all. Yet private property must still heap the purchasing power upon the few rich and withdraw it from the many poor. So that, in the end, the subject of the one boast that private property can make—the great accumulation of so-called "wealth" which it points so proudly to as the result of its power to scourge men and women daily to prolonged and intense toil, turns out to be a simulacrum. With all its energy, its Smilesian "self-help," its merchant-princely enterprise, its ferocious sweating and slave-driving, its prodigality of blood, sweat and tears, what has it heaped up, over and above the pittance of its slaves? Only a monstrous pile of frippery, some tainted class literature and class art, and not a little poison and mischief. This, then, is the economic analysis which convicts Private Property of being unjust even from the beginning, and utterly impossible as a final solution of even theindividualist aspect of the problem of adjusting the share of the worker in the distribution of wealth to the labor incurred by him in its production. All attemps yet made to con struct true societies upon it have failed: the nearest things to societies so achieved have been civilizations, which have rotted into centers of vice and luxury, and eventually been swept away by uncivilized races. That our own civilization is already in an advanced stage of rottenness may be taken as statistically proved. That further decay instead of improvement must ensue if the institution of private property be maintained, is economically certain. Fortunately, private property in its integrity is not now practicable. Although the safety valve of emigration has been furiously at work during this century, yet the pressure of population has forced us to begin the restitution to the people of the sums taken from them for the ground landlords,holders of tenant right, and capitalists, by the imposition of an income tax, and by compelling them to establish out of their revenues a national system of education, besides imposing restrictions—as yet only of the forcible-feeble sort—on their terrible power of abusing the wage contract. These, however, are dealt with by Mr. Sidney Webb in his historic essay. I should not touch upon them at all, were it not that experience has lately convinced all economists that no exercise in abstract economics, however closely deduced, is to be trusted unless it can be experimentally verified by tracing its expression in history. It is true that the process which I have presented as a direct development of private property between free exchangers had to work itself out in the Old World indirectly and tortuously through a struggle with political and religious institutions and survivals quite antagonistic to it. It is true that cultivation did not begin in Western Europe with the solitary emigrant pre-empting his private property, but with the tribal communes in which arose subsequently the assertion of the right of the individual to private judgment and private action against the tyranny of primitive society. It is true that cultivation has not proceeded by logical steps from good land to less good; from less good to bad; and from bad to worse: the exploration of new countries and new regions, and the discovery of new uses for old products, has often made the margin of cultivation more fruitful than the center, and, for the moment (while the center was shifting to the margin), turned the whole movement of rent and wages directly counter to the economic theory. Nor is it true that, taking the world as one country, cultivation has yet spread from the snowline to the water's edge. There is free land still for the poorest East End match-box maker if she could get there, reclaim the wilderness there, speak the language there, stand the climate there, and be fed, clothed, and housed there while she cleared her farm; learned how to cultivate it; and waited for the harvest. Economists have been ingenious enough to prove that this alternative really secures her independence; but I shall not waste time in dealing with that. Practically, if there is no free land in England, the economic analysis holds good of England, in spite of Siberia, Central Africa, and the Wild West. Again, it is not immediately true that men are governed in production solely by a determination to realize the maximum of exchange value. The impulse to production often takes specific direction in the first instance; and a man will insist on producing pictures or plays although he might gain more money by producing boots or bonnets. But, his specific impulse once gratified, he will make as much money as he can. He will sell his picture or play for a hundred pounds rather than for fifty. In short, though there is no such person as the celebrated "economic man," man being willful rather than rational, yet when the willful man has had his way he will take what else he can get; and so he always does appear, finally if not primarily, as the economic man. On thewhole, history, even in the Old World, goes the way traced by the economist. In the New World the correspondence is exact. The United States and the Colonies have been peopled by fugitives from the full-blown individualism of Western Europe, pre- empting private property precisely as assumed in this investigation of the conditions of cultivation. The economic relations of these cultivators have not since put on any of the old political disguises. Yet among them, in confirmation of the validity of our analysis, we see all the evils of our old civilizations growing up; and though with them the end is not yet, still it is from them to us that the great recent revival of the cry for nationalization of the land has come, articulated by a man who had seen the whole tragedy of private property hurried through its acts with unprecedented speed in the mushroom cities of America. On Socialism the analysis of the economic action of Individualism bears as a discovery, in the private appropriation of land, of the source of those unjust privileges against which Socialism is aimed. It is practically a demonstration that public property in land is the basic economic condition of Socialism. But this does not involve at present a literal restoration of the land to the people. The land is at present in the hands of the people: its proprietors are for the most part absentees. The modern form of private property is simply a legal claim to take a share of the produce of the national industry year by year without working for it. It refers to no special part or form of that produce; and in process of consumption its revenue cannot be distinguished from earnings, so that the majority of persons, accustomed to call the commodities which form the income of the proprietor his private property, and seeing no difference between them and the commodities which form the income of a worker, extend the term private property to the worker's subsistence also, and can only conceive an attack on private property as an attempt to empower everybody to rob everybody else all round. But the income of a private proprietor can be distinguished by the fact that he obtains it unconditionally and gratuitously by private right against the public weal, which is incompatible with the existence of consumers who do not produce. Socialism involves discontinuance of the payment of these incomes, and addition of the wealth so saved to incomes derived from labor. As we have seen, incomes derived from private property consist partly of economic rent; partly of pensions, also called rent, obtained by the subletting of tenant rights; and partly of a form of rent called interest, obtained by special adaptations of land to production by the application of capital: all these being finally paid out of the difference between the produce of the worker's labor and the price of that labor sold in the open market for wages, salary, fees, or profits. The whole, except economic rent, can be added directly to the incomes of the workers by simply discontinuing its exaction from them. Economic rent, arising as it does from variations of fertility or advantages of situation, must always be held as common or social wealth, and used, as the revenues raised by taxation are now used, for public purposes, among which Socialism would make national insurance and the provision of capital matters of the first importance. The economic problem of Socialism is thus solved; and the political question of how the economic solution is to be practically applied does not come within the scope of this essay. But if we have got as far as an intellectual conviction that the source of our social misery is no eternal well-spring of confusion and evil, but only an artificial system susceptible of almost infinite modification and readjustment—nay, of practical demolition and substitution at the will of Man, then a terrible weight will be lifted from the minds of all except those who are, whether avowedly to themselves or not, clinging to the present state of things from base motives. We have had in this century a stern series of lessons on the folly of believing anything for no better reason than that it is pleasant to believe it. It was pleasant to look round with a consciousness of possessing a thousand a year, and say, with Browning's David, "All's love; and all's law." It was pleasant to believe that the chance we were too lazy to take in this world would come back to us in another. It was pleasant to believe that a benevolent hand was guiding the steps of society; overruling all evil appearances for good; and making poverty here the earnest of a great blessedness and reward hereafter. It was pleasant to lose the sense of worldly inequality in the contemplation of our equality before God. But utilitarian questioning and scientific answering turned all this tranquil optimism into the blackest pessimism. Nature was shown to us as "red in tooth and claw": if the guiding hand were indeed benevolent, then it could not be omnipotent; so that our trust in it was broken: if it were omnipotent, it could not be benevolent; so that our love of it turned to fear and hatred. We had never admitted that the other world, which was to compensate for the sorrows of this, was open to horses and apes (though we had not on that account been any the more merciful to our horses); and now came Science to show us the corner of the pointed ear of the horse on our own heads, and present the ape to us as our blood relation. No proof came of the existence of that other world and that benevolent power to which we had left the remedy of the atrocious wrongs of the poor: proof after proof came that what we called Nature knew and cared no more about our pains and pleasures than we know or care about the tiny creatures we crush underfoot as we walk through the fields. Instead of at once perceiving that this meant no more than that Nature was unmoral and indifferent, we relapsed into a gross form of devil worship, and conceived Nature as a remorselessly malignant power. This was no better than the old optimism, and infinitely gloomier. It kept our eyes still shut to the truth that there is no cruelty and selfishness outside Man himself; and that his own active benevolence can combat and vanquish both. When the Socialist came forward as a meliorist on these lines, the old school of political economists, who could see no alternative to private property, put forward in proof of the powerlessness of benevolent action to arrest the deadly automatic production of poverty by the increase of population, the very analysis I have just presented. Their conclusions exactly fitted in with the new ideas. It was Nature at it again—the struggle for existence—the remorseless extirpation of the weak—the survival of the fittest —in short, natural selection at work. Socialism seemed too good to be true: it was passed by as merely the old optimism foolishly running its head against the stone wall of modern science. But Socialism now challenges individualism, skepticism, pessimism, worship of Nature personified as a devil, on their own ground of science. The science of the production and distribution of wealth is Political Economy. Socialism appeals to that science, and, turning on Individualism its own guns, routs it in incurable disaster. Henceforth the bitter cynic who still finds the world an eternal and unimprovable doghole, with the placid person of means who repeats the familiar misquotation, "the poor ye shall have always with you," lose their usurped place among the cultured, and pass over to the ranks of the ignorant, the shallow, and the superstitious. As for the rest of us, since we were taught to revere proprietary respectability in our unfortunate childhood, and since we found our childish hearts so hard and unregenerate that they secretly hated and rebelled against respectability in spite of that teaching, it is impossible to express the relief with which we discover that our hearts were all along right, and that the current respectability of to-day is nothing but a huge inversion of righteous and scientific social order weltering in dishonesty,uselessness, selfishness, wanton misery, and idiotic waste of magnificent opportunities for noble and happy living. It was terrible to feel this, and yet to fear that it could not be helped—that the poor must starve and make you ashamed of your dinner—that they must shiver and make you ashamed of your warm overcoat. It is to economic science—once the Dismal, now the Hopeful—that we are indebted for the discovery that though the evil is enormously worse than we knew, yet it is not eternal—not even very long lived, if we only bestir ourselves to make an end of it.

The type of socialism that the Fabian Society advocated was purely state-run socialism. The theorists of the Fabian Society present their proposed political theory of socialism while simultaneously rejecting other non-Marxist alternative socialist concepts (eg: imaginative socialism, anarchist socialism, syndicalist socialism, guild socialism). Fabian socialism emphasized the control of the entire society in terms of industry. The Fabian leaders never wanted the workers employed in that industry to have total control over the management of any industry. As such, they strongly believed that workers employed in coal mines or iron mines should not have full power to produce, distribute or determine the market price of coal or iron, and that the entire society should have control over such resources. And for the same reason it seemed ridiculous to them that the power of control over the sewage system should rest solely in the hands of the laborers employed in that work. Fabian theorists were never in favor of giving control power to the workers. Because, they felt that if this kind of power was given to the working class, the trade unions would take the form of the central offices of the big companies and there would be no overall control in the hands of the society.

Few of the defects of guild socialism were detected by the Fabian leaders –

First, the consumers of the goods produced in the guild socialist system would have almost no control;

Second, producer control would not be feasible in practical economics;

Thirdly, when compared with democratic collectivism (democratic collectivism), guild socialism does not have any special appeal of its own;

Fourthly, the experience of social evolution shows that there is very little chance of social development along the path of guild socialism.

The measures emphasized in the primary activities of Fabian collectivism are:

(1) fixing a national minimum wage for the working class and introducing this wage into the socio-economic production system;

(2) establishing 'urban socialism' as an essential component of decentralization in socialist states and bringing special-purpose bodies under the control of democratic local governance;

(3) gradual expansion of the state's regulatory powers in the economic sphere, and the bringing under the control of the central government or local governments, as necessary, of important industries and public welfare services at the national level;

(4) enforcing social control over the banking system and national credit policy, and finally

(5) Establishment of state ownership in mines and mineral production, railways, port administration etc. and formation of representative bodies for proper social management of the former owners after compensation.

So it appears that there are two aspects of collectivism in Fabian theory:

First, to establish organized state authority in the place of individual chauvinistic administration in important national industries and services, and secondly, to watch closely that the atmosphere of freedom is not lost in the socialist state system. On the one hand, the Fabian leaders avoided the idealistic socialist ideals, while on the other hand, they did not accept that only the producer would have full rights in the production process. They wanted to build a decentralized state and local municipal government framework within the democratic state structure. They fully supported the right of the working class to organize in their own organizations, but were not in favor of giving full control to institutions such as trade unions. They believed that if the state system and the administration could be freed from the small-minded and exploitative influence of capitalism and organized on a democratic basis, then it would be possible for the common man to enjoy freedom and people would be able to make their free time more creative outside of their work.

Economic Theory of Fabian Socialism*

The only recourse to establishing justice in society is to determine the precise economic theory of democratic socialism, In 1884-85, Reverend Philip Wickstead, a follower of the economist Stanley Jevons, had a long discussion on economics with Bernard Shaw and Sidney Webb. In the pages of the socialist magazine Today, Wicksteed was attracted to Bernard Shaw and Sidney Webb's critique of Marxian economic theory, and Bernard Shaw found Wicksteed's views more acceptable than Marx's. As a result, doubts appear in the minds of Fabian socialists about the acceptability of Marx's labor theory of value. Wicksteed did not find the Marxian interpretation of "surplus value" acceptable. He wants to show that the value of 'labour force' is not determined by the amount of labor employed in the production of a commodity, so when a buyer in a pujabist system of production buys a product for the price of 'labour force', the buyer by consuming that product Enjoying 'surplus value' is not proved. This criticism of Wicksteed influenced the economic ideas of Fabian theorists such as Bernard Shaw.

And so the Fabians decided to reject the Marxist economic concept.

On the other hand, the economic ideas of David Ricardo, John Stuart Mill and Henry George were widely accepted in the intellectual circles of Britain during this period. Ricardo and Mill's economic ideas appear to be more acceptable to Fabian society theorists as an economic argument for socialism. Their ideas were strongly opposed to the Marxist theory of establishing a socialist system by seizing state power under the leadership of the working class. But in order to prove the superiority of Socialism over Pujism, they have to show that under the Pujism system the laborer is deprived of the full value of his production. Therefore, even if they do not accept Marx's statement, they feel the need for some kind of 'surplus value' related theory.

The theory of 'marginal utility' (marginal utility) of economists like Javems did not seem acceptable to Fabian theorists. Because, according to the theory of marginal utility, it is believed that both capital and labor as factors of production earn interest and wages respectively in proportion to their respective contributions in the production of wealth in a particular situation. Accepting this kind of theory does not prove the exploitation of workers in the capitalist system of production and distribution. So they drew on the concept of 'rent' in economic discussions to develop the economic theory of Fabian society, and using the Ricardo-introduced 'rent theory' in capitalist industrial production, the Fabian theorists came up with their own 'Theory of Rent'.

Theory of Rent (Theory of Ricardian): David Ricardo, a classical economist developed a theory in 1817 to explain the origin and nature of economic rent. Rent is the payment made to landlord for the use of land. Ricardo was of the view that rent is paid for the fertility of land. Ricardo stated "Rent is the portion of the produce of the earth which is paid to landlord for the use of the original and indestructible powers of the soil."

ASSUMPTIONS-

1. Rent of land arises due to the differences in the fertility of the soil.
2. Law of diminishing marginal returns. As the different plots of land differ in fertility, the produce from the inferior plots of land diminishes though the total cost of production in each plot of land is the same.
3. Rent accrues only to land i.e. none of the other factors of production earn rent. However later on Modern economists disagreed on it.
4. There is tendency to move from most fertile land to the less fertile one.
5. Land on which no rent is earned is known as marginal land.

6.   Total cost spent on each piece of land is same.

According to Ricardo rent arises as the difference between production of Marginal land (On which zero rent accrues) and superior land. As there is general tendency to move from most fertile land (Attracts highest rent) to the less fertile land, a point comes where no rent accrues to what is called a Marginal land. So in this way Ricardo classified land into various grades according to their fertility. The most fertile land will attract highest rent and Marginal land will attract no rent indicating the land to be the infertile one.

EXAMPLE

There are 6 grades of land – I, II, III, IV, V, VI. The classification is on the basis of fertility. A is most fertile. The fertility of soil is known by its production. Most fertile soil will have more production and consequently more value of output. So the column of value of output is indicator of fertility of the soil. As mentioned in assumption total cost remains same. Say here total cost = 1000.

RENT EARNED

GRADES OF LAND	AMOUNT SPENT (cost) (Rs.)	VALUE OF OUTPUT (Rs.)	RENT (VALUE OF OUTPUT- AMOUNT SPENT)
I	1000	5000	5000-1000= 4000
II	1000	4000	4000-1000= 3000
III	1000	3000	3000-1000= 2000
IV	1000	2000	2000-1000= 1000
V	1000	1000	1000-1000= 0
VI	1000	NIL	-

RENT EARNED

As can be seen that Grade I is the most superior land producing maximum output of 5000 on which Rent earned is 4000. Similarly Grade II land earns 3000 and so on. This shows direct relation between the value of output and rent earned thereof keeping the amount spent on land same on every piece of land . On Grade V land Amount spend = Value of output i.e. Total rent is 0. This is Marginal land. Grade VI land will never be cultivated as the Value of Output is NIL. Highest Rent = On Grade I land i.e. Most superior piece of land Marginal land = Grade V land where Amount spend and Value of Output is Equal

i.e. ZERO RENT

Land left uncultivated = Grade VI land as the value of output is nil and Amount spent is 1000 so it is irrational to cultivate it.

Ricardo further said that arising of rent is not static but dynamic i.e. it can change according to time and circumstances. Say in above example if the value of output changes then Marginal land, Rent etc. will change Ricardo said that "Corn is high not because rent is high but rent is high because corn is high". He changed popular belief that rent does not affect the price of product but is affected by it. If price remains high, cost will also remain high resulting in high residual income and increase in price.

This "Theory of Rent" introduced by Ricardo can be presented to you in another way so that we develop a clear understanding of the serious issues related to it. Dear friends, Although today we generally use the term 'rent' for any contractual payment for use of an asset, say, rent for a shop, a house, a piece of land or a machine etc., economists have traditionally associated rent with the use of services of land only.

David Ricardo's idea was that 'nature has been very generous to human beings and has endowed the land with some 'original and indestructible powers' for their use. Due to those powers, output from the land would exceed the total of payment to all kinds of inputs. Thus, after compensating all other factors of production involved in agriculture, there would remain a surplus. The owner of the land can rightfully claim that 'surplus'. Thus we can show this kind of rent as surplus arising from agricultural activities.

We can show it in two ways:

i) Intensive Cultivation and

ii) Extensive Cultivation

i) Intensive Cultivation: A farmer with a given piece of land keeps on engaging more and more workers as long as the marginal revenue product (MRPL) exceeds market wage rate.

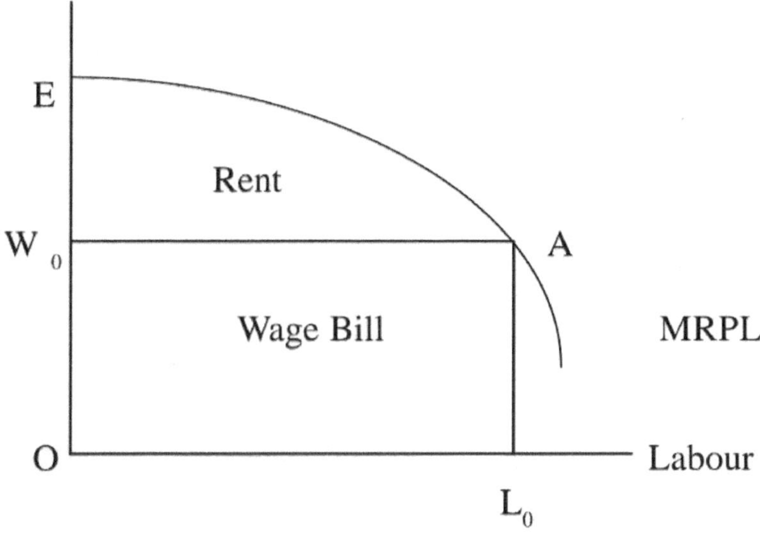

Fig.1

In Fig.1, O L0 is the number of workers employed at market wage rate of O W0. Therefore, total product of labour equals O E A L0. But, the wage will be equal to the rectangle O W0 A L0 only. Thus, when worker are paid at the going market rate, the landlord is still left with a surplus equal to W0 E A. This will be regarded as share of land – the rent.

ii) Extensive cultivation: This approach to the determination of rent is significantly different from that of intensive cultivation example seen above. Suppose we have land of different grades, say, A, B, C, D and E. Initially, the farmer will plough the best grade land. As the population rises, demand for the farm produce grows. Therefore, inferior grade land is also brought under the plough, gradually. Suppose, value of the produce from the E grade is barely equal to input costs. Then we can say that plot E generates no surplus. Hence, it is called marginal piece of land. Rest of the pieces marked A, B, C and D generate output greater then the costs –

which are same for all the pieces. This excess of value of output over and above the costs is rent.

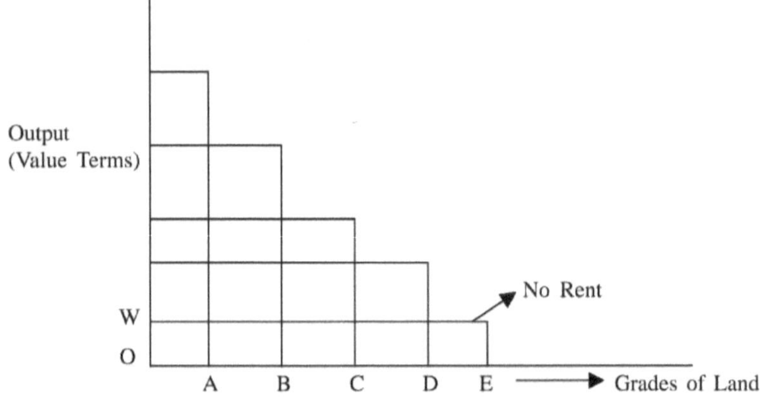

Fig.2

In Fig.2: We have 5 pieces of land, A, B, C, D and E. The piece A is of the best grade, B is inferior to A, C is inferior to B and so on. Thus, the piece E is of the worst grade. Heights of bars above A, B, C, D and E indicate the value of output produced on the respective pieces. We find that value of output on piece E is just enough to cover the cost of cultivation. Also note that this cost = OW is same for each of the pieces. So the Grade E land generates no surplus, while grade A generates the maximum. Such surplus is appropriated as rent.

Hence, it can be said that superior grade land generates a surplus. That surplus is called a rent and is claimed by owners of land as differential surplus. If market value of produce on the marginal land E increases above the cost of cultivation, the farmer will have an incentive to move on to the so far sub-marginal land F as well – thus extending the cultivation. If, on the other hand, market value falls below cost of cultivation, the farmer may be forced to stop using the marginal land. Therefore, we can say that only the lands superior to the marginal land can generate surplus or rent. Ricardo asserted that rent of land tended to depend upon the price of the produce of land. Rent was not regarded as a cost of production for the farm output, as wage bill represented the labour cost.

Essentially, through mutual discussions between Bernard Shaw, Sidney Webb, Graham Wallace and Sidney Olivier, the core of Fabian economic theory was developed between 1886 and 1888. Among them, Bernard Shaw and Wallace were initially somewhat influenced by Marxian theory, but Sidney Webb was early on in favor of adopting John Stuart Mill's theory of value. Of course, they were all motivated to provide some sort of theoretical explanation of 'surplus value', as they needed to prove that no section of society was getting its due under capitalism and that social justice was to be achieved by establishing socialism. need Sidney Webb's essay on economic theory in favor of the Fabian Society was published in the London Quarterly Journal of Economics (January 1888). Later Fabian economic theory was explained in a simple, comprehensible form by Bernard Shaw in a chapter of his edited book Fabian Essays in Socialism (1889). Bernard Shaw explained Fabian economic theory in a simple, universally understandable form in a chapter of his edited book Fabian Essays in Socialism (1889). In the introduction to the 1920 edition of this book, Sidney Webb commented that Fabian economic theory was very useful for the country and the time. His statement on this matter: "The part of the book that comes most triumphantly through the ordeal.is... the economic analysis. Tested by a whole generation of further experience and criticism, I conclude that in 1889, we knew our Political Economy, and that our Political Economy was sound."

Fabian Society's 'Theory of Rent'

The core of Fabian economic theory is his 'theory of rent', credited to Sidney Webb and Sidney Olivier, and this theory was recognized by the Fabian Society in 1888. "Webb, Bernard Shaw, and Wallace considered the 'Theory of Rent' of the Fabian Society to be a special addition to the history of socialist economic thought."

The Theory of Rent developed by the Fabian Society is an influential concept in economics, particularly in the context of land rent.

- Theory of Rent by Fabian Society

The Theory of Rent as discussed by the Fabian Society is rooted in the economic ideas of David Ricardo and further developed by the Society's members. It addresses the nature and economic implications of rent in a capitalist system.

1. Concept of Economic Rent: Economic rent refers to the income derived from the ownership of a resource (in this case, land) that is in fixed supply. Unlike wages or profits, which are determined by the cost of production, rent is determined by the scarcity of the resource.

2. Land as a Special Factor: The Fabian Society, building on Ricardo's work, argues that land is a unique factor of production due to its fixed supply. As the population grows and demand for land increases, the value of land rises. This increase in value is what constitutes economic rent.

3. Differential Rent: Differential rent arises from variations in the quality of land. Land that is more productive or better located will command higher rents compared to less productive or poorly located land. This differentiation creates a system where rent is determined by the relative advantages of the land.

4. Rent and Property Ownership: The Fabian Society highlights the social implications of rent. As land is owned by a small fraction of the population, the rent collected is seen as a form of unearned income. This income does not result from individual effort but from the scarcity and productivity of land, raising questions about social justice and equity.

5. Policy Implications: The Fabian Society advocates for reforms to address the inequality created by the current system of land

ownership and rent. Proposals include land taxation or the public ownership of land to ensure that the economic benefits of land are more widely distributed and to reduce the speculative element in land ownership.

According to Fabian theorists, the injustice and deprivation faced by the common people in the capitalist socio-economic system is at the root of "unearned income" in the hands of a small number of people. Explaining the concept of unearned income, they show that the idle owner of property enjoys such income only because of his personal ownership; the owner does not have to make any effort or effort to earn this income. "According to Ricardo and Mill, this" "unearned income" "is called" "rent" "in Fauboyan economic theory." Since this income or revenue is basically a kind of social revenue, they thought that the entire society has a right over this surplus revenue generated for social reasons and to establish this right in the hands of the society means to establish socialism.

In his discussion of economic theory, Bernard Shaw was the first to cite some of the then-current definitions of economic rent. For example, John Stuart Mill's definition: "the rent of land consists of the excess of its return above the return to the worst land in cultivation" (Principles of Political Economy, 1865 edition, vol. I) Second, Henry Fawcett's definition: The rent of land represents the pecuniary value of the advantages which such land possesses over the worst land in cultivation (Manual of Political Economy, 1876) Third, Alfred Marshall's definition: The rent of a piece of land is the excess of its produce over the produce of an adjacent piece of land which would not be cultivated at all if the rent were paid for it (Economics of Industry, 1879, Book II, ch. Basically all these definitions of rent are the modified and refined form of the definition given by Ricardo. According to Ricardo, rent is that portion of the produce of the earth which is paid to the landlord for the use of the original and indestructible powers of the soil (Principles of Political Economy and Taxation, 1817, ch. ii). Then Bernard Shaw said that then in the case of capitalist enterprise, profit can be considered as the rent of ability, that is, profit must be understood as the excess of the product of ability over that of ordinary stupidity. But in the capitalist system profit means the difference between the cost of production of a commodity and its market price. That is, profit is not synonymous with rent in the economic sense and is not comparable to the output of marginal land. In the capitalist system profit is regulated simply by the capitalists eagerness to be idle, on the one hand, and the proletarian's need of subsistence, on the other. "

In this type of society, the supply of labor is more than the demand for labor. So, The worker does not receive wages in proportion to his labour power. If the worker's wage is less than his "rent of ability," he is said to be exploited. There is no end to the greed of the lazy, rich owner class. In the capitalist system the owners collectivize and increase the market price by reducing the supply of goods for their profit. They want to enjoy the benefits of ownership unconditionally because of private ownership without considering the social good. Socialism is the name given to the abolition of this kind of unearned income of the owners, and the wealth thus accumulated must be added to the production of labour in the society. The part which is economic rent in the real sense should be social property, and should be used in the general interest of the society. That's what socialism does. So the Fabian theorists did not accept what Marx called surplus value or mehrworth. They wanted to understand the inherent deprivation and injustice of the capitalist system by applying Ricardo's concept of rent to the industrial sector.

Bernard Shaw explains the economic goals of Fabian socialism in his inimitable language as follows: "What the achievement of Socialism involves economically is the transfer of rent from the class which now appropriates it to the whole people. Rent being that part of the produce which is individually unearned, this is the only equitable method of disposing of it. There is no means of getting rid of econo- mic rent, So long as the fertility of land varies from acre to acre, and the number of persons passing by a shop window per hour varies from street to street, with the result that two farmers or two shopkeepers of exactly equal intelligence and industry will reap unequal returns from their year's work, so long will it be equitable to take from the richer farmer or shopkeeper the excess over his fellow's gain which he owes to the bounty of Nature or the advantage of situation, and divide that excess or rent equally between the two. If the pair of farms or shops be left in the hands of a private landlord, he will take the excess, and, instead of dividing it between his two tenants, live on it himself idly at their expense. "The economic object of Socialism is not, of course, to equalize farmers and shopkeepers in couples, but to carry out the principle over the whole community by collecting all rents and throwing them into the national treasury. As the private proprietor has no reason for clinging to his property except the legal power to take the rent and spend it on himself-this legal power being in fact what really constitutes him into a proprietor -its abrogation would mean his expropriation. The socializa- tion of rent would mean the socialization of the sources of production by the expropriation of the present private proprie- tors, and the transfer of their property to the entire nation, This transfer, then, is the subject-matter of the transition to Socialism..."

Thus, it appears that by applying Ricardo's 'rent theory', which is mainly applied to land, to industry, Fabian theorists want to show that the owner of capital in the capitalist economic system is enjoying 'unearned income' and only by ending it can equality be established in society. In their speech, they were influenced by the ideas of neo-classical economists like John Stuart Mill, Alfred Marshall and Henry Sedgewick about rent. Because no man can produce all the things he needs by his own labor, exchange system is prevalent in human society and this exchange is done through gold or money. Wind and sunlight are essential but not exchangeable, as they are inexhaustible and freely available. According to Bernard Shaw, the exchange value of a commodity is not determined by the amount of labor used in its production. This did not seem acceptable to Fabian theorists like Marx. The market price of a commodity in a capitalist system depends on the owner of capital, market conditions and the marginal utility of the commodity. Industries, like agriculture, produce goods and sell them later, and whatever is left over after paying the workers a minimum wage goes into the pocket of the industrial owner. In other words, from a practical point of view, it can be said that the share owner (shareholder) in the field of industry and the owner (landlord) of the land in the field of agriculture similarly live on the wealth produced by the labor of the proletariat from their property. Fabian economic theory is tried to be built around this type of concept of 'surplus value'. In a capitalist system of production in a democratic country the "skilled and organized" industrial worker may get some of this surplus value but does not get his full due, he remains deprived, and the owner enjoys 'unearned income'.

The Fabian leaders especially drew attention to the unequal distribution that existed in the capitalist social system. Their argument is that the efficiency of the elements employed in the production process (eg labour, skill, initiative, capital) depends on appropriate education, but this opportunity is not equally available to all in the capitalist system. As a result, what is received as compensation for participation in production remains exploitation. In other words, the seeds of inequality lie within the social structure of capitalism. Fabian theorists did not deny the need for capital and its associated accumulation in the production process, but they did not agree to the need for private ownership. According to them, the accumulation of capital required for production can be done by the whole society collectively and the responsibility for overseeing and managing the production process can be separated from the ownership of capital! And so it should.

Fabian theorists believed that it was possible to analyze the character of capitalism by explaining the theory of rent. Here they had a great difference of opinion with Mark's taste. Moreover, he considered the application of rent theory to industry as a significant contribution to the theoretical discussion of economics. They create a 'theory of exploitation' which can be compatible with any theory of value. This is because Fabian deprivation theory states that none of the various factors involved in production in a capitalist system are paid or rewarded in proportion to their efforts in creating wealth, as a portion of the "unearned income" always goes into the owner's pocket. The principle is that there is always a division in capitalist society. (difference) remains between the rich minority and the poor majority. This division cannot be eliminated through the price mechanism, because the position of the beneficiary is always strengthened in the capitalist system. To introduce social justice against it, the state-power It must be used, otherwise it will not be possible to have any effect. So the Fabian theorists were in favor of the state's intervention in the economic field. Instead of the capitalist, they expressed the opinion in favor of the nationalization of industrial enterprises Industry was run by professionally skilled administrators and managers, as they did not want to entrust the management of industry to the working class or introduce democracy into industry.

Applying Ricardo's theory of rent to capitalist industry, Fabian theorists interpret 'surplus value' as the difference between the average productivity of labor and the marginal productivity of labour. As the productive power of labor as a factor of production diminishes, the average product of labor tends to fall. Thus the rate of decline of the productive forces rapidly depends on the elasticity of average production, and this elasticity ultimately determines the volume of "surplus value." An analysis of this "surplus value" reveals that it consists of the following categories:

(a) economic rent, i.e. the share of production due to geography;

(b) rent of ability, i.e. the share of production which is added due to the efficiency of skilled labor over unskilled labour;

(c) economic interest, i.e. the portion added to production as a result of the use of more and better quality;

(d) Opportunity rent (rent of opportunity) or profit (profit), i.e. the portion added to production due to an external or sudden advantage in the production process.

All of the above can be considered as some form of "rent". In capitalist industry the owner of the production process pockets these 'taxes' simply by claiming ownership. This type of owner is described by Bernard Shaw as 'idle rich'. Fabian socialism seeks to end the unearned income of these 'lazy rich'. To achieve this goal, it is necessary to establish the authority of the state over the production process and only in this way justice will be established in the social system. The economic theory of the Fabian society thus presents an intelligent holistic analysis.

An important part of Fabian economic theory is the explanation of the origin of financial inequality. As incomes fall due to capitalist deprivation, the 'effective demand' of the working class or middle class weakens, and this weakened demand leads to a crisis in the production system, as the market shrinks. But the solution, in Fabian's theory, is state intervention, not working-class revolution. There is a difference between Marxian socialism and Fabian socialism.

As eternal worshipers of democratic socialism, here is the article "Exchange Value" of the Fabian Society so that my fellow readers can understand their ideology properly -

Exchange Value.

It is evident that the custom of exchange will arise in the first instance as soon as men give up providing each for his own needs by his own labor. A man who makes his own tables and chairs, his own poker and kettle, his own bread and butter, and his own house and clothes, is jack of all trades and master of none. He finds that he would get on much faster if he stuck to making tables and chairs, and exchanged them with the smith for a poker and kettle, with bakers and dairymen for bread and butter, and with builders and tailors for a house and clothes. In doing this, he finds that his tables and chairs are worth so much—that they have an exchange value, as it is called. As a matter of general convenience, some suitable commodity is set up to measure this value. We set up gold, which, in this particular use of it, is called money. The chairmaker finds how much money his chairs are worth, and exchanges them for it. The blacksmith finds out how much money his pokers are worth, and exchanges them for it. Thus, by employing money as a go-between, chairmakers can get pokers in exchange for their chairs, and blacksmiths chairs for their pokers. This is the mechanism of exchange; and once the values of the commodities are ascertained it works simply enough. But it is a mere mechanism, and does not fix the values or explain them. And the attempt to discover what does fix them is beset with apparent contradictions which block up the right path, and with seductive coincidences which make the wrong seem the more promising. The apparent contradictions soon show themselves. It is evident that the exchange value of anything depends on its utility, since no mortal exertion can make a useless thing exchangeable. And yet fresh air and sunlight, which are so useful as to be quite indispensable, have no exchange value; while a meteoric stone, shot free of charge from the firmament into the back garden, has a considerable exchange value, although it is an eminently dispensable curiosity. We soon find that this somehow depends on the fact that fresh air is plenty and meteoric stones scarce. If by any means the supply of fresh air could be steadily diminished, and the supply of meteoric stones, by celestial cannonade or otherwise, steadily increased, the fresh air would presently acquire an exchange value which would gradually rise, while the exchange value of meteoric stones would gradually fall, until at last fresh air would be supplied through a meter and charged for like gas, and meteoric stones would be as unsalable as ordinary pebbles. The exchange value, in fact, decreases with the supply. This is due to the fact that the supply decreases in utility as it goes on, because when people have had some of a commodity, they are partly satisfied, and do not value the rest so much. The usefulness of a pound of bread to a man depends on whether he has already eaten some. Every man wants a certain number of pounds of bread per week: no man wants much more; and if more is offered he will not give much for it—perhaps not anything. One umbrella is very useful: a second umbrella is a luxury: a third is mere lumber. Similarly, the curators of our museums want a moderate collection of meteoric stones; but they do not want a cartload apiece of them. Now the exchange value is fixed by the utility, not of the most useful, but of the least useful part of the stock. Why this is so can readily be made obvious by an illustration. If the stock of umbrellas in the market were sufficiently large to provide two for each umbrella carrier in the community, then, since a second umbrella is not so useful as the first, the doctrinaire course would be to ticket half the umbrellas at, say, fifteen shillings, and the other half at eight and sixpence. Unfortunately, no man will give fifteen shillings for an article which he can get for eight and sixpence; and when the public came to buy, they would buy up all the eight and sixpenny umbrellas. Each person being thus supplied with an umbrella, the remainder of the stock, though marked fifteen shillings, would be in the position of second umbrellas, only worth eight and sixpence. This is how the exchange value of the least useful part of the supply fixes the exchange value of all the rest. Technically, it occurs by "the law of indifference." And since the least useful unit of the supply is generally that which is last produced, its utility is called the final utility of the commodity. If there were but one umbrella in the world, the exchange value of its total utility would be what the most delicate person would pay for it on a very wet day sooner than go without it. But practically, thanks to the law of indifference, the most delicate person pays no more than the most robust: that is, both pay alike the exchange value of the utility of the last umbrella produced—or of the final utility of the whole stock of umbrellas. These terms—law of indifference, total utility, and final utility—though admirably expressive and intelligible when you know beforehand exactly what they mean, are, taken by themselves, failures in point of lucidity and suggestiveness. Some economists, transferring from cultivation to utility our old metaphor of the spreading pool, call final utility "marginal utility." Either will serve our present purpose, as I do not intend to use the terms again. The main point to be grasped is, that however useful any commodity may be, its exchange value can be run down to nothing by increasing the supply until there is more of it than is wanted. The excess being useless and valueless, is to be had for nothing; and nobody will pay anything for a commodity as long as plenty of it is to be had for nothing. This is why air and other indispensable things have no exchange value, while scarce gewgaws fetch immense prices. These, then, are the conditions which confront man as a producer and exchanger. If he produces a useless thing, his labor will be wholly in vain: he will get nothing for it. If he produces a useful thing, the price he will get for it will depend on how much of it there is for sale already. If he increases the supply by producing more than is sufficient to replace the current consumption, he inevitably lowers the value of the whole. It therefore behooves him to be wary in choosing his occupation as well as industrious in pursuing it. His choice will naturally fall on the production of those commodities whose value stands highest relatively to the labor required to produce them—which fetch the highest price in proportion to their cost, in fact. Suppose, for example, that a maker of musical instruments found that it cost him exactly as much to make a harp as to make a pianoforte, but that harps were going out of fashion and pianofortes coming in. Soon there would be more harps than were wanted, and fewer pianofortes: consequently the value of harps would fall, and that of pianofortes rise. Since the labor cost of both would be the same, he would immediately devote all his labor to pianoforte making; and other manufacturers would do the same, until the increase of supply brought down the value of pianofortes to the value of harps. Possibly fashion then might veer from pianofortes to American organs, in which case he would make less pianofortes and more American organs. When these, too, had increased sufficiently, the exertions of the Salvation Army might create such a demand for tambourines as to make them worth four times their cost of production, whereupon there would instantly be a furious concentration of the instrument-making energy on the manufacture of tambourines; and this concentration would last until the supply had brought down the profit to less than might be gained by gratifying the public craving for trombones. At last, as pianofortes were cheapened until they were no more profitable than harps; then American organs until they were no more profitable than pianos; and then tambourines until they were level with American organs; so eventually trombones will pay no better than tambourines; and a general level of profit will be attained, indicating the proportion in which the instruments are wanted by the public. But to skim off even this level of profit, more of the instruments may be produced in the ascertained proportion until their prices fall to their costs of production, when there will be no profit. Here the production will be decisively checked, since a further supply would cause only a loss; and men can lose money, without the trouble of producing commodities, by the simple process of throwing it out of the window. What occurred with the musical instruments in this illustration occurs in practice with the whole mass of manufactured commodities. Those which are scarce, and therefore relatively high in value, tempt us to produce them until the increase of the supply reduces their value to a point at which there is no more profit to be made out of them than out of other commodities. The general level of profit thus attained is further exploited until the general increase brings down the price of all commodities to their cost of production, the equivalent of which is sometimes called their normal value. And here a glance back to our analysis of the spread of cultivation, and its result in the phenomenon of rent, suggests the question: What does the cost of production of a commodity mean? We have seen that, owing to the differences in fertility and advantage of situation between one piece of land and another, cost of production varies from district to district, being highest at the margin of cultivation. But we have also seen how the landlord skims off as economic rent all the advantage gained by the cultivators of superior soils and sites. Consequently, the addition of the landlord's rent to the expenses of production brings them up even on the best land to the level of those incurred on the worst. Cost of production, then, means cost of production on the margin of cultivation, and is equalized to all producers, since what they may save in labor per commodity is counterbalanced by the greater mass of commodities they must produce in order to bring in the rent. It is only by a thorough grasp of this leveling-down action that we can detect the trick by which the ordinary economist tries to cheat us into accepting the private property system as practically just. He first shows that economic rent does not enter into cost of production on the margin of cultivation. Then he shows that the cost of production on the margin of cultivation determines the price of a commodity. Therefore, he argues, first, that rent does not enter into price; and second, that the value of commodities is fixed by their cost of production, the implication being that the landlords cost the community nothing, and that commodities exchange in exact proportion to the labor they cost. This trivially ingenious way of being disingenuous is officially taught as political economy in our schools to this day. It will be seen at once that it is mere thimblerig. So far from commodities exchanging, or tending to exchange, according to the labor expended in their production, commodities produced well within the margin of cultivation will fetch as high a price as commodities produced at the margin with much greater labour. So far from the landlord costing nothing, he costs all the difference between the two.This, however, is not the goal of our analysis of value. We now see how Man's control over the value of commodities consists solely in his power of regulating their supply. Individuals are constantly trying to decrease supply for their own advantage. Gigantic conspiracies have been entered into to forestall the world's wheat and cotton harvests, so as to force their value to the highest possible point. Cargoes of East Indian spices have been destroyed by the Dutch as cargoes of fish are now destroyed in the Thames, to maintain prices by limiting supply. All rings, trusts, corners, combinations, monopolies, and trade secrets have the same object. Production and the development of the social instincts are alike hindered by each man's consciousness that the more he stints the community the more he benefits himself, the justification, of course, being that when every man has benefited himself at the expense of the community,the community will benefit by every man in it being benefited. From one thing the community is safe. There will be no permanent conspiracies to reduce values by increasing supply. All men will cease producing when the value of their product falls below its cost of production, whether in labour or in labour plus rent. No man will keep on producing bread until it will fetch nothing, like the sunlight, or until it becomes a nuisance, like the rain in the summer of 1888. So far, our minds are at ease as to the excessive increase of commodities voluntarily produced by the labour of man.

Dear readers so we understand that, The economic theory of Fabian socialism is closely linked to its political theory. Like other forms of socialism, Fabian socialism advocates for public ownership of key industries and services, such as healthcare, education, transportation, and utilities. However, the Fabians were not opposed to the existence of private enterprise, particularly in areas that they believed were not essential to the functioning of society. Instead, they argued for a mixed economy, in which both public and private sectors would coexist, but where the state would have the power to regulate and control private enterprise in the public interest.

One of the key economic policies advocated by the Fabians was progressive taxation. They believed that a progressive tax system, in which those with higher incomes and greater wealth paid a larger share of their income in taxes, was essential for reducing inequality and funding social welfare programs. The Fabians were also early advocates of the welfare state, arguing that the state had a responsibility to provide for the basic needs of its citizens, such as healthcare, education, and housing. These services, they argued, should be provided universally and funded through taxation, rather than being left to the private market.

In addition to advocating for public ownership and welfare programs, the Fabians also supported policies aimed at regulating the economy and preventing the excesses of capitalism. This included measures such as minimum wage laws, labor protections, and antitrust regulations to prevent the concentration of economic power in the hands of a few large corporations. The Fabians believed that by regulating capitalism and ensuring that the benefits of economic growth were more evenly distributed, it was possible to create a more just and equitable society without the need for revolution.

As we have seen, Fabian socialism represents a distinctive approach within the broader socialist tradition, one that emphasises gradual, reformist change through democratic means, rather than revolution. While it shares some common goals with other forms of socialism, such as the desire for greater social and economic equality, it differs in its emphasis on the role of the state, the importance of education and expertise, and the rejection of class struggle as the primary driver of social change.

• • •

CHAPTER XXIII

Nehru: A True Democratic Socialist

"Political Democracy has no meaning if it does not embrace economic democracy . And economic democracy is nothing but socialism. " - Jawaharlal Nehru

One of the main exponents of Democratic Socialism in India was the former Indian Prime Minister J L Nehru .

Finding the truth from various research papers –

1. Jawaharlal Nehru argued that Democratic Socialism could mitigate the evils of all the third world countries.

2. 'Democratic Socialism' where 'equality' in the words of the late Prime Minister Nehru- 'means not merely the equality of possessing a vote, but economic and social equality.' It is basically accepted that neither of the equalities can be fully achieved without the help of the other. It is under this impression that Pandit Nehru declared, "Political Democracy has no meaning if it does not embrace economic democracy. And economic democracy is nothing but socialism."

3. Nehru said: We have to plan at both ends . We have to stop the cumulative forces that make the rich richer and we have to start the cumulative forces which enable the poor to get over the barrier of poverty .

4. "Socialism is the inevitable outcome of democracy. Political democracy has no meaning if it does not embrace economic democracy. And economic democracy is nothing but socialism. Monopoly is the enemy of socialism. To that extent it has grown during the last few years, we have drifted away from the goal of socialism."-Jawaharlal Nehru

5. "I think it is possible to establish socialism by democratic means provided, of course, the full democratic process is available." -Jawaharlal Nehru

6. "We have to plan at both ends. We have to stop the cumulative forces that make the rich richer and we have to start the cumulative forces which enable the poor to get over the barrier of poverty." -Jawaharlal Nehru

---

- Nehru emphasised on free and fair elections where the suffrage for the citizens is a must, for example, the goal of democratic socialism also encompasses the issues pertaining to the nationalisation of means of production . They also include steps like raising the minimum wages, removal of poverty, securing a national health plan, checking the concentration of economic power and demanding passage of welfare legislations for the workers.

(References:http://www.yourarticlelibrary.com/essay/nehrus-views-on-democratic-socialism/40303/)

- Nehru has recalled: "My outlook was wider, and nationalism by itself seemed to me definitely a narrow and insufficient creed. Political freedom, independence, were no doubt essential, but they were steps only in the right direction; without social freedom and a socialistic structure of society and the state, neither the country nor the individual could develop much."

(References: http://inc.in/CongressSandesh/123/Socialism-of-Jawaharlal-Nehru-and-Indian-National-Congress)

Peaceful solution to class conflict:

In a democratic socialist setup, Nehru opined that class conflict should be ended by peaceful solution. He never believed in the Marxian idea of class struggle or communist – policy of 'ruthless suppression'. On a democratic set – up, due caution should be taken to put an end to the class conflicts inside the society .

Another significant aspect of Nehru's Model of Economic Development was the creation of Consciousness of Economic Planning. The First Five Year Plan (1951 – 56), the Second Five Year Plan (1956 -61) and the Third Five Year Plan (1961 – 66) galvanised Nehru's democratic socialism.

References:

R.C. Pillai; Political Thought in Modern India p-26

http://www.preservearticles.com/201106238420/nehru-and-democratic-socialism.html

---

- Nehru wanted the model of Democratic Socialism which suits Indian traditions and ethos. He was influenced by the Fabian Socialism of Britain. He was of the opinion that Parliamentary politics is the means of achieving socialism. Multiple social groups and ideological groups will strengthen Indian democracy. Pluralism will become the ideological foundation of individual liberty and societal demands must have a beautiful reconciliation.

The espousal of socialism as the Congress goal was most difficult to achieve.Nehru was opposed in this by the right wing Congressmen Sardar Patel, Dr.Rajendra Prasad and Chakravarthi Rajagopalachari. He had the support of the left wing Congressmen Maulana Azad and Subhas Chandra Bose.The trio combined to oust Dr.Prasad as Congress President in 1936. Nehru was elected in his place and held the presidency for two years (1936 – 37).

Nehru was then succeeded by his socialist colleagues Bose (1938 –39) and Azad (1940 – 46). After the fall of Bose from the mainstream of Indian politics (due to his support of violence in driving the British out of India), the power struggle between the socialists and conservatives balanced out. However, Sardar Patel died in 1950, leaving Nehru as the sole remaining iconic national leader, and soon the situation became such that Nehru was able to implement many of his basic policies without hindrance. The conservative right wing of the Congress (comprising India's upper class elites) would continue opposing the socialists until the great schism in 1969 . Nehru's daughter, Indira Gandhi, was able to fulfil her father's dream by the 42nd amendment (1976) of the Indian constitution by which India officially became "socialist" and "secular".

It must be said that Jawaharlal Nehru fully realised the difficulties inherent in seeking radical change through democratic processes. In thinking of a form of socialism suited to our national needs and national genius, Nehru envisaged a limited place for the private sector, but he was quite clear about the framework. "I think it is possible to establish socialism by democratic means provided, of course, the full democratic process is available".

Nehru was a firm believer in parliamentary democracy. He had full faith in the ruling party and healthy opposition. He believed in universal adult suffrage for the success of democracy. For the success of parliamentary democracy, he put emphasis on the rule of majority, methods of discussion, negotiation, persuasion and so on. The press, judiciary and public opinion will have a check on the legislators and will be the guard in checking corruptions in parliamentary democracy .

Nehru contended that liberty and democracy had no significance except in the context of equality . In his presidential address to the Indian National Congress at Lahore in 1929 Nehru declared, 'Today politics have ceased to have much meaning, and the most vital question is that of social and economic equality" Laying stress on the importance of equality Nehru asserted, "Democracy means equality and democracy can only flourish in an equal society".

He realised that political liberty brought the vote but was of little use when society was riddled with poverty and economic inequality. Long back Nehru stated, "There cannot be ups and downs and social inequalities in this country. These must be gotten rid of. We have to build up a new social order in which everyone will have the fullest opportunity for development, no exploitation, and in which there will not be merely political democracy, but economic democracy, which means economic equality without which political democracy will be a hoax . What does it matter to one whether he has a vote or not, when he is hungry and starving."

Nehru's acceptance of political democracy was not unqualified. As he considered it to mean the end of social democracy. "I am perfectly prepared to accept political democracy," he said, "only in the hope that this will lead to social democracy." He was clear in his mind that political democracy "is only the way to the goal and is not the final objective". He saw clearly that if profound economic changes did not take place fast enough, the political structure would be rendered unstable. If political or social institutions stand in the way of such change, they have to be removed .

* ***The Truth***

Pt . Jawaharlal Nehru was a great Indian Democratic Socialist. He was the harbinger of the socialist trend in Indian National Movement and, indeed, was instrumental in making India embark upon the path of socialism. However, he wanted to achieve the objectives of socialism gradually within the democratic framework. He was one of the few who did not take democracy for granted but sought to explain his conception and show how it could be brought into harmony with his conception of socialism and how it could be implemented. In this connection, he was very much influenced by the British socialists of his days. (Nehru became interested in the philosophy of socialism from an early period in his life, while studying law in London, he was "vaguely attracted to the Fabians and socialistic ideas.") Nehru was very much moved when he saw his countrymen suffering from poverty, ignorance and disease . He thought socialism was the only panacea for all ills prevalent in the Indian Society.

• • •

1. (References:https://www.jstor.org/stable/)
2. (References:https://www.jstor.org/stable/418540)
3. (References:iosrjournals.org/iosr-jhss/papers/Vol19-issue7/Version-3/L01973103105.pdf)
4. (References:shodhganga.inflibnet.ac.in/bitstream/10603/49272/8/08_chapter%202.pdf)

CHAPTER XXIV

The Human Economy

The Human Economy questions established capitalist models that give profit and expansion top priority over human well-being, fairness, and sustainability. Rooted in the conviction that economies should serve the people rather than the other way around, the Human Economy promotes a system that advances the 99% rather than a small elite. This economy is one in which the well-being of all individuals is the fundamental measure of success, and it promotes concepts like as inclusion, fairness, democratic involvement, environmental sustainability, and social justice. In a time of rising inequality, climate change, and economic uncertainty, the Human Economy presents a bold vision for reorganising society and putting people first in economic life.

The all-encompassing approach to development of a Human Economy appeals to me. Unlike the present neoliberal economic model that gives GDP growth top priority as the only indicator of development, the Human Economy broadens the definition of economic success to include human flourishing, fair access to resources, and environmental health. It values social fairness and sustainability to try to change systems that uphold environmental damage and inequity. The Human Economy invites us to reconsider our relationship with employment, consumption, production, and commerce and to develop institutions that put the communal benefit over individual wealth growth. In this enlarged research, I will look at the fundamental ideas of the Human Economy, underline actual cases of its implementation, and investigate policies meant to help the change to a more compassionate economic system. I will evaluate how these concepts might be integrated into local, national, and global frameworks to support an economy that benefits the 99%.

The previous two decades have seen the entrenchment of neoliberal economic policies across the globe, typified by deregulation, privatisation, tax cuts for companies, and austerity measures. For most people, these policies have increased poverty and inequality; they have disproportionately helped the rich. Not only is the growing disparity of income and wealth a social concern but also a structural weakness in the economic system itself. The 2008 global financial crisis was a wake-up call for many, highlighting the inherent flaws of a system built to serve the interests of corporations and the rich elite.

Neoliberalism operates on the idea that free markets are the most efficient and effective ways of allocating resources, but in fact, it has concentrated wealth in the hands of the few while pulling away social safety nets and protections for the most vulnerable. This strategy has destroyed public services, reduced labour rights, and exacerbated the precariousness of work. It has also fueled environmental damage by prioritising short-term profitability over long-term sustainability. In contrast, the Human Economy offers an alternative to this extractive model, providing a system that focusses human dignity, fairness, and sustainability.

The Occupy Wall Street movement in 2011 was one of the most conspicuous protests against the shortcomings of neoliberalism, particularly in the wake of the 2008 financial crisis. With its rallying cry of "We are the 99%," Occupy Wall Street intended to call attention to the massive inequalities fostered by the global banking system. The movement was not simply a critique of economic inequality but also a call for a new economic system that would suit the needs of the people. While the movement gradually faded, its message and effect remained on, spurring a broader discourse about the need for systemic reform.

Core Principles of the Human Economy

Equity and Justice: An Economy for All

Equity is the idea that everyone should have equal access to the resources and chances they need to live a full life. It is at the heart of the Human Economy. This is more than just making sure everyone has the same chances; it also means getting rid of systemic barriers to success and making sure that the economy works for everyone, not just the lucky few. Policies like progressive taxation, universal healthcare, free education, and living wages that aim to reduce differences in income and wealth are at the heart of this effort. Finland's approach to education, for example, shows how to be fair in real life. In Finland, all children, no matter their family's income, get a good education because the system is fully paid for by the government. This means that kids from all walks of life go to the same schools—not just those with lots of money. Finland consistently ranks high in global education rankings, and this system is one reason for that. It also shows how policies that focus on fairness can lead to more fair results.

Sustainability: Protecting the Planet for Future Generations

The Human Economy also emphasises environmental sustainability, recognizing that economic systems must operate within the limits of the natural world. This means transitioning away from fossil fuels and other extractive industries toward renewable energy, regenerative agriculture, and sustainable consumption patterns. It also means respecting the rights and knowledge of Indigenous communities, who have long practised stewardship of the land in ways that modern economies are only beginning to understand. Denmark offers a compelling example of sustainability in action. The country has made significant strides toward transitioning to renewable energy, particularly wind power, and has set ambitious targets to reduce carbon emissions. Denmark's energy policies are driven by a recognition that environmental sustainability is not just an economic necessity but a moral imperative. This shift to renewable energy has created new jobs, reduced the country's reliance on fossil fuels, and made Denmark a global leader in the fight against climate change. The Human Economy sees sustainability not as a burden but as an opportunity to create an economy that benefits both people and the planet.

Democratic Participation: Giving Power to the People

A key principle of the Human Economy is democratic participation — the idea that all citizens should have a say in the economic decisions that affect their lives. This requires shifting power away from corporations and financial elites and toward workers, consumers, and communities. Worker-owned cooperatives provide a practical example of how economic democracy can be achieved. In these cooperatives, workers have a direct stake in the success of the business and participate in decision-making processes, ensuring that profits are distributed more equitably. The Mondragon Corporation in Spain is a shining example of economic democracy in action. Founded in the Basque region in 1956, Mondragon has grown into one of the largest cooperatives in the world, with over 80,000 employees. The cooperative operates in various industries, from manufacturing to finance, and has demonstrated that businesses can be both profitable and democratic. At Mondragon, workers elect their managers, and profits are reinvested in the company or distributed to the workers, ensuring that the wealth generated by the business benefits those who create it.

• • •

In this exploration of a humane economy, Now I will focus on two key areas: *pre-distribution* and *redistribution*. Pre-distribution aims to create an economy that is fairer before government intervention is required, ensuring that the rules and structures in place produce more equitable outcomes. Redistribution, on the other hand, addresses the inequalities that arise through taxation and social welfare programs.

Pre-Distribution: Creating an Economy Designed for Fairness

Pre-distribution is a concept that aims to reduce inequality at its root by structuring the economy in such a way that wealth is distributed more fairly before any government interventions, such as taxes or social welfare programs, are implemented. This approach seeks to ensure that the economic system itself produces fairer outcomes. In today's global economy, wealth distribution is heavily skewed toward the top, with a small percentage of people controlling the vast majority of wealth. This concentration of wealth is largely a result of how the current economic system is structured, with policies favouring corporate profits and deregulation at the expense of workers' rights, fair wages, and environmental sustainability.

Regulating Globalization for Equity

Neoliberal policies that stress deregulation, free trade, and the opening up of capital markets have often been used to push for globalisation, which has linked economies all over the world. Globalisation has helped many people get out of poverty and has helped many economies grow, but it has also made inequality worse within and between countries. The richest people and companies have gotten the most out of globalisation. On the other hand, workers and small businesses have often had to deal with its worst effects, like job losses, stagnant wages, and damage to the environment. But globalisation doesn't always mean that rules need to be loosened. Countries can still trade with each other around the world and benefit from having economies that are linked together, as long as the rules that govern that trade are fair, protect workers' rights, and put environmental sustainability first. South Korea is a good example of a country that has been able to join the global economy and reduce inequality at the same time. South Korea has rules that protect domestic industries, regulate multinational corporations, and help social welfare programs. The country's economy has grown thanks to these policies, which have also made sure that the benefits of that growth are shared more fairly. In the same way, Brazil has taken a more controlled approach to globalisation, with policies that protect the environment and encourage social inclusion. Millions of people have been lifted out of poverty and social conditions have been improved thanks to Brazil's Bolsa Família program, which gives cash to families based on certain conditions. Brazil has been able to reduce inequality while still growing its economy by putting limits on how it interacts with the global economy and putting money into social welfare programs. A new way of thinking about globalisation should focus on making the world's system more fair and balanced. This would mean putting in place rules that make sure big businesses and rich people pay their fair share of taxes, protect workers' rights, and stop environmental damage as much as possible. Also, international trade agreements should have parts that put human rights, worker safety, and environmental protections first.

The Role of Technology in Driving Inequality

Although it has been a main engine of economic development, technology has also helped to create growing disparity. While the fast growth of digital platforms, artificial intelligence, and automation presents fresh chances for wealth creation, it has also displaced many people, especially those in low-skill employment. Many workers are left without employment or with positions paying less as computers and algorithms get increasingly ability of completing tasks typically done by humans. Dealing with the disparity brought about by technology developments revolves mostly on the topic of "who owns the robots?" Should the advantages of technology and automation only be experienced by a tiny set of owners, the disparity between the rich and the poor will keep widening. Conversely, if ownership of technology is more generally dispersed, the advantages can be divided more fairly. Policies encouraging worker ownership of technology and enterprises help to solve this in one sense. Business models such cooperatives, employee-owned companies, and social entrepreneurs help to more fairly share ownership and profits among employees. These approaches can serve to lower inequality and guarantee more general sharing of the advantages of technology by including employees in the success of the company. Policies that control technology and guarantee worker protection help governments also be of influence. Governments might, for instance, legislate that businesses offer retraining and assistance for employees whose jobs are destroyed by automation. Particularly for people in the gig economy, they may also support laws guaranteeing that technology firms pay fair salaries and give their employees benefits. Governments might also fund public ownership of important technology so that every person benefits from technical developments. Furthermore helping to guarantee that new technologies are created with the public good in mind rather than only for profit is public investment in research and development.

Strengthening Labor Rights and Promoting Fair Wages

One of the key ways to create a more humane economy is by strengthening labour rights and ensuring that workers are paid fair wages. In many countries, labour rights have been eroded over the past few decades, with policies favouring employers over workers. This has led to a decline in union membership, weaker worker protections, and stagnant wages. Rebuilding labour rights and promoting fair wages are essential to reducing inequality and ensuring that workers share in the benefits of economic growth. Strong labour unions can help negotiate better wages and working conditions for workers, while laws that protect workers' rights, such as minimum wage laws, can help ensure that all workers are paid a living wage.

The gig economy, which has grown rapidly in recent years, presents a particular challenge for labour rights. Gig workers, who are often classified as independent contractors rather than employees, do not have the same protections as traditional employees, such as minimum wage laws, overtime pay, or access to benefits like health insurance and retirement plans. To address this, governments can implement policies that extend labour protections to gig workers, ensuring that they are paid fair wages and have access to benefits. For example, California's Assembly Bill 5 (AB5) requires companies like Uber and Lyft to classify their drivers as employees rather than independent contractors, granting them access to employee protections and benefits. Other countries, such as the United Kingdom, have also implemented regulations aimed at protecting gig workers. Additionally, governments can promote policies that ensure that workers are paid a living wage. The concept of a living wage goes beyond the minimum wage, ensuring that workers earn enough to cover their basic needs, such as housing, food, and healthcare. By raising the minimum wage and implementing living wage laws, governments can help reduce poverty and inequality.

Reinventing the Private Sector: Business Models for Equality

The private sector plays a crucial role in shaping the economy, and current business practices have contributed significantly to rising inequality. Corporations have increasingly focused on maximising shareholder returns, often at the expense of workers, the environment, and society as a whole. This focus on short-term profits has led to practices such as offshoring jobs, cutting wages, and avoiding taxes, all of which have contributed to the growing gap between the rich and the poor.

To create a more humane economy, we need to reinvent the private sector, promoting business models that prioritise social and environmental goals alongside profits. This can be achieved through the promotion of cooperatives, employee-owned businesses, social enterprises, and other models that distribute ownership and profits more fairly among workers and communities.

Cooperatives: Sharing Ownership and Profits

Cooperatives are businesses that are owned and controlled by their members, who share in the profits and decision-making. Unlike traditional corporations, where ownership and control are concentrated in the hands of shareholders, cooperatives distribute ownership more broadly, ensuring that workers and communities benefit from the success of the business.

One of the most famous examples of a successful cooperative is Mondragon Corporation, a worker-owned cooperative based in the Basque region of Spain. Mondragon was founded in 1956 and has since grown into one of the largest and most successful cooperatives in the world, with over 80,000 employees and operations in more than 30 countries.

Mondragon's success is built on its commitment to democratic decision-making, social responsibility, and equitable income distribution. Workers at Mondragon have a say in the decisions that affect the business, and the company prioritises the well-being of its employees and the communities in which it operates. Mondragon's cooperative model has allowed it to weather economic downturns better than many traditional corporations, as its workers are more invested in the long-term success of the business.

Governments can support the growth of cooperatives by providing access to capital, technical assistance, and favourable regulatory environments. By promoting cooperatives, governments can help create an economy that is more inclusive and equitable, where workers have a greater stake in the success of the businesses they work for.

Employee-Owned Businesses: Empowering Workers

Employee-owned businesses are another model that distributes ownership and profits more fairly among workers. In an employee-owned business, workers own shares in the company and have a say in the decisions that affect the business. This can lead to better wages, benefits, and working conditions, as workers have a direct interest in the success of the company. One example of a successful employee-owned business is the John Lewis Partnership, a UK-based retailer that is owned by its employees. The company, which operates John Lewis department stores and Waitrose supermarkets, has over 80,000 employees, all of whom are partners in the business.

The John Lewis Partnership is not only a prominent example of how employee ownership can work on a large scale, but also demonstrates how such businesses can flourish by aligning the interests of workers with the broader goals of the company. Employees (or "partners," as they are called within the company) share in the company's profits through annual bonuses and have a voice in the governance of the company, including electing representatives to serve on various boards. This system has allowed John Lewis to maintain a high level of employee engagement, productivity, and satisfaction while also ensuring fairer income distribution.

Governments can encourage the development of employee-owned businesses by providing tax incentives, grants, and technical support to companies that transition to employee ownership. This can be particularly useful in cases where businesses are at risk of closure due to retirement or economic downturns. By transitioning to employee ownership, such businesses can remain open, preserve jobs, and create a more equitable distribution of profits.

The rise of employee-owned businesses could also address some of the issues stemming from corporate monopolies. As employees share in ownership and decision-making, they are less likely to engage in practices that exploit workers or degrade the environment in the pursuit of short-term profits. This creates a more sustainable and ethical business model that benefits not just the owners, but all stakeholders.

Social Enterprises: Balancing Profit with Social Impact

Social enterprises are businesses that prioritise social and environmental goals alongside financial performance. These organisations seek to address societal challenges—such as poverty, inequality, and environmental degradation—through market-based solutions. Rather than focusing solely on maximising shareholder returns, social enterprises reinvest their profits into initiatives that benefit the community, support marginalised groups, or promote sustainability.

An example of a successful social enterprise is Grameen Bank in Bangladesh, which pioneered the concept of microcredit. Founded by Nobel laureate Muhammad Yunus, Grameen Bank provides small loans to poor and marginalised individuals, particularly women, who are often excluded from traditional banking systems. The bank's model has helped millions of people lift themselves out of poverty by enabling them to start small businesses and become financially independent.

Grameen Bank's success highlights how businesses can be structured to serve both social and financial goals. By targeting underserved populations and reinvesting profits into programs that support the community, social enterprises can create a more humane and equitable economy.

Governments can support the growth of social enterprises by providing access to capital, reducing regulatory barriers, and offering tax incentives to businesses that prioritise social and environmental impact. Additionally, governments can promote policies that encourage traditional businesses to adopt social responsibility initiatives, such as implementing fair labour practices, reducing carbon emissions, or investing in community development.

Redistribution: Addressing Inequality through Taxation and Social Welfare

While pre-distribution focuses on creating fairer outcomes within the economy itself, redistribution involves the use of government policies—such as taxation and social welfare programs—to address the inequalities that arise within the system. Redistribution is a key tool in creating a humane economy because it ensures that wealth is more evenly distributed across society, and that vulnerable populations are supported through public services.

Progressive Taxation: Ensuring Fairness in Wealth Distribution

One of the most effective ways to address economic inequality is through progressive taxation, where individuals with higher incomes and wealth pay a larger share of taxes than those with lower incomes. Progressive taxation ensures that the burden of funding public services and social welfare programs is more equitably distributed and that the wealthiest individuals contribute their fair share to society.

Many countries have implemented progressive tax systems to varying degrees of success. For example, the Scandinavian countries—such as Denmark, Norway, and Sweden—are known for their highly progressive tax systems, which help fund comprehensive social welfare programs, including universal healthcare, free education, and robust social safety nets. These programs have contributed to low levels of poverty and inequality in these countries while also promoting social cohesion and economic stability.

In contrast, countries like the United States have a less progressive tax system, with many tax loopholes and deductions benefiting the wealthy, leading to higher levels of inequality. By reforming the tax system to close these loopholes and increase taxes on the wealthiest individuals, governments can generate more revenue to fund social programs that benefit all citizens.

Another important aspect of progressive taxation is the taxation of wealth and capital gains. In many countries, income from investments and assets is taxed at lower rates than income from wages and salaries, exacerbating inequality. By increasing taxes on capital gains, dividends, and inherited wealth, governments can reduce the concentration of wealth at the top and ensure that the tax system is more equitable.

Universal Basic Income: Providing a Safety Net for All

Universal Basic Income (UBI) is a policy proposal that has gained increasing attention in recent years as a potential solution to poverty and inequality. UBI involves providing all citizens with a regular, unconditional cash payment, regardless of their income or employment status. Proponents argue that UBI can provide a safety net for those who are unemployed or underemployed, reduce poverty, and give people the freedom to pursue education, entrepreneurship, or caregiving without the pressure of financial insecurity.

Several pilot programs have tested the concept of UBI with promising results. For example, in Finland, a two-year UBI experiment provided 2,000 unemployed individuals with a monthly payment of €560. Participants reported lower levels of stress, improved mental health, and greater life satisfaction, even though the program did not significantly increase employment. Similar experiments in Canada, Kenya, and the United States have shown that UBI can reduce poverty, improve well-being, and increase economic stability.

Critics of UBI argue that it is too expensive and could disincentivize work. However, proponents counter that UBI can be funded through progressive taxation, reductions in other forms of social welfare, or the implementation of wealth taxes. Moreover, evidence from pilot programs suggests that UBI does not significantly reduce work effort and may even encourage people to pursue more meaningful or productive work.

UBI is not a panacea, but it could play a key role in creating a more humane economy by ensuring that all citizens have a basic level of financial security. Combined with other policies, such as progressive taxation and social welfare programs, UBI could help reduce inequality and promote greater economic stability.

Strengthening Social Safety Nets: Reducing Poverty and Promoting Social Mobility

In addition to progressive taxation and UBI, strengthening social safety nets is essential for reducing poverty and promoting social mobility. Social safety nets include programs such as unemployment insurance, food assistance, housing subsidies, and healthcare coverage. These programs provide crucial support to individuals and families who are struggling to make ends meet, particularly during times of economic hardship or personal crisis.

Countries with strong social safety nets tend to have lower levels of poverty and inequality. For example, in Germany, the welfare state provides a wide range of benefits to citizens, including healthcare, unemployment insurance, parental leave, and pensions. These programs have helped reduce poverty and promote social mobility, allowing individuals from disadvantaged backgrounds to access education, healthcare, and other opportunities that can improve their economic prospects.

Strengthening social safety nets can also contribute to economic stability by preventing poverty and hardship from spiralling into broader economic problems, such as increased crime or social unrest. Governments can support social safety nets by ensuring that they are adequately funded, accessible to all who need them, and designed to promote long-term economic security rather than simply providing temporary relief.

Integrating Ecological Responsibility into Economic Policy

A humane economy cannot be achieved without addressing the pressing environmental challenges facing the world today. Climate change, resource depletion, and environmental degradation pose significant threats to human well-being and the stability of economies around the world. Therefore, integrating environmental sustainability into economic policy is crucial for creating an economy that is not only fair and just but also capable of supporting future generations.

Green New Deal:
The concept of a Green New Deal has gained traction in recent years as a comprehensive plan to address climate change while also promoting economic justice. A Green New Deal involves massive public investments in renewable energy, sustainable infrastructure, and green jobs, with the goal of transitioning to a low-carbon economy while also reducing inequality and creating new economic opportunities.

For example, the Green New Deal proposal in the United States, championed by progressive lawmakers like Alexandria Ocasio-

Cortez and Bernie Sanders, calls for investments in clean energy technologies, such as wind and solar power, as well as energy efficiency, public transportation, and sustainable agriculture. The plan also includes provisions for job creation, worker protections, and social justice initiatives to ensure that the benefits of the green transition are shared equitably.

Implementing a Green New Deal would require significant public investment, but it also has the potential to create millions of new jobs in industries such as renewable energy, energy efficiency, and sustainable transportation. Moreover, by reducing reliance on fossil fuels and mitigating the impacts of climate change, a Green New Deal could prevent the costly economic disruptions associated with environmental disasters, such as floods, droughts, and extreme weather events.

Countries like Germany and Denmark have already made significant progress in transitioning to renewable energy and sustainable infrastructure through government investment and policy incentives. These countries have shown that it is possible to decouple economic growth from carbon emissions while also promoting social equity and job creation.

Circular Economy:

Another key component of a humane and sustainable economy is the transition to a circular economy, which aims to minimise waste and maximise the reuse and recycling of resources. In a circular economy, products are designed to last longer, be easily repaired, and eventually be recycled or repurposed at the end of their lifecycle. This stands in contrast to the current "linear" economic model, which is based on the extraction of resources, production of goods, and disposal of waste.

Transitioning to a circular economy can reduce the environmental impact of production and consumption while also creating new economic opportunities in industries such as recycling, repair, and remanufacturing. For example, the Netherlands has set an ambitious goal of becoming fully circular by 2050. To achieve this goal, the government has implemented policies that encourage companies to design products with circularity in mind, invest in recycling infrastructure, and promote sustainable consumption patterns among consumers.

A circular economy can also contribute to economic resilience by reducing dependence on finite resources and mitigating the risks associated with resource scarcity or supply chain disruptions. By prioritising the efficient use of materials and the regeneration of natural systems, a circular economy promotes long-term sustainability and reduces the environmental costs of economic growth.

Governments can support the transition to a circular economy by implementing policies that promote product design for longevity, incentivize recycling and reuse, and discourage wasteful consumption practices. For example, extended producer responsibility (EPR) policies require manufacturers to take responsibility for the disposal or recycling of their products at the end of their lifecycle, encouraging them to design products that are easier to recycle or repair.

Carbon Pricing:

Carbon pricing is another important policy tool for promoting environmental sustainability within the framework of a humane economy. By putting a price on carbon emissions, governments can incentivize businesses and consumers to reduce their carbon footprint and invest in cleaner, more sustainable alternatives. Carbon pricing can take the form of a carbon tax, which imposes a fee on each ton of carbon dioxide emitted, or a cap-and-trade system, which sets a limit on emissions and allows companies to buy and sell emission allowances.

Countries like Sweden, Canada, and the European Union have implemented carbon pricing mechanisms with varying degrees of success. In Sweden, for example, a carbon tax has been in place since 1991, and it has contributed to a significant reduction in carbon emissions while also promoting economic growth.

Carbon pricing not only helps reduce greenhouse gas emissions but also generates revenue that can be reinvested in renewable energy projects, infrastructure improvements, and social programs. In Canada, the federal government has implemented a carbon pricing system that includes rebates for citizens to offset increased energy costs. This approach demonstrates how carbon pricing can be used not only as a disincentive for polluting activities but also as a means of redistributing wealth and promoting social equity.

One of the challenges of implementing carbon pricing is ensuring that it does not disproportionately impact low-income households, who may spend a larger share of their income on energy and transportation. To address this issue, governments can design carbon pricing systems that include rebates or subsidies for low-income families, as well as targeted investments in public transportation, energy efficiency, and renewable energy projects in underserved communities. This ensures that the transition to a low-carbon economy is both just and equitable.

Additionally, carbon pricing can drive innovation in clean energy technologies by creating a financial incentive for businesses to invest in low-carbon solutions. As companies seek to reduce their carbon footprint and avoid paying higher taxes or buying emission allowances, they are likely to invest in research and development of renewable energy sources, energy storage systems, and energy-efficient products. This can accelerate the transition to a low-carbon economy and create new economic opportunities in the growing green technology sector.

However, carbon pricing alone is not sufficient to achieve the deep emissions reductions needed to mitigate climate change. It must be complemented by other policies, such as renewable energy subsidies, stricter environmental regulations, and investments in green infrastructure. Together, these policies can create a comprehensive framework for reducing emissions, promoting sustainability, and ensuring that the benefits of the low-carbon transition are shared by all members of society.

Financial Inclusion: Expanding Access to Banking and Credit

Financial inclusion should also be given top priority in a humane economy so that every person, from all backgrounds or income level, has access to dependable and reasonably priced financial services. Reducing poverty, advancing entrepreneurship, and letting people save for the future, invest in education, or launch small businesses all depend on financial inclusion.

About 1.7 billion adults worldwide are unbanked, so lacking access to conventional banking products including credit cards, loans, or savings accounts. Many of these people live in underdeveloped nations or underprivileged areas where financial institutions are few. People who lack access to these services sometimes find themselves caught in debt and poverty by depending on unofficial or predatory lending methods.

Growing mobile banking and digital financial services is one way to support financial inclusion. By letting people move money, pay bills, and save using their mobile phones, mobile banking systems like M-Pesa have transformed access to financial services in nations like Kenya. M-Pesa has given millions of Kenyans—especially those living in rural areas—access to once out-of-reach basic financial products. For many low-income people, this has helped to raise living standards, boost financial stability, and stimulate economic activity.

By investing in digital infrastructure, encouraging financial literacy, and building regulatory environments that support the growth of inclusive financial products, governments and international organisations can support financial inclusion. Particularly among women in developing nations, microfinance organizations—which offer small loans to people without access to conventional banking services—have been effective in encouraging entrepreneurship and economic empowerment.

Apart from increasing access to credit and banking, financial inclusion also entails making sure people have access to reasonably priced insurance products, retirement savings plans, and other financial tools meant to help them control risks and over time create wealth. Promoting financial inclusion helps a humane economy enable people to take charge of their financial futures, lower poverty, and generate more fair economic opportunities.

Education and Job Training: Preparing Workers for the Future Economy

Driven by technological developments, globalisation, and changing labour markets, access to high-quality education and job training becomes more important as the global economy keeps changing. To guarantee that every person has the tools and knowledge required to thrive in the modern economy, a humane economy has to give education and workforce development top priority.

Access to education is still uneven in many nations, and people from low-income or marginalised backgrounds sometimes encounter major obstacles to get a quality education. Because those without access to education are less likely to find well-paying employment or pursue additional education and training, this fuels cycles of poverty and inequality.

Governments can invest in universal access to high-quality education—from early childhood education to higher education and vocational training—to help to solve this problem. This covers making sure public schools have enough money, making sure teachers are fairly paid and well-trained, and correcting racial, gender, income, or geographic location differences in educational outcomes.

Apart from conventional education, job training initiatives are indispensable for equipping employees for the upcoming economy. Workers will have to change by learning new skills and moving to different sectors as automation and artificial intelligence transform sectors and upend established job markets. Investing in job training and reskilling initiatives that enable workers—especially those in sectors vulnerable to automation— acquire the skills required to flourish in growing sectors including renewable energy, healthcare, and technology helps governments support this transition.

Germany's dual education system, which combines classroom instruction with vocational training, for instance, has been effective in both lowering young unemployment and preparing workers for a variety of sectors. This approach could be modified to fit other nations so that workers are ready to satisfy the needs of the future economy and help close the skill gap.

Moreover, lifelong learning initiatives can give people continuous chances to improve their knowledge and abilities over their employment. Workers must keep competitive in the labour market by means of constant education as the speed of technological development quickens. Working together, governments and companies can provide easily available, reasonably priced, flexible lifelong learning opportunities so that every employee has the means to thrive in an economy undergoing fast change.

Global Cooperation: Building a Humane Economy on an International Scale

Creating a humane economy is not only a national endeavour but also a global one. In an increasingly interconnected world, global cooperation is essential for addressing the economic, social, and environmental challenges that transcend national borders. Issues such as climate change, economic inequality, and global health require coordinated efforts and shared responsibility among nations.

International organisations, such as the United Nations, the World Bank, and the International Monetary Fund, play a crucial role in promoting global cooperation on economic and social issues. These organisations can help facilitate dialogue between countries, provide financial assistance to developing nations, and promote policies that support sustainable development, poverty reduction, and economic justice.

One key area of global cooperation is the implementation of the United Nations Sustainable Development Goals (SDGs), a set of 17 goals aimed at addressing global challenges such as poverty, inequality, climate change, and peace and justice. Achieving these goals will require collaboration between governments, businesses, civil society, and international organisations to create a more equitable and sustainable global economy.

For example, Goal 8 of the SDGs focuses on promoting sustained, inclusive, and sustainable economic growth, full and productive employment, and decent work for all. Achieving this goal will require policies that promote fair labour practices, protect workers' rights, and ensure that economic growth benefits all members of society, particularly the most vulnerable.

In addition to global efforts to reduce poverty and inequality, international cooperation is essential for addressing climate change and promoting environmental sustainability. The Paris Agreement, an international treaty aimed at limiting global warming to well below 2 degrees Celsius above pre-industrial levels, represents a significant step toward global climate action. However, achieving the goals of the Paris Agreement will require continued cooperation between countries, as well as investments in renewable energy, green technology, and climate adaptation measures.

Conclusion: Toward a More Humane Economy ---

An economy that is humane places the well-being of all individuals as its top priority, advocates for social and economic justice, and guarantees that economic growth is both sustainable and fair. To realise this vision, a comprehensive strategy is necessary, encompassing pre-distribution policies to tackle economic inequalities, redistribution policies to ensure equitable wealth distribution, and environmental sustainability policies to safeguard the planet for future generations. Global collaboration is indispensable for establishing a compassionate economy that effectively tackles the issues of poverty, inequality, and climate change at a global level, alongside national policies. Through collaboration, governments, corporations, civil society, and international organisations have the ability to construct a fair and impartial global economy that advantages all individuals in society. The pursuit of a compassionate economy will be challenging, yet it is indispensable in order to establish a global society where all individuals have the chance to prosper. This vision necessitates courageous measures, inventive strategies, and a dedication to fairness and environmental responsibility. In essence, a compassionate economy goes beyond simply attaining economic expansion, but rather focusses on guaranteeing that this expansion is accessible, fair, and enduring for everyone.

• • •

CHAPTER XXV

A Roadmap for Reducing Inequality in India

India, a rapidly growing economy, has witnessed significant progress in recent years. However, this growth has not been evenly distributed. Economic inequality continues to rise, with the gap between the rich and the poor widening at an alarming rate. A 2023 report from Oxfam revealed that the richest 1% of Indians now own more than 60% of the country's total wealth, further exacerbating the economic divide. The staggering concentration of wealth among the elites has led to increased calls for policies that can address the imbalance, foster social justice, and generate much-needed revenue for the country. One effective method to combat this inequality is through the introduction of an inheritance tax and a revised wealth tax. These measures can help redistribute wealth, encourage more equitable economic practices, and generate additional resources for the government.

Introducing an Inheritance Tax and Raising the Wealth Tax

India's rising inequality has made it imperative to address the accumulation of wealth in the hands of a few. An inheritance tax, though controversial, holds the potential to break cycles of entrenched wealth. The core philosophy behind this tax is the idea that wealth should be created through effort and innovation rather than inherited across generations.

Studies have shown that once significant wealth is amassed, it tends to grow at a pace far exceeding the average returns available to the majority of the population. This perpetuates a cycle of wealth concentration where the rich get richer, solidifying economic inequality. For example, according to the Forbes 2023 Billionaire List, there are now over 2,600 billionaires globally, collectively controlling more than $12 trillion in wealth—a sum that dwarfs the combined wealth of the bottom 80% of the world's population. Furthermore, nearly 60% of this wealth is either inherited or the result of crony capitalism, rather than entrepreneurship or innovation.

In developing nations like India, the situation is more pronounced. By 2023, nearly 75% of billionaire wealth in India had either been inherited or linked to government connections. A UBS study projected that over the next two decades, an estimated $4 trillion of global wealth will be passed on to the next generation, with a large portion of this transfer happening in developing economies, including India.

India's Inheritance Tax and Wealth Tax Potential

India's direct tax revenue remains relatively low compared to other G20 and BRICS nations, where wealth taxes contribute significantly to public finances. In the fiscal year 2022-23, wealth taxes constituted a mere 0.05% of India's total gross tax revenue, even lower than the previous decade. In contrast, inheritance and wealth taxes in countries such as Germany, France, and the United States generate substantial revenues that help mitigate social disparities.

Recent studies suggest that implementing an inheritance tax and revising the wealth tax could increase India's tax revenue by nearly 1.0% of GDP. This figure is even more significant when considering the rapid increase in private wealth in the country. From $3.6 trillion in 2013, private wealth had surged to over $9 trillion by 2023.

Despite this growth, wealth remains concentrated in the hands of a few. By 2023, the richest 10% of Indian households held more than 77% of the nation's wealth. The number of billionaires in India had increased to 166, their combined wealth equaling nearly 14% of the country's GDP. A 2022 study by economists Gandhi and Walton showed that nearly half of this wealth was inherited, further highlighting the role of generational wealth in perpetuating inequality.

The Impact of Hidden Wealth and Tax Havens

Income inequality in India is further exacerbated by hidden wealth, a significant portion of which is held by the richest Indians in offshore tax havens. These tax shelters obscure the true extent of inequality. In 2023, India's Ministry of Finance estimated that at least $250 billion of Indian wealth is held in offshore accounts. This wealth largely evades taxation, depriving the government of revenue that could be used to fund public services.

A 2023 report by the Tax Justice Network estimated that globally, between $10 and $12 trillion of private wealth is hidden in tax havens, with India's share estimated to be between $200 billion and $250 billion. Much of this wealth is untaxed, contributing to both global and national inequality while simultaneously depriving governments of essential revenue.

The Importance of Inheritance and Wealth Taxes in India

Given the vast amount of wealth being accumulated and inherited by a small elite, implementing an inheritance tax and increasing the wealth tax could significantly bolster India's tax revenue. The government could then allocate these funds toward programs aimed at reducing inequality, improving social services, and fostering broader economic growth. Many G20 and BRICS countries have already developed robust wealth tax systems, contributing significantly to their tax revenues. In contrast, India's wealth tax system remains underdeveloped, with its revenue contribution being negligible. By reforming this system and introducing an inheritance tax, the Indian government could take significant steps toward closing the wealth gap and ensuring that the benefits of economic growth are more evenly distributed.

Not Reducing Corporate Tax Rates and Eliminating Tax Exemptions for Corporations

Another essential step in addressing inequality in India is maintaining current corporate tax rates and eliminating unnecessary tax exemptions for corporations. The global trend of lowering corporate tax rates to attract investment has led to a race to the bottom, severely undermining governments' ability to fund critical social services. The belief that lower corporate tax rates spur investment and economic growth is widely debated. For example, in 2023, analysis of Australia's planned corporate tax cut from 30% to 25% revealed that the policy would likely result in only a modest increase in GDP (0.03% annually over 20 years) and negligible improvements in employment and wage growth. Nobel laureate Joseph Stiglitz has argued that lowering corporate tax rates does little to stimulate meaningful investment. Instead, he notes that companies prioritise other factors, such as the quality of the workforce, infrastructure, and political stability, when making investment decisions. Thus, reducing corporate taxes ultimately harms a country's ability to fund public services, which are crucial for fostering long-term economic growth.

The Role of Corporate Tax Incentives in Inequality

Despite evidence suggesting limited benefits from corporate tax incentives, many developing countries, including India, continue to offer extensive exemptions to corporations. In the 2022-23 fiscal year, India provided over Rs 7 lakh crore (approximately $86 billion) in tax breaks to corporations. These incentives primarily benefit large, profitable companies while depleting the government's ability to finance essential public services. The aggregate revenue lost to corporate tax incentives is staggering. In 2023, India's 'Revenue Forgone Statement' revealed that the government had forfeited Rs 6.4 lakh crore (about $77 billion) in tax incentives. This amounted to nearly 45% of the country's total tax revenue, a figure that could otherwise be used to improve healthcare, education, and infrastructure for the population.

Rationalizing Corporate Tax Policy in India

With India's corporate tax incentives contributing to vast revenue losses, it is crucial for the government to reevaluate its approach. The Finance Minister, Nirmala Sitharaman, announced a reduction in corporate tax rates in 2022, with the lowest rate dropping to 15% for new manufacturing companies. While this move aimed to attract foreign direct investment (FDI) and stimulate industrial growth, it also risks further reducing corporate tax revenue at a time when the nation faces significant fiscal challenges. A 2023 report by the IMF noted that downward pressure on corporate tax revenues is more pronounced in developing economies than in developed ones. This trend is particularly concerning as it undermines the ability of countries like India to finance critical public goods and services that promote broader economic development.

Cracking Down on Corporate Tax Dodging and Ending the Era of Tax Havens

Corporate tax avoidance remains a significant challenge in India. Many Indian companies continue to use tax havens like Mauritius, Cyprus, and Singapore to shelter their profits. The 2021 Pandora Papers, following the earlier Panama Papers, revealed how Indian elites, including business leaders and politicians, use offshore structures to hide wealth and avoid taxes. The Tax Justice Network's 2023 report estimated that India loses over Rs 75,000 crore annually due to corporate tax avoidance schemes. These losses represent funds that could otherwise be invested in improving the country's education, healthcare, and infrastructure, all of which are vital for reducing inequality.

Strategies for Addressing Corporate Tax Avoidance

To effectively combat corporate tax dodging, India must strengthen its domestic tax enforcement mechanisms and collaborate with international partners to clamp down on tax havens. The OECD's 2022 BEPS (Base Erosion and Profit Shifting) framework has been a significant step in curbing tax avoidance, but more work is needed to ensure compliance. Additionally, India should focus on closing tax loopholes and imposing stricter penalties for tax evasion. Tax evasion and avoidance remain prevalent in India, with practices such as transfer pricing and profit shifting allowing corporations to reduce their tax burdens at the expense of public funds. Ending tax dodging and fostering a fairer tax system requires decisive action. Governments must commit to reforming their tax codes and eliminating harmful corporate practices that erode tax bases and perpetuate inequality.

• • •

Inequality in India remains among the most urgent problems of our day. The Indian government can start to close the widening disparity between the rich and the poor by including inheritance and wealth taxes, keeping corporate tax rates, and doing away with ineffective tax exemptions. Together with a crackdown on corporate tax avoidance, these policies will assist to build a more fair society. Fostering social cohesiveness, boosting economic growth, and making sure that every person gains from development depend on a more equitable distribution of wealth. India has to solve the ingrained inequality that could compromise its development even as it develops as a major worldwide economic actor.

• • •

Definition And Terminology

- **Imperialism**: A policy or ideology in which a nation expands its power and influence through methods such as military force, colonisation, or other means. Imperialism frequently leads to the exploitation and dominance of one nation by another.
- **Colonialism**: The act of a country acquiring and maintaining colonies or territories, in which the colonising power exerts control over the local population and exploits the resources. The economic and political structures of the colonised regions have been long-lastingly influenced by colonialism.
- **Neocolonialism**: The act of utilising economic, political, cultural, or other pressures to directly or indirectly control or influence other countries, particularly former colonies, without the use of military or political force. Multinational corporations and international financial institutions are frequently implicated in neocolonialism.
- **Hegemony**: The possession of a dominant position in the political, economic, or cultural spheres by a single country or group or over others. Hegemony can be achieved through economic dominance, military force, or cultural influence.
- **Ethnocentrism**: The conviction that one's own ethnic group or culture is inherently superior, which frequently results in prejudice and discrimination against other peoples. Social conflict and exclusion may be exacerbated by ethnocentrism.
- **Populism**: A political strategy that endeavours to advocate for the interests and concerns of the general populace, frequently in opposition to the elite or establishment. Populism is a political ideology that is present in all political spectrums and may involve economic protectionism, nationalism, and anti-elitism.
- **Nationalism**: A political ideology that prioritises the interests, culture, and identity of a specific nation or group of

individuals. Often, nationalism is characterised by a sense of pride and loyalty to one's country, but it can also result in exclusionary policies and conflict with other nations.

- **Xenophobia**: The fear or hatred of individuals from other cultures or foreigners. Discrimination, violence, and exclusionary policies towards immigrants and other minority groups may result from xenophobia.

- **Racism**: The conviction that one race is superior to others, resulting in discrimination and prejudice based on its race. Systemic inequalities, institutional practices, and individual attitudes are all potential manifestations of racism.

- **Patriotism**: A sentiment of pride, loyalty, and devotion towards one's country. Although patriotism is frequently perceived as a positive expression of national identity, it can occasionally be employed to substantiate exclusionary or aggressive policies.

- **Totalitarianism**: A political system in which the state maintains complete control over all facets of public and private life, frequently under the leadership of a single leader or ruling party. The suppression of dissent, censorship, and the utilisation of propaganda are the hallmarks of totalitarian regimes.

- **Authoritarianism**: A political system in which a single leader or small group holds concentrated power, with very little or no opposition and limited political freedoms. Repression, censorship, and a robust military or police presence are frequently employed by authoritarian regimes.

- **Oligarchy**: A government in which a small number of individuals hold power, frequently as a result of their wealth, family connections, or military control. Oligarchies are frequently linked to corruption and inequality and can be found in both democratic and authoritarian systems.

- **Plutocracy**: A society or system in which the wealthy are in control, and economic power is translated into political influence. Plutocracy frequently leads to policies that exacerbate economic inequality and benefit the wealthy.

- **Meritocracy**: A system in which individuals are rewarded and promoted based on their abilities, talent, and effort, rather than their social class or background. Although meritocracy is frequently perceived as a fair system, it can also exacerbate existing inequalities if opportunities are not equally accessible to all.
- **Bureaucracy**: A form of government or organisation in which state officials or administrators make decisions rather than elected representatives. Formal rules, procedures, and hierarchical structures are frequently indicative of bureaucracies.
- **Patronage**: The act of providing government jobs, contracts, or other benefits to individuals or groups in exchange for political support. Corruption, nepotism, and inefficiency in government may result from patronage.
- **Clientelism**: A political system in which politicians provide goods or services to individuals or groups in exchange for political support. Politicians and their supporters frequently engage in a reciprocal relationship known as clientelism, which can result in inequality and corruption.
- **Corporatism**: A political and economic system in which business, labour unions, or other organisations, as well as interest groups, have a formal role in the decision-making process. The concentration of power among specific groups and the potential undermining of democratic representation are potential consequences of corporatism.
- **Demagogue**: A political leader who aims to acquire power by appealing to the emotions, desires, and prejudices of the populace, rather than relying on rational arguments or policies. Rhetoric that incites fear, anger, and division is frequently employed by demagogues.
- **Propaganda**: Information, particularly that which is biassed or deliberately misleading, that is employed to advance a specific political cause or perspective. Propaganda is frequently employed by governments or political organisations to maintain

control and influence public opinion.

- **Censorship**: The act of suppressing or prohibiting speech, writing, or other forms of expression that are determined to be politically inconvenient, harmful, or objectionable. Authoritarian regimes frequently implement censorship as a means of managing information and controlling dissent.
- **Surveillance State**: A government that employs technology and mass surveillance to extensively monitor and collect information on its citizens. Authoritarian regimes are frequently linked to surveillance states, which can result in the violation of civil liberties and privacy.
- **Civil Liberties**: The fundamental rights and freedoms that are legally guaranteed to individuals, including the right to privacy, freedom of speech, and freedom of assembly. In order to safeguard individuals from government overreach and guarantee democratic governance, civil liberties are indispensable.
- **Humanitarianism**: The philosophy and practice of advancing human welfare and social reform, frequently through public policy, advocacy, or charitable work. Humanitarianism prioritises the safeguarding of human rights, empathy, and compassion.
- *Social Contract**: A theoretical agreement among individuals in a society to establish a government and adhere to its regulations in exchange for protection and the advantages of living in a community. In political theory and philosophy, the social contract is a fundamental concept.
- *Civil Society**: The collection of associations, community groups, and non-governmental organisations that operate independently of the state and advocate for the interests of citizens. The promotion of democracy, social justice, and human rights is significantly influenced by civil society.
- **Social Capital**: The networks, relationships, and norms of trust and reciprocity that exist within a community or society. Social capital is indispensable for the cultivation of collective

action, social cohesion, and cooperation.

- **Civic Engagement**: The involvement of individuals in the decision-making processes that impact their communities and public life. Civic engagement encompasses activities such as volunteering, voting, and engaging in social movements.
- **Political Participation**: The engagement of individuals in the political process, which includes activities such as political discourse, campaigning, voting, and attending rallies. For a democracy to function effectively, political participation is indispensable.
- **Public Opinion**: The collective beliefs, attitudes, and preferences of the general public regarding political, social, or economic matters. Government policies, elections, and social movements may be affected by public opinion.
- **Political Socialisation**: The process by which individuals acquire and cultivate their political beliefs, values, and behaviours. Political socialisation is facilitated by a variety of agents, such as family, education, media, and peer groups.
- **Ideology**: A set of beliefs, values, and ideas that influence the political and social actions of an individual or group and shape their worldview. From conservative to liberal, socialist to capitalist, and everything in between, ideologies can be found.
- **Conservatism**: A political ideology that prioritises the preservation of established institutions, social stability, and tradition. Conservatives frequently advocate for a strong emphasis on individual responsibility and limited government intervention in the economy.
- **Liberalism**: A political ideology that prioritises individual rights, freedoms, and equality, frequently advocating for government intervention to safeguard civil liberties and advocate for social justice. Liberals generally advocate for policies that advance economic regulation, environmental protection, and social welfare.
- **Socialism**: A collective ownership and control of the means of production and distribution of goods and services, which is

a political and economic ideology. Socialists advocate for the equitable distribution of wealth and the reduction of economic inequality.

- **Communism**: Economic and political ideology that promotes a classless society in which the state collectively owns and controls all property and resources. Communism endeavours to abolish private ownership and establish a society that is founded on communal welfare and equality.
- **Anarchism**: A political philosophy that promotes the elimination of all forms of government and hierarchical authority, with the objective of establishing a society that is based on self-governance, mutual aid, and voluntary cooperation.
- **Libertarianism**: A political philosophy that promotes the minimal infiltration of government into the personal lives and economy of individuals. Libertarians prioritise individual liberty, free markets, and restricted government.
- **Environmentalism**: A social and political movement that aims to safeguard and preserve the natural environment from exploitation, degradation, and pollution. Environmentalists are proponents of the preservation of natural resources, sustainable development, and conservation.
- **Green Politics**: A political ideology that prioritises grassroots democracy, social justice, and environmental sustainability. Green politics frequently promotes policies that mitigate climate change, safeguard ecosystems, and advance renewable energy.
- ** Feminism**: A social and political movement that challenges gender-based discrimination and oppression and advocates for the rights and equality of women. Feminists endeavour to resolve concerns such as gender pay disparities, reproductive rights, and gender-based violence.
- **Intersectionality**: A theoretical framework that considers the intersection of various forms of social identity, including race, gender, class, and sexuality, to establish overlapping systems of discrimination and oppression. Intersectionality

underscores the interconnectedness of social inequalities.

- **Gender Equality**: The condition in which all individuals, regardless of their gender, have equal access to resources, opportunities, and rights. Addressing disparities in areas such as education, employment, and political representation is a critical component of gender equality.

- **LGBTQ+ Rights**: The movement that promotes the equality, dignity, and rights of individuals who identify as lesbian, gay, bisexual, transgender, queer, or other sexual and gender minorities. LGBTQ+ rights encompass concerns such as the recognition of gender identity, anti-discrimination protections, and marriage equality.

- **Social Mobility**: The capacity of individuals or families to ascend or descend the social and economic ladder within a society.. Factors such as education, income, and social networks frequently impact social mobility.

- **Economic Justice**: The endeavour to ensure that wealth, income, and opportunities are distributed fairly and equitably within a society. Economic justice entails the resolution of issues such as poverty, inequality, and access to resources.

- **Distributive Justice**: The ethical principle that resources and benefits within a society should be distributed fairly and equitably for all. Need, merit, and equality are frequently taken into account in distributive justice.

- **Restorative Justice**: A justice system that prioritises the repair of the harm caused by criminal behaviour through reconciliation, restitution, and rehabilitation, as opposed to punitive measures. Restorative justice prioritises the requirements of both victims and offenders.

- **Criminal Justice System**: The network of institutions, laws, and processes that are responsible for the enforcement of laws, the preservation of public order, and the administration of justice. Law enforcement, courts, and correctional facilities comprise the criminal justice system.

- **Penal System**: The set of laws, institutions, and practices that regulate the rehabilitation and punishment of individuals who have been convicted of crimes. Prisons, probation, and parole programs comprise the penal system.

- **Recidivism**: The propensity of individuals who have been convicted of crimes in the past to reoffend and engage in criminal activity. Recidivism rates are frequently employed to evaluate the efficacy of rehabilitation programs and the criminal justice system.

- **Police Brutality**: The use of excessive force by law enforcement officers against civilians, frequently inflicting injury or death. In discussions of civil rights, justice, and law enforcement reform, police brutality is a significant issue.

- **Mass Incarceration**: The act of incarcerating a significant number of individuals, frequently with a disproportionate impact on marginalised communities. Systemic racism, overcriminalization, and the privatisation of prisons are all associated with mass incarceration.

- **Private Prisons**: Prisons that are managed by private companies rather than the government. Private prisons are frequently criticised for prioritising profit over the welfare of inmates and for contributing to mass incarceration.

- **Judicial Review**: The authority of courts to review and, if justified, invalidate laws and government actions that are deemed unconstitutional. Judicial review is a critical mechanism for safeguarding individual rights and maintaining the rule of law.

- *Separation of Powers**: The process of dividing government responsibilities into three distinct branches—legislative, executive, and judicial—in order to prevent any one branch from acquiring an excessive amount of power. The separation of powers is a fundamental principle of democratic governance.

- **Checks and Balances**: A system in which each branch of government has the authority to monitor and restrict the actions of the other branches, thereby preventing any single branch from becoming excessively powerful. Maintaining the rule of law and safeguarding democracy necessitates the maintenance of checks and balances.

- **Constitutionalism**: The principle that the structure, functions, and boundaries of government authority should be established by a constitution, which restricts the power of the government. Constitutionalism is a critical component of democratic governance and the safeguarding of individual rights.
- **Federalism**: A form of government in which the authority is divided between a central authority and smaller political units, such as states or provinces. Federalism enables the division of authority and obligations among various levels of government.
- **Decentralisation**: The process of transferring power, authority, and responsibility from the central government to regional or local governments. Decentralisation is frequently pursued in order to enhance governance, enhance public participation, and mitigate regional disparities.
- **Devolution**: The transfer of authority from a central government to regional or local governments, frequently within a federal or unitary framework. The purpose of devolution is to provide regions with a greater degree of autonomy in managing their own affairs.
- **Autonomy**: The capacity of a region or group to independently govern itself and make decisions without the guidance of a central authority. Regions or minority groups that desire increased self-determination frequently pursue autonomy.
- **Sovereignty**: The paramount authority of a state to govern itself and make decisions without external interference. International law's fundamental principle of sovereignty is frequently referenced in discussions of self-determination and national independence.
- **Nation-State**: A political entity in which the boundaries of a nation and a state are congruent, resulting in a unified and sovereign nation. The modern world is characterised by the

nation-state as the predominant form of political organisation.

- **Multilateralism**: A diplomatic and international relations approach in which multiple countries collaborate to resolve global issues and make decisions through international organisations and agreements. Cooperation, consensus-building, and collective action are the primary objectives of multilateralism.

- **Bilateralism**: A diplomatic and international relations approach in which two countries work together to address specific issues and make agreements. Bilateralism often involves direct negotiations and cooperation between two states.

- **Unilateralism**: A diplomatic and international relations strategy in which a single nation acts autonomously, without requesting the approval or cooperation of other nations. International tensions and conflicts may result from unilateralism.

- **Economic Integration**: The process by which countries reduce trade barriers and coordinate economic policies to establish a more interconnected and comprehensive global economy. Increased trade, investment, and economic growth may result from economic integration.

- **Free Trade**: A policy in which countries reduce or eliminate tariffs, quotas, and other trade barriers to facilitate the unrestricted flow of goods and services across borders. Free trade is frequently advocated as a method to enhance consumer choice and economic efficiency.

- **Protectionism**: A policy in which a nation implements tariffs, quotas, and other trade barriers to safeguard its domestic industries and restrict imports. Protectionism is frequently implemented to bolster local businesses and employment opportunities; however, it can result in increased consumer prices and trade disputes.

- **Trade Liberalisation**: The process of fostering a more competitive and open global economy by reducing or eliminating trade barriers, such as tariffs and quotas.

International trade agreements and organisations are frequently employed to promote trade liberalisation.

- Big Data: The extensive and intricate datasets that are produced by digital technologies, social media, and other sources. Patterns, trends, and insights that inform decision-making in business, government, and other sectors can be uncovered through the analysis of big data.

- Smart Cities: Urban areas that optimise city services, improve sustainability, and enhance the quality of life by utilising digital technologies, data, and IoT devices. The objective of smart cities is to establish urban environments that are more resilient, livable, and efficient.

- Carbon Footprint: The aggregate quantity of greenhouse gases, particularly carbon dioxide, that an organisation, individual, or product emits. Addressing climate change and fostering sustainability necessitates a reduction in carbon footprints.

- Carbon pricing is an economic policy instrument that motivates the reduction of greenhouse gas emissions by assigning a cost to carbon emissions, typically through a carbon tax or cap-and-trade system. The objective of carbon pricing is to redirect the economy towards low-carbon alternatives.

- Circular Economy: An economic model that prioritises the sustainable utilisation of resources by reducing waste, repurposing materials, and recycling products. The circular economy endeavours to establish a closed-loop system that minimises environmental impact and conserves resources.

- Green Economy: An economic model that emphasises economic growth, social equity, and environmental sustainability. The green economy is dedicated to the promotion of green technologies and industries, the conservation of natural resources, and the reduction of carbon emissions.

- Environmental Justice: The equitable treatment and substantive participation of all individuals, irrespective of their race, nationality, or income, in the process of environmental decision-making. Environmental justice aims to rectify disparities in environmental impacts and guarantee that all individuals have access to a healthy environment.

- Diversity: The diversity of life on Earth, which encompasses a wide range of species, ecosystems, and genetic diversity. The provision of ecosystem services that support human well-being, as well as the health and resilience of ecosystems, are contingent upon biodiversity.

- Conservation: The sustainable management, preservation, and protection of natural resources, ecosystems, and wildlife. The objective of conservation efforts is to safeguard endangered species, preserve biodiversity, and guarantee the long-term health of the planet's ecosystems.

- Radical Nationalism**: A more extreme form of nationalism that frequently entails the implementation of aggressive policies and procedures to achieve national objectives, such as the exclusion of minorities, xenophobia, and intolerance towards other nations.

- Historical Revisionism**: The re-interpretation of historical events, frequently in order to advance a political agenda. In numerous instances, historical revisionism entails the downplaying or alteration of facts in order to reshape the narrative in a manner that is advantageous to a specific group or ideology.

- Fascism**: A political ideology that is far-right and authoritarian, exalting nation and often race above the individual. It is characterised by the forcible suppression of opposition, dictatorial power, and the significant regimentation of society and the economy.

- Dictatorship**: A government in which a single leader or a small clique possesses absolute power. The suppression of political opposition and the centralisation of power are the hallmarks of dictatorships, which frequently emerge during periods of social or economic instability.

- Capitalism**: An economic system that is predicated on the private ownership of the means of production and their operation for profit. Competitive markets, private property, and the pursuit of profit as a driving force are among the key features.

- Inequality in the Economy**: The unequal distribution of wealth, income, and opportunity among various groups within society. Economic inequality is frequently associated with social stratification and can result in substantial disparities in the availability of resources and services.
- Wealth Concentration**: The process by which wealth is concentrated in the hands of a small fraction of society. This can result in the affluent gaining more social and economic power, frequently at the expense of the general populace.
- Unemployment**: The condition of being actively seeking employment and currently unemployed. Various factors, such as economic downturns, technological changes, and shifts in industry, can influence unemployment, which is frequently a critical indicator of economic health.
- Fake Economic Growth**: An apparent increase in economic activity that does not result in genuine improvements in living standards or economic sustainability. Short-term gains that are not indicative of long-term economic health are frequently associated with fake economic growth.
- Real Economic Growth**: Sustainable economic growth that results in long-term enhancements in living standards, increased employment opportunities, and a fair distribution of wealth.
- Democratic Socialism**: A political ideology that promotes political democracy in conjunction with social ownership of the means of production, combining elements of democracy with socialist principles. The objective of democratic socialism is to mitigate inequality by means of government intervention in the economy.
- Fabian Socialism**: A form of socialism that promotes gradual, rather than revolutionary, changes to achieve a socialist society. The Fabian Society, which was established in the United Kingdom, advocated for this ideology and had a significant

impact on various aspects of British politics.

- BJP (Bharatiya Janata Party)**: A right-wing political party in India that is currently one of the two major political parties in the country. The BJP has been criticised for its role in promoting radical nationalism and authoritarian practices, and it is associated with Hindu nationalism.

- Human Economy**: An economic system that places a higher value on the well-being of individuals and the promotion of social justice than on economic growth and profit. A human economy prioritises the welfare of all members of society, guaranteeing that economic policies are intended to benefit the majority, rather than the minority.

- Inequality**: The unequal distribution of resources, rights, and opportunities among individuals. Inequality can take on a variety of forms, such as economic, social, and political disparities, which frequently result in systemic disadvantages for specific groups.

- Corruption**: The misuse of power for personal gain, frequently involving bribery, embezzlement, and other forms of dishonest or fraudulent behaviour by those in positions of authority. Corruption can exacerbate inequality and social injustice and undermine trust in institutions.

- Dictatorial Power**: The unbridled authority of a dictator, in which all decisions are made without democratic processes or checks and balances. The suppression of human rights and political freedoms is frequently the result of dictatorial power.

- Capitalist Interest**: The motivations and objectives of individuals and entities that benefit from the capitalist system, frequently emphasising the preservation of the status quo to safeguard their economic advantages, wealth accumulation, and profit maximisation.

- Nexus**: A connection or series of connections that connect two or more entities. A nexus is frequently used to describe the interrelationship between power structures in the context of politics and economics, such as the connection between capitalist interests and dictatorial power.

- Jawaharlal Nehru** has been a central figure in Indian politics both before and after independence. He was the first Prime Minister of India. Nehru was a proponent of democratic socialism and was instrumental in the development of India's secular and democratic institutions.

- Rabindranath Thakur (Tagore)**: A Bengali polymath who was a prolific writer, composer, philosopher, painter, and poet. Tagore's perspective on nationalism was critical; he argued that extreme nationalism could result in intolerance and conflict, and he favoured a more inclusive and humanistic approach.

- Fabian Society**: A British socialist organisation initiated in 1884, the Fabian Society promoted the gradual implementation of socialist principles through democratic means. The society played a crucial role in the establishment of the Labour Party in the United Kingdom.

- Hindutva**: A term that refers to the Hindu nationalism ideology in India, which promotes the importance of Hindu culture and values in the governance and society of the country. Hindutva has been linked to intolerance and exclusionary practices towards non-Hindu communities.

- Secularism**: The principle of distancing religion from the governance of a nation. Secularism guarantees that government policies are not influenced by religious beliefs, thereby enabling a more neutral and inclusive state.

- Public Services**: The government's provision of essential services to its citizens, such as healthcare, education, transportation, and social welfare. Public services are frequently funded through taxation and are intended to benefit the general public.

- Geopolitical Tensions**: Political and strategic disputes between nations, frequently centred on ideological differences, resource competition, and territorial disputes. Global economic and security conditions can be influenced by geopolitical tensions, which can result in instability.

- Energy Insecurity**: The inability of a nation to sustain economic growth and meet the needs of its population due to the absence of reliable access to affordable energy sources. Geopolitical tensions, market volatility, and environmental concerns are frequently associated with energy insecurity.
- Net Zero Emissions**: The equilibrium between the quantity of greenhouse gases released into the atmosphere and the quantity that is captured. It is imperative to combat climate change by achieving net-zero emissions, which necessitates substantial reductions in carbon output.
- Environmental Sustainability**: The process of preserving ecological equilibrium by preventing the depletion of natural resources. sustainable practices are designed to satisfy the requirements of the present without jeopardising the capacity of future generations to satisfy their own needs.
- Social Ownership**: A concept in socialism in which the community as a whole owns or regulates the means of production, distribution, and exchange, frequently through the state or cooperatives. Social ownership is perceived as a means of guaranteeing that the advantages of economic activity are distributed more equitably.
- Labour Party**: A significant political party in the United Kingdom that has been historically associated with left-wing politics and the advocacy of social justice, workers' rights, and public ownership of strategic industries.
- Warm Home Discount**: A UK government initiative that offers eligible low-income households a reduction in their electricity bills during the winter months. The initiative is a component of a more comprehensive initiative to address fuel poverty.
- Energy Regulator (Ofgem)**: The Office of Gas and Electricity Markets, or Ofgem, is the regulatory body responsible for the electricity and downstream natural gas markets in Great Britain. Ofgem is responsible for safeguarding the interests of consumers, fostering competition, and guaranteeing the reliability of energy supplies.

- Prepayment Meters**: A type of energy meter that necessitates users to prepay for their energy prior to consumption, frequently through a pay-as-you-go system. Prepayment meters are frequently utilised in low-income households; however, they may occasionally result in increased energy expenses.
- Universal Credit (UC) is a social security benefit in the United Kingdom that is designed to simplify the welfare system by replacing six older benefits with a single monthly payment. Universal Credit is intended for individuals who are either unemployed or have a low income and are of working age.
- Employment and Support Allowance (ESA)**: A benefit provided by the United Kingdom government to individuals who are unable to work due to an illness, health condition, or disability. ESA offers personalised assistance and financial assistance to individuals who require it.
- Child Tax Credit (CTC)**: A government benefit in the United Kingdom that is designed to assist families with children. It offers financial assistance to low-income families to assist with the expenses associated with raising children.
- Pension Credit**: A means-tested benefit in the United Kingdom that is intended to provide additional funds to elderly individuals with low incomes. Guarantee Credit and Savings Credit are the two components of Pension Credit, both of which are designed to guarantee that pensioners receive a minimum income.
- Social Welfare**: Government initiatives that are intended to enhance the welfare of citizens, with a particular emphasis on those who are financially disadvantaged. Unemployment benefits, housing assistance, and healthcare subsidies are all potential components of social welfare programs.
- Food Insecurity**: The condition of not having consistent access to an adequate supply of nutritious, affordable food. Poverty, unemployment, and economic instability are frequently associated with food insecurity.
- Living Wage**: The minimum income required for an employee to satisfy their basic necessities, such as food, housing, and other

necessities. The living wage is generally set at a higher rate than the legal minimum wage in order to guarantee a satisfactory standard of living.

- Fuel Poverty**: The inability to maintain a sufficient level of heating in one's residence. Fuel poverty is frequently the result of a combination of low income, high energy costs, and inadequate energy efficiency in residential buildings.
- Economic Policy**: The actions that governments take in the economic field, including taxation, government budgets, the money supply, interest rates, and labor markets. The economic performance of a nation is influenced by economic policies.
- Social Mobility**: The ability of individuals or families to move up or down the social ladder within a society. Income, education, and occupation fluctuations across generations are frequently employed as indicators of social mobility.
- Public Finance**: The examination of the methods by which governments generate and allocate funds, including taxation, government expenditures, budgeting, and public debt. Public finance is essential for comprehending the allocation of resources within a society.
- Austerity**: Economic policies that are designed to decrease government deficits by means of tax increases, spending cuts, or a combination of the two. Austerity measures are frequently the subject of controversy due to their potential to result in diminished public services and social welfare.
- Taxation**: The process by which a government collects money from individuals and businesses to finance public services and infrastructure. Income tax, sales tax, and property tax are among the many forms of taxes.
- Social Security**: A government program that offers financial assistance to individuals who have insufficient or no income. Examples of social security benefits include pensions, disability payments, and unemployment benefits.
- Public Sector**: The government-run portion of the economy, which encompasses public services, state-owned enterprises,

and government agencies. The provision of essential services to citizens is significantly influenced by the public sector.

- Private Sector**: The portion of the economy that is owned and operated by private individuals and companies. Profit motivations are the primary motivator for the private sector, which operates in competitive markets.

- Market Economy**: An economic system in which production and prices are determined by unrestricted competition between privately owned businesses. Supply and demand, with minimal government intervention, are the defining characteristics of market economies.

- Mixed Economy**: An economic system that integrates aspects of both capitalism and socialism. In a mixed economy, the production and distribution of goods and services are significantly influenced by both the private and public sectors.

- Progressive Taxation**: A tax system in which the tax rate increases in proportion to the increase in the taxable amount. Progressive taxation is intended to guarantee that individuals with higher incomes contribute a greater proportion of their income to taxes.

- Regressive Taxation**: A tax system in which the tax rate decreases as the taxable amount increases. Regressive taxes are frequently criticised for their disproportionate impact on low-income individuals and for contributing to inequality.

- Universal Basic Income (UBI)**: A social security model in which all citizens receive a consistent, unconditional sum of money from the government, irrespective of their income or employment status.

- Minimum Wage**: The lowest legal wage that employers are permitted to pay their employees. The minimum wage is designed to guarantee a basic standard of living and safeguard workers from exploitation.

- Collective Bargaining**: The process by which workers, through their unions, negotiate with employers to secure improved wages, working conditions, and benefits. Collective bargaining is a critical element of labour rights.

- Labour Rights**: The rights and protections that are granted to workers, such as the right to safe working conditions, fair wages, and the ability to organise and join unions.
- Economic Growth**: The prolonged expansion of an economy's production of goods and services. Changes in Gross Domestic Product (GDP) are the main indicator of economic growth.
- GDP (Gross Domestic Product)**: The aggregate value of all goods and services produced within a country's borders during a specific period, typically measured annually. GDP is a critical metric for evaluating economic performance.
- Inflation**: The rate at which the general level of prices for goods and services increases, thereby diminishing purchasing power. Various factors, such as demand-pull inflation, cost-push inflation, and built-in inflation, can contribute to inflation.
- Recession**: A temporary economic downturn that is characterised by a decrease in trade and industrial activity, commonly characterised by two consecutive quarters of negative GDP growth.
- Monetary Policy**: The process by which a central bank regulates a country's money supply and interest rates to achieve economic objectives, including the stabilisation of the currency, the maintenance of employment, and the control of inflation.
- Fiscal Policy**: Government policies that pertain to borrowing, taxation, and government spending. The economy is influenced by fiscal policy, which involves the adjustment of revenue and expenditure levels.
- Public Debt**: The aggregate sum of money that a government owes to its creditors. Public debt is frequently employed to fund government expenditures that surpass revenue, regardless of whether they are domestic or foreign.
- Deficit Spending**: A budget deficit occurs when a government spends more money than it receives in revenue. During a recession, deficit spending is frequently implemented to stimulate economic growth.

- Privatisation**: The process of transferring ownership of public assets or services to private entities. In an effort to enhance efficiency and mitigate government debt, privatisation is frequently pursued.
- Nationalisation**: The process of transferring private sector assets to public ownership. Nationalisation is frequently pursued to guarantee public oversight of critical industries and services.
- Social Insurance**: A government-mandated program that offers financial assistance to individuals during periods of unemployment, illness, or retirement. Payroll taxes are the primary source of funding for social insurance.
- Poverty Line**: The minimum income that is considered sufficient in a specific country. Individuals who are living below the poverty line are frequently eligible for government assistance and are considered to be impoverished.
- Social Determinants of Health**: The circumstances in which individuals are born, grow, live, work, and age, which affect their health outcomes. Income, education, and social support are among the social determinants of health.
- Income Distribution**: The manner in which a nation's total income is allocated to its citizens. An analysis of income distribution can be conducted to comprehend economic inequality.
- Gini Coefficient**: A quantifier of income inequality within a population, with a range of 0 (perfect equality) to 1 (perfect inequality). The Gini coefficient is employed to evaluate the distribution of wealth or income.
- Wealth Tax**: A tax that is imposed on an individual's net worth, which includes the value of assets such as stocks, bonds, and property. Wealth taxes are frequently suggested as a method of reducing inequality.
- Estate Tax**: A tax imposed on the transfer of property upon the owner's death. Estate taxes are frequently imposed on substantial inheritances with the objective of reducing the concentration of wealth.

- Carbon Tax**: A tax on carbon emissions that is designed to decrease the production of greenhouse gases. Carbon taxes are a component of a more comprehensive initiative to address climate change.

•••